Thomas Hardy and Women

Thomas Hardy and Women

Sexual Ideology and Narrative Form

Penny Boumelha
Lady Margaret Hall, Oxford

THE UNIVERSITY OF WISCONSIN PRESS

Published in the United States of America in 1985 by
The University of Wisconsin Press
114 North Murray Street
Madison, Wisconsin 53715

First published in Great Britain in 1982 by
The Harvester Press Limited

Printed in Great Britain by
Whitstable Litho Ltd., Whitstable, Kent

LC 84–19663
ISBN 0-299-10244-0

Library of Congress Cataloging in Publication Data

Boumelha, Penny.
   Thomas Hardy and women
   Reprint. Originally published: Sussex:Harvester
Press; Totowa, N.J.:Barnes & Noble, 1982.
   Bibliography: pp.157–173.
   Includes index.
   1. Hardy, Thomas, 1840-1928—Characters—Women.
2. Women in literature.   3. Sex role in literature.
4. Feminism and literature.   I. Title
PR4757.W6B63   1985   823′.8   84–19663
ISBN 0-299-10244-0

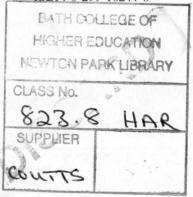

For Connie Burden and Katy Boumelha

Contents

Preface

Throughout this book, except where a different edition or version of the text is specified, I have used the fourteen-volume New Wessex Edition of Hardy's novels, published by Macmillan in 1975–6, and the three-volume New Wessex Edition of the Stories (Macmillan, 1977). References to these editions are given in parentheses in the text. The short titles *Early Life* and *Later Years* refer, of course, to what is for the most part Hardy's autobiography, dictated to his second wife: that is, to *The Early Life of Thomas Hardy, 1840–1891* (London, 1928) and *The Later Years of Thomas Hardy, 1892–1928* (London, 1930), both published under the name Florence Emily Hardy.

During the years that I have spent writing this book, I have inevitably incurred more debts of gratitude than I can hope to settle here. I am particularly indebted to Mary Jacobus, of Cornell University, for generously sharing with me the results of her own scholarship and her critical acuity, and for her kindness and encouragement over a long period. Among the many friends who have assisted me by their interest, support, discussion, or invaluable help with childcare, I should like to thank Homi Bhabha, Maud Ellmann, Tadhg Foley, Felix Thompson, Helen Trilling, and Mary Wilkins. Finally, I must thank Susan Saunders, an understanding and expert typist.

Introduction

From the early stages of his career, Hardy was associated with the portrayal of female characters. Interestingly, it was as a misogynist – or, in the latter stages of his career, at least as an anti-feminist – that he was most often perceived and enlisted in one party or another. The rabidly anti-feminist Charles G. Harper, for instance, singles out Hardy for the accuracy of his portraiture of women. Edmund Gosse flatly asserts that 'Men have made Mr. Thomas Hardy, who owes nothing to the fair sex; if women read him now, it is because the men have told them that they must.' The feminist Clementina Black, reviewing *Tess of the d'Urbervilles*, gives Gosse the lie, and claims Hardy as 'one of that brave and clear-sighted minority' who have drawn a distinction between 'moral worth' and simple chastity in women.[1] A somewhat quaintly written piece in the *Westminster Review*, on the other hand, implicitly discerns the influence of Schopenhauer on Hardy's women (a comparison that will recur), and suggests that a more varied depiction could help to effect a transformation in the imperfectly evolved female nature:

> His women are always of the same order. Why is that? He has chosen a type of woman, too, which is not attractive. . . . Why does not such artist [sic] more devotedly study the woman-nature in its depth and fervour; expand the horizon of the womankind he portrays in completing his literary structures? There is a lack of tenderness, of strength, of passion, where you look for them the most! . . . Caprice, whim, irony, rivalry, jealousy as the sole leverage! Mr Hardie [sic] ought to know these most admirable traits of disposition are not the exclusive heritage and valued possessions of women. Granting the debatement that may be made, that women generally are defective in the ability of seeing and judging life broadly, therefore justly, in its multiform complexity, in view of that admission, we look to the artist as an effective teacher to aid in the adjustment of that deficiency.[2]

Elizabeth Chapman sees Hardy as a prime instance of what her essay calls 'The Disparagement of Women in Literature':

[In] Mr Thomas Hardy – we find a general view of woman which is the reverse of exhilarating to believers in her advancing development and brighter future. I do not think it would be very wide of the mark to describe the abstract being masquerading in Mr Hardy's work as woman as a compound three-parts animal and one-part fay; or, as one might put it, with *Jude the Obscure* fresh in one's memory, three-parts Arabella and one part Sue.[3]

This extract illustrates very clearly how often exception is taken, above all, to what is seen as an excessive emphasis on sexuality (most often translated as 'sensuality') in his women. Richard Le Gallienne, reviewing *Life's Little Ironies*, finds Hardy unduly coarse in this respect:

There is one fault in Mr Hardy's work that still jars in his *Life's Little Ironies*, but which he can hardly be expected to eradicate, as it is temperamental – a certain slight coarseness of touch in his lovemaking. There is always something of the sensualist about his heroes. When they are not cads they are apt to be prigs, and his women and men alike are always somewhat too obviously animal.[4]

Many of the more recent critics have followed one of two paths: either they have accused Hardy of entrapment in conventional views of women's character and sphere of action, or else they have remarked on his particular interest in and sympathy with women. It is perhaps not surprising that women predominate among the first group, and men among the second. Virginia Woolf anticipated the modern feminist criticisms in her comments on the basic conventionality of his concept of sexual difference:

However lovable and charming Bathsheba may be, still she is weak; however stubborn and ill-guided Henchard may be, still he is strong. This is fundamental; this is the core of Hardy's vision, and draws from the deepest sources of his nature. The woman is the weaker and the fleshlier, and she clings to the stronger and obscures his vision.

Kathleen Rogers, in the same vein, concludes from her study of Hardy's women that 'these novels show the tenacity of sexist assumptions even in so humane and enlightened a man as Hardy'. Patricia Stubbs, though she introduces the idea of specifically fictional conventions, makes what is basically a very similar point:

But though the overall tendency and meaning of his work is critical, even subversive in the depth of its alienation from orthodox values, Hardy's radicalism is often attenuated by the weight of received assumptions and literary forms. This is particularly the case in his portrayal of women, where his powerful moral iconoclasm is often in conflict with the use of essentially traditional character types, which either cannot comfortably accomodate his ideas or, alternatively, place a sharp limitation on his thinking.[5]

To set against this view of the insufficiently radical or pion-eering Hardy is a second strain of critical comment, in which he figures as a novelist notable for his peculiarly acute empa-thy with women. Geoffrey Thurley has written of Hardy's 'feminine vision of sexual relations', inherited, he claims, from the Brontës, while Irving Howe has remarked upon Hardy's 'gift for creeping intuitively into the emotional life of women' and his 'openness to the feminine principle'.[6]

More recent feminist critics have suggested that the 'women' in the works of a male writer find their significance primarily as a means to the representation of maleness. They can provide an image of what is missing, or lost, or repressed, in the acquisition of masculinity. This is most evident, as Elaine Showalter's persuasive reading has shown, in *The Mayor of Casterbridge*. Michael Henchard, in selling his wife and daughter to the sailor Newson, repeats in a startlingly blatant form the definitive patriarchal act of exchange. More than this, however, he attempts in that act to extirpate at a stroke all the elements in himself that might be called 'feminine', the bonds of love and family loyalty and nurturance that fall outside the sphere of commerce. He enters, instead, into the 'masculine' world of contracts, competition, and technology, all of which are displayed in the arena of the marketplace that dominates the central part of the novel. But each of the women of the novel, from Susan to Lucetta to the furmity-woman, comes back; this return of the repressed initiates what Showalter calls an 'un-manning', as Henchard loses progressively all the signs and symbols of his ascent to power and authority (as mayor, as employer, as father). The women of *The Mayor of Casterbridge* are at once the instruments for the probing of the significance of patriarchal power for the male, and 'idealised and melancholy projections of a repressed male self'.[7]

Rosalind Miles, rather similarly, concludes that Hardy's imagination was particularly fired by the eroticised appeal of the 'otherness' of an experience that eludes him:

Hardy *used* women, fictionally, because of their combination of weakness with strength, fragility with capacity for suffering, endurance with so much to endure. . . . A woman in Hardy's hands could be made to bear a weight of suffering whose inflictions transcend the personal and move through human to sublime; he never found the same true of a male character.[8]

This notion of a sublimity of suffering draws quite evidently upon the long-standing convention of the moral superiority of women – a convention which, according to Patricia Stubbs, focuses a double-bind pervasive in Hardy's presentation of women:

This is a contradiction which lies at the heart of the novel and of women's predicament in Hardy's society, for the very qualities which in contemporary belief made women morally superior, once internalized, as they are in Tess, also left them defenceless and vulnerable to sexual exploitation. Tess's whole history suggests that Hardy understands the crippling effect of such 'qualities' of character, but he never really rejects them.[9]

If, for some, Hardy's women are pre-eminently sublime victims, however, for others they are above all sexual destroyers: 'In his major novels Hardy ascribes much of the unhappiness of human life to the character of women, who more than men are "tools of the life force", and though destroyed are also the causes of men's destruction.'[10]

But from all the critical comments in this brief survey, there arise (all the more urgently in that they are not asked) a number of questions. What, first, is the relationship between the women that we are and the woman-as-sign that figures in the novels? How is it that 'received assumptions' and 'contemporary belief' – or, for that matter, a 'critical' and 'subversive' challenge to 'orthodox moral values' – enter into works of fiction? And – a related question – what is the status for his fiction of Hardy's personal views on such issues as the double standard, or the laws of divorce? What, more generally, can it mean for a male writer to represent 'women' in a novel? I cannot hope here to give full attention or satisfactory answers to these problems, but they will provide the starting-point for a brief outline of the critical presuppositions from which my analysis of Hardy's fiction proceeds.

That analysis will be largely concerned with the relation of Hardy's fiction to contemporary ideologies of sexual difference and of the nature of woman, and it is important, therefore, to indicate briefly in what sense the term 'ideology' is used. It is to be understood, throughout this book, neither in the liberal sense of a body of more or less consciously held, overtly political beliefs, nor in the 'vulgar' marxist sense of 'false consciousness', illusion at the level of ideas, either deliberately fostered and manipulated by certain individuals, groups, or classes with the conscious motivation of self- or class-interest, or as 'a spontaneous precipitate of one's position within the class-structure', in Eagleton's phrase. Rather, 'ideology' will be used in the sense made familiar by Althusser and some subsequent marxist theorists: that is, as a complex system of representations by which people are inserted as individual subjects into the social formation.[11] Its role – which is not to say that is governed by any intention – is to offer a false resolution of real social contradictions by repressing the questions that challenge its limits and transposing, displacing, or eliding the felt contradictions of lived experience in a way that will permit of an apparent resolution. It is not illusory, for it is the condition of the way in which people experience their relation to the social relations of production; nor does it consist of a set of ideas. While ideology is real, then, in that it is compounded of lived experience, it is simultaneously 'false', in that it obscures the nature of that experience, by representing as obvious and natural what is partial, factitious, and ineluctably social. That is not to say that it 'expresses' or 'embodies' class-interest, nor does it stand in any direct or spontaneous relation to modes or relations of production. Eagleton has argued that ideology 'encodes the *class-struggle*';[12] in my use of the term, however, it will also encode other relations of power and dominance, and principally that of male dominance. But ideology is not a homogeneous and overarching unity which is somehow *imposed* upon a passive or an acquiescent working class, or female sex. Such categories are themselves constituted in ideology. There is, at any historical moment and in any domain of discourse, at least the possibility of a number of ideologies that may stand in contradiction or even conflict with one another, and it is in the confrontation and interrogation of these contradictions within and between ideologies that there inheres the possibility of change, as the primacy of the unified subject is unsettled by their evident partiality.

How, then, do these ideologies bear upon the literary text? The text does not 'express' ideology; rather, it produces, re-produces and transforms elements of ideology into its own literary effects. The 'history' of the text is not a reflection or a doubling of real history, but it represents an ideologically constituted experience of real history. In this will consist the ideological project of the work (which may or may not have some correspondence with the views and intentions of its writer). The classic, readable, realist text has as its project to effect an imaginary resolution of actual (but displaced) social contradictions. A hierarchy of discourses establishes a dominant perspective, and it is in the process of identification with that 'point of view' that the reader is called upon to become an ideological subject and to experience that resolution. But that does not mean that the text's project will be simply or uniformly fulfilled. There may emerge contradictions which cannot be reconciled, and the reader may be called upon to identify with conflicting perspectives that cannot be rendered coherent.

It is here that the importance of form, of genre and of narrative voice, comes into play. The writer does not make a free choice among 'empty' genres. While genre does not in itself determine that a text must be read in a certain way, it brings with it a history of reading, a set of conventions and of specifically aesthetic ideologies. The expectations engendered by the genre can enter into a relation of tension and opposition with the author's sense of an intention and, more significantly, with the project of the text, as Catherine Belsey has noted:

> There may be a direct contradiction between the project and the formal constraints, and in the transgression thus created it is possible to locate an important object of the critical quest. . . . The unconscious of the work (*not*, it must be noted, of the author) is constructed in the moment of its entry into literary form, in the gap between the ideological project and the specifically literary form.[13]

The formal coherence of the genre may be disrupted, ironised, or subverted by elements that cannot be contained within the limits of its ideology; in the case of Hardy, this can be seen most clearly in the anxieties and ambiguities of his relation to the pastoral mode.[14] In *Under the Greenwood Tree*, there is a relatively straightforward (if strained and uneasy) use of the pastoral. Progressively, however, the pastoral is thrown into question as other genres and modes of writing enter more deeply into the fiction. The pastoral is disrupted by tragedy, and the tragedy subverted by elements of realism that cannot be stabilised within its mythical perspective. With *Tess of the d'Urbervilles* and *Jude the Obscure*, realism in turn is pushed against its limits by the disintegration of the cohering power of character and by the radical dissonances of narrative voice and point of view. The disjunction of such varied modes resists the organisation into a hierarchy of discourses that would endorse a particular ideological position. Hardy was experimental as a novelist, not only with genres and modes of narration, but also with the ways in which they could be made to confront and play off against one another. They enter into a relation of interrogation that refuses not only closure, but also enclosure by the authority of a 'placing' discourse. I shall go on to argue, in the course of this book, that the formal dislocations and discontinuities are at their sharpest and most unsettling in the depiction of sexual and marital relationships, and that the radicalism of Hardy's representation of women resides, not in their 'complexity', their 'realism' or their 'challenge to convention', but in their resistance to reduction to a single and uniform ideological position. The experimentalism of Hardy's novels would make it all too easy to see him as a lonely pioneer in the field of fiction, or, equally, to assimilate him into a distinguished company of (male) 'major' writers who turned to the exploration of women's experience at this time. His novels display their textuality in an unusually overt fashion, in their quotations, allusions and echoes of the traditions of 'fine writing', and in what has been called their thematic obsession with literary culture.[15] The open dialogues in which his texts engage (with Arnold, Shelley, and Wordsworth, among others), and the patient transcribing of extracts into his Notebooks, to some degree demonstrate Hardy's anxious and displaced relation to his own sense of a predominantly metropolitan and intellectual literary culture (and audience). But for all that, he did not altogether serve this distinction between 'major' and 'minor' fiction, and was always aware of the developments in fiction during the period of his own writing career. Although Hardy was cautious in his public comments on the New Fiction, it nevertheless proved an enabling and fruitful development for him as a novelist, in both its formal experimentation and its increasingly explicit concern with sexual and marital themes.

But if Hardy's radicalism is to be read correctly, it must be situated historically: that is, not in a context of simple contemporaneity, but in relation to the shifts and mutations of contemporary ideologies which the fiction itself produces and transforms. The 'sexuality', the 'women', the 'marriage' and the 'non-marriage' which it represents are all constituted in an ideology of sexual difference that was transformed, at this period, by the impact of biologistic interpretations of Darwinism (itself, of course, constituted within a 'science' that was not the objective and incontrovertible discourse it proclaimed itself to be). This book is an attempt to examine Hardy's fiction, not as the product of personal temperament or sensibility, nor in the light of his own sexual pathology, his unfortunate marital history, and his personal views concerning women, or sex, or marriage and divorce, but in the historical situation that was a vital determination of his radicalism.

NOTES

1 See respectively, Charles G. Harper, *Revolted Woman: Past, Present, and to Come* (London, 1894), p. 19; Edmund Gosse, 'The Tyranny of the Novel,' *National Review*, 19 (1892), 163–75, rpt. in *Questions at Issue* (London, 1893), p. 14; and Clementina Black, rev. of *Tess of the d'Urbervilles*, *Illustrated London News*, 9 January 1892, p. 50.

2 'E. V. Ingram' [Caradoc Granhim], 'Art Literature,' *Westminster Review*, 142 (1892), 399–400.

3 Elizabeth R. Chapman, *Marriage Questions in Modern Fiction, and Other Essays on Kindred Subjects* (London, 1897), p. 80.

4 Richard Le Gallienne, *Retrospective Reviews. A Literary Log II 1893–1895* (London, 1896), pp. 80–3.

5 See, respectively, Virginia Woolf, 'Thomas Hardy's Novels,' *Times Literary Supplement*, 19 January 1928, p. 33; Kathleen Rogers, 'Women in Thomas Hardy,' *Centennial Review*, 19 (1975), 257; and Patricia Stubbs, *Women and Fiction: Feminism and the Novel 1880–1920* (Brighton, 1979), p. 81.

6 Geoffrey Thurley, *The Psychology of Hardy's Novels: The Nervous and the Statuesque* (St. Lucia, Queensland, 1975), p. 23; Irving Howe, *Thomas Hardy* (London, 1968), p. 109.

7 Elaine Showalter, 'Towards a Feminist Poetics,' in *Women Writing and*

Writing about Women, ed. Mary Jacobus (London, 1979), p. 27. See also her 'The Unmanning of the Mayor of Casterbridge,' in *Critical Approaches to the Fiction of Thomas Hardy*, ed. Dale Kramer (London, 1979), pp. 99–115.

8 Rosalind Miles, 'The Women of Wessex,' in *The Novels of Thomas Hardy*, ed. Anne Smith (London, 1979), pp. 38–9.

9 Stubbs, *Women and Fiction*, pp. 82–3.

10 Clarice Short, 'In Defense of *Ethelberta*,' *Nineteenth-Century Fiction*, 13 (1958), 50.

11 See, particularly, Louis Althusser, 'Ideology and Ideological State Apparatuses,' in *Lenin and Philosophy and Other Essays*, trans. Ben Brewster (London, 1970), pp. 121–73; Pierre Macherey, *A Theory of Literary Production*, trans. Geoffrey Wall (London, 1978); Terry Eagleton, *Criticism and Ideology: A Study in Marxist Literary Theory* (London, 1976); and Steve Burniston and Chris Weedon, 'Ideology, Subjectivity and the Artistic Text,' in *Working Papers in Cultural Studies*, 10 (1977), rpt. as *On Ideology*, Centre for Contemporary Cultural Studies (London, 1978), pp. 199–229.

12 Terry Eagleton, rev. of *Truth and Ideology*, by Hans Barth, *Notes and Queries*, NS 25 (1978), 362.

13 Catherine Belsey, *Critical Practice*, New Accents (London, 1980), pp. 107–8.

14 Cf. Eagleton, *Criticism and Ideology*, pp. 94–5.

15 Eagleton, *Criticism and Ideology*, p. 131.

CHAPTER 1

Sexual Ideology and the 'Nature' of Woman, 1880–1900

The sexual ideology and practices of the English bourgeoisie in the second half of the nineteenth century have been widely documented and examined by twentieth-century sociologists and historians.[1] They have shown basic agreement about certain features: the polarisation of women into the chaste and the depraved, the virgin and the whore; the virginity ethic, manifested alike in the fierceness with which 'innocence' was protected in the young and adult woman, and in the 'defloration mania' which dominated English brothels in the 1880s, occasioning widespread child prostitution and a flourishing trade in the surgical reconstruction of the hymen;[2] the double standard; the interdependence of monogamous marriage and the prevalence of prostitution. The general picture emerges of a sexuality at once furtive and dismal, in which wives submit pleasurelessly to the act of procreation in darkened rooms, while men seek sexual gratification in fantasy and with prostitutes:

> It was a morality which fostered prurience and hypocrisy. From the stronghold of the chaste, monogamous family it enabled the individual to fulminate against all vicious living while clandestinely he sowed his wild oats. It encouraged wives to become sexual ninnies while their husbands contracted venereal disease. It hounded "fallen" women to become whores in the name of God.[3]

In such a view, sexuality is not merely unspoken, but literally unspeakable; prudery, hypocrisy, and pruriently excessive linguistic delicacy have repeatedly been identified as the hallmarks of Victorian debate on the issues of sex and marriage, and fiction has been frequently advanced in evidence of such an interpretation.[4]

And yet, during the later part of the century, there was an enormous growth in the amount of public discussion concerning these supposedly taboo subjects: the debate over the

Matrimonial Causes Act and the subsequent detailed reporting
of divorce cases; the Campaign for the Repeal of the Contagious
Diseases Acts; the issue of child prostitution, Stead's 'Maiden
Tribute' articles, and the raising of the age of consent; the
'marriage question' and the problem of 'surplus' women; the
Wilde trial and the free union fiction of the 1880s and 1890s – in
all these instances, the debate was open and prolonged, in
newspapers, essays and fiction, in the courts and the Houses of
Parliament, in public meetings and organisations. By the end of
the century, the period is notable not so much for the avoidance
of such subjects, as for the way in which private sexual
experience comes to be publicly spoken. Michel Foucault has
characterised 'Walter', the unidentified pseudonymous author
of *My Secret Life*, as the Victorian *par excellence*, compulsively
doubling his sexual life through narration.[5] It is important,
however, to notice that this 'speaking' of sexuality takes
particular, well-defined forms: this period represents the decisive shift of sexuality from the area of moral discourse to that of
the scientific, a shift which has brought sexuality in the
twentieth century under the dominance of the psychoanalytic.
A growing medicalisation of sexuality interacted with the
far-reaching influence of Darwin's accounts of evolution and its
agents to make of science an instrument of social intervention
which apparently offered its own guarantees of success. The
seeming dispassionate incontrovertibility of scientific law
afforded a deceptively simple means of social progress: it would
suffice to act in harmony with that which was biologically
ordained. There emerged with increasing prominence an ideology of the 'natural' whose workings provide an ironic contrast
to the naive optimism of such contemporary apostrophes to
science as this by Ellis Ethelmer:

> Source of the Light that cheers this later day,
> Science calm moves to spread her sovereign sway;
> Research and Reason, ranged on either hand,
> Proclaim her message to each waiting land;[6]

The transfer from biological law and organisation to social,
which seems so obviously metaphorical, is sometimes made
with a directness so explicit as to make 'organicism' a barely
adequate characterisation:

As, however, we cannot always calculate, before deciding on any course of action, what will be the best for the community, in general it is safest to be guided by our healthy natural instincts, and to do the work we wish to do. . . . Our instincts have been given us by Nature, and Nature always knows what is best for us. There are cases of course, in which these instincts have been perverted by the influence of civilisation. These must be corrected by education; and here science comes in.[7]

The emergence of the medicalisation of sexuality can be traced back to the eighteenth century, and seems to have begun with the presentation of masturbation as a disease, or at the least, a symptom. The earliest known work to connect masturbation and organic disease, *Onania: or, the Heinous Sin of Self-Pollution, And all its Frightful Consequences, in Both Sexes consider'd, &c* (1710?) makes no attempt at a medical account of the connection, but rather, as its title indicates, treats disease as a kind of secular equivalent of punishment for sin.[8] Later works, such as Samuel Tissot's *L'onanisme* (1760), try to trace the connection in somewhat random pseudo-scientific ways. By the first half of the nineteenth century, the link between sexuality and medicine has been firmly established, and manifests itself in various ways. It reinforces, for example, the institutionalising of childbirth, with the female midwife giving way to the male technician, the obstetrician, and the vast battery of instruments available to the newly established specialist.[9] The medical establishment came to combine the moral authority of the church with the apparent irrefutability of the scientist. A corresponding sexualisation of medical practice sometimes accompanied this medicalisation of sexuality: the dangers inherent in intimately physical contact between male specialist and female patient exercised some authorities; one medical textbook solemnly warns of the corrupting effect of internal examination:

> I have, more than once, seen young unmarried women, of the middle-classes of society, reduced, by the constant use of the speculum, to the mental and moral condition of prostitutes; seeking to give themselves the same indulgence by the practice of solitary vice; and asking every medical practitioner, under whose care they fell, to institute an examination of the sexual organs.[10]

A further manifestation of this medicalisation is the emergence of a whole technology of sexuality: anti-masturbation devices for males, such as cages lined with spikes or locked by parents, contraceptive devices for women like the Vertical and Reverse Current Vaginal Tube or the Irrigator, and the number of patent cures available to treat all manner of sexual problems.[11]

Science could bring ostensibly neutral and dispassionate observation to bear on the vexed issues of the female 'nature' and role; it is no coincidence that in doing so it frequently confirmed not only the long-standing diagnosis of irrationality, pettiness, vanity and inconsequentiality, but also the necessity of confining women to their traditional spheres of activity, home and family. The particular ideological strength of medical expertise was that it was able effortlessly to turn the normative into the rigidly prescriptive; the classic instance is Acton's often cited assertion, in 1862, of female sexual anaesthesia;

> . . . there can be no doubt that sexual feeling in the female is in abeyance . . . and even if roused (which in many instances it never can be) is very moderate compared with that of the male. . . . The best mothers, wives, and managers of households, know little or nothing of sexual indulgences. Love of home, children, and domestic duties, are the only passions they feel.
>
> As a general rule, a modest woman seldom desires any sexual gratification for herself. She submits to her husband, but only to please him; and, but for the desire of maternity, would far rather be relieved from his attentions.[12]

The normative generalisations ('in many instances', 'as a general rule') shade over into explicitly moral norms ('the best mothers', 'a modest woman'). It is worth noting that, although Acton's works on genital and venereal disease and on prostitution were long considered authoritative and were still being reprinted in the 1890s, there was at no stage unanimity among the medical establishment on this issue; a reviewer of Acton's works called attention to his account of female sexuality as

> 'unphysiological in the first place, and, moreover, experience proves the contrary; for, putting aside . . . the case of courtezans whose desires are a trade, there can be no doubt that both in the human subject and in the lower animals the female *does* participate fully in the sexual passion.'[13]

Indeed, Acton himself seems to have been half aware that there was something wrong with this account, for the paragraph I have quoted concludes soothingly: 'No nervous or feeble young man need, therefore, be deterred from marriage by any exaggerated notion of the duties required from him. The married woman has no wish to be treated on the footing of a mistress.' This version of woman's insensibility is quite evidently constructed by a male writer to allay the fears of a male readership – fears of sexual inadequacy, and of immoderate demands on the part of the woman, at least if she be of the 'mistress' variety. Underlying these fears is the sense of female insatiability as the obverse of female unresponsiveness, in the characteristically Victorian polarisation of women into Virgin and Whore, Lily and Rose, wife and mistress.

A similarly transparent ideological version of female sexuality can be seen in the other *locus classicus* of pre-Darwinian sexology, an anonymous article on prostitution in 1850. The writer argues for a more humane treatment and view of prostitutes, on the grounds that their very 'nature' shows them to be victims rather than debauched:

> In men, in general, the sexual desire is inherent and spontaneous, and belongs to the condition of puberty. In the other sex, the desire is dormant, if not non-existent, till excited; always till excited by undue familiarities; almost always till excited by actual intercourse. . . . Women whose position and education have protected them from exciting causes, constantly pass through life without ever being cognizant of the promptings of the senses. Happy for them that it is so! We do not mean to say that uneasiness may not be felt – that health may not sometimes suffer; but there is no consciousness of the cause.[14]

The writer at once denies and concedes the existence of sexual desire in women: it is absent, but it can cause 'uneasiness' and deterioration of the health. It is evidently not desire that does not exist, but recognition or acceptance of it, 'consciousness of the cause'. After this initial confusion, he is able to assert that there is no struggle for virtue in women: modesty, decency, chastity, are *inherent* female characteristics.[15] The ideal of innocence – protected by 'position and education', the attributes pre-eminently of the bourgeois woman – reveals itself as an ideal of ignorance and repression.

Darwinism, with the *Origin of Species* (1859), but more particularly with *The Descent of Man* (1871), imparted a new momentum to biologically deterministic views of the female 'nature'. Darwin's account of sexual selection worked from the basis of a fixed polarity of male and female characteristics, at the level of physiology (the controversial question, for example, of absolute and relative difference of brain weight) and, by an unargued extension, at the level of mental characteristics:

> It is generally admitted that with woman the powers of intuition, of rapid perception, and perhaps of imitation, are more strongly marked than in man; but some, at least, of these faculties are characteristic of the lower races, and therefore of a past and lower state of civilisation.[16]

The use of phrases such as 'generally admitted' and 'perhaps', the blurring of social and biological causation implicit in the 'therefore', the use of unsupported empirical observation, and, elsewhere, of simple analogy between bodily and mental structures, are all typical of Darwin's method of argument in this account of mental sexual differences.[17]

Darwinism came fairly rapidly to dominate Victorian biology, but in doing so it posed certain problems for contemporary social theory and sociology. Sociologists from Spencer and Comte worked with biological models of social organisation clearly in mind, but laid a greater stress on environmental factors, or acquired characteristics, than the Darwinian emphasis on inherited characteristics would support. Thereafter, the newly dominant scientificism established a new ultimate authority, the ratification of the social *status quo* by the appeal to 'objective' and 'universal' physiological laws. The appeal to science shifts the site of the disabilities of women from history to nature, and in doing so, it undercuts the struggle of women against their oppression. It became necessary, in order to substantiate this appeal to scientific 'law', to supply the link, untheorised in Darwin, between physiological and psychological organisation. Weismann's influential notion of the 'germ-plasm', first available in English in 1882, was one attempt to do so, but it did not identify the locus of the differentiation of male and female mind and temperament. It distinguished, rather, between the unvarying transmissible characteristics of the 'germ-plasm' and the physiologically individualised 'soma', and this distinction was to lend weight to the claims of hereditarian eugenists that reforms in welfare and social environment could not improve the nation's breeding-stock. Geddes and Thomson ascribed maleness and femaleness to a differentiation of cell-metabolism, between the *'katabolic'* (energy-dispersing) sperm and the *'anabolic'* (energy-con-serving) ovum, a difference which exercised a determining force over the development of body and mind.[18] Alternatively, the periodicity of the female physiological processes of men-struation, pregnancy and lactation could act as the site of differentiation; Frederic Harrison, in an address on the anniversary of the death of Comte, cites menstruation as the reason for the disqualification of women from participation in some aspects of public life:

> But there is one feature in the feminine organisation which, for industrial and political purposes, is more important than all. It is subject to functional interruption absolutely incompatible with the highest forms of continuous pressure. . . .
>
> Supposing all other forces equal, it is just the five per cent. of periodical unfitness which makes the whole difference between the working capacity of the sexes.[19]

This urge to find a biological origin and function for the difference between the sexes and for their differing social roles can be seen in works which attempt an ambitious synthesis of physiology, psychology and sociology, such as Ferrerro's *The Problem of Woman from a Bio-Sociological Point of View* (Turin, 1893) or Lombroso and Ferrerro's *La donna delinquente, la prostituta, e la donna normale* (1893). The best-known English exponent is Havelock Ellis, whose organicist understanding of the connection between biological laws and social institutions finds lyrical expression in the invocation to science in the introduction to *The New Spirit* (1890):

> We know that wherever science goes the purifying breath of spring has passed and all things are re-created. . . . We know at last that it must be among our chief ethical rules to see that we build the lofty structure of human society on the sure and simple foundations of man's organism.[20]

When he comes, in *Man and Woman* (1894), to attempt a close analysis of the physiological foundations of that 'lofty struc-ture', he devotes a chapter to the different mental capacities of men and women. His conclusions are predictable – women are more diligent but less rational, quicker and more precocious, but much given to impulse and vanity. His method, however, is interesting – an extraordinary farrago of anthropological, sociological and physiological data. A symptomatic example is account, based on *La donna delinquente*, of the female tendency to deceitfulness: its causes include menstruation, which is disgusting and so obliges women to learn to conceal it, and the duties of maternity, since much of the education of the young consists in skilful lying.[21]

Some feminists, accepting the principle of inherent sexual differentiation, argued a different version of evolution (all too often echoing Darwin's cavalier use of 'fact' and evidence, however). Eliza Burt Gamble reviews Darwin's evidence and accepts unchallenged only his statement that pairing arouses distate in females; so she stresses the active role of females in the process of sexual selection in these terms: 'The female made the male beautiful that she might endure his caressess [sic].'[22] She concludes, in Lamarckian rather than Darwinian vein, that 'the diseases and physical disabilities of women' – presumably including menstruation – 'are due to the overstimulation of the animal instincts in her male mate' (p. 45). Ellis Ethelmer puts the same view more succinctly:

> Action repeated tends to rhythmic course,
> And thus the mischief, due at first to force,
> Brought cumulative sequence to the race,
> Till habit bred hereditary trace;[23]

Edward Carpenter, too, argued that 'There is little doubt that menstruation, as it occurs today in the vast majority of cases, is somehow pathological and out of the order of nature.'[24]

The attempt to isolate biologically determined and innately differing male and female natures gave a spurious scientific underpinning to the double standard of sexual morality. Clement Scott, writing in 1894, can argue that men are 'born animals' and women 'angels', so that it is in effect only 'natural' for men to indulge their sexual appetites and, hence, perverse – 'unnatural' – for women to act in the same way.[25] By the end of the century, defenders of the double standard (heavily under attack from feminists of various kinds) were justifying it by the appeal to the laws of biology rather than the laws of property and inheritance which had figured prominently in, for example, debates over the grounds for divorce in the Matrimonial Causes Act of 1857.[26]

The Darwinistic evolutionary perspective is the impulse behind the widespread and growing concern, towards the end of the century, with eugenics. The choice of a sexual partner, when biological inheritance is all and environment nothing, becomes a matter, not of personal emotion, but of public concern, for upon it depends the continuation and evolutionary progress of 'the race'. Eugenics seemed to offer a truly scientific method of social reform – and (an added advantage for reformists) one which posed no threat to existing institutions and practices; it held out the hope of simply breeding out mental and physical handicap, and such socially undesirable 'strains' as the criminal, the prostitute, even the idle and vicious. Existing kinds of social reform, on the other hand, could be seen as affording unnatural protection to inferior stock which would otherwise die out. Despite the progressive tinge it gained from its alliance with some sections of the contraceptive movement against religious orthodoxy, the reactionary nature of the eugenics movement is clear. It is rooted in the moral and political economy of Malthusianism, a doctrine whose class-interest is self-evident; some early propagandists for contraception argued that it could supplement or even replace trades unions by restricting the available supply of labour and so forcing up wages. Conversely, some eugenists argued for tax relief as an incentive for middle-class (and biologically superior) couples to breed.[27] Nevertheless, for some, the eugenics movement appeared compatible with certain kinds of socialism. Edward Aveling, for example, draws a distinction between 'The poor who are thus from their own fault', and 'earnest workers' whose efforts to limit their family size are 'hindered . . . by Conservatives and Christians'. For him, any system of state aid to the poor is a misplaced endeavour:

> But, one dreads whether there may not be to the end some few, that may in time come to be regarded as monsters, who finding they can obtain the necessities of life . . . with scarcely any exertion on their own behalf, will prefer, as to-day millions and millions prefer to remain stupid and vicious, and therefore poor. The whole of our criminal classes illustrate on an awful scale to-day that which I mean.[28]

'Stupid and vicious, and *therefore* poor': the phrase encapsulates a widespread argument of the eugenists – an argument which contains nothing of socialism – that British society of the time offered so much scope for social mobility that a stubborn refusal to rise to fame, fortune, or at least respectability could be ascribed only to the vices of indolence and stupidity. In effect, this is to displace the whole class-system of the period from economics to nature; it is no more than a biological justification for capitalism.

And yet, incongruously enough, it is an argument employed by Karl Pearson in support of a call for socialism:

> I believe in the efficiency of society largely depending on the selection of better stocks, the removal or destruction of the less fit stocks. . . . Now my grave difficulty about Neo-Malthusianism is this: it tends to act in the better, in the physically or mentally fitter, ranks of society among the educated and thrifty of the middle and working classes. . . . While limiting the population we must, at the same time, ensure that the worst stock is the stock which is first and foremost limited. . . . I do not see how, without a strong Socialistic State, it will be possible.[29]

Elsewhere, he provides a clue as the nature of those 'less fit stocks' that are to be removed or destroyed:

> Shall those who are diseased, shall those who are nighest to the brute, have the right to reproduce their like? Shall the reckless, the idle, be they poor or wealthy, those who follow mere instinct without reason, be the parents of future generations? Shall the consumptive father not be socially branded when he hands down misery to his offspring, and inefficient citizens to the state?[30]

This 'branding', at first sight so obviously metaphorical, takes on a more sinister air when compared to the suggestion of Lady Cook (better known as Tennessee Claflin) that libertines and syphilitics should be branded or tattooed as a warning sign to innocent women.[31]

Such 'socialism' was double oppressive to women, placing a duty to breed on some women, and a duty not to on others, all on criteria of 'fitness' which are at best only a transparent disguise for the socio-economic characteristics of the bourgeoisie. Further, the preoccupation with biological inheritance and transmission tended also towards the containment of sexuality, and especially though not exclusively of female sexuality, within the area of procreation. This is manifested in the legislation of 1885 which criminalised even private sexual acts between adult males; in the subsequent hysteria of the Wilde trial; and in the reinforcement of opposition in some members of the medical establishment to contraception and abortion, insofar as they involved any degree of choice for women. Even compulsory sterilisation for the 'unfit' was sometimes seen as justified.[32] An interventionist approach to fertility, whether legally or medically effected, could go no further.

Eugenics appealed, nevertheless, to many feminists, offering as it seemed a vital new channel for that 'influence' which women had long been supposed to exercise, however deviously or indirectly, over public events. The 'New Woman' fiction of the 1880s and 1890s is often concerned with the new mission of women, the moral reform of society by race-improvement. This eugenic mission promises a consoling fantasy of power without an unsettling challenge to the existing separation of male and female spheres of influence, in which the woman is consigned exclusively to marriage and motherhood. Such a view could only subvert, and not confront, the sexual double standard. Women had already been held responsible for the continuing existence of the double standard – by William Logan, for example:

> And *how* is the vice of unchastity confined within boundaries so rigid in the case of the female sex? . . . it is because *even an unchaste man will marry none but a chaste woman.* . . . Let women in England look upon a proposal of marriage from a profligate man as men in England would regard a proposal of marriage with a Haymarket outcast . . . and unchastity in men will become as rare as it is in women.[33]

Such exhortations are moral; woman's mission to overthrow the double standard becomes in the last twenty years of the century almost a crusade, but the ground has again shifted from the moral to the scientific. If the eugenic work of race-progress by the careful choice of a marriage partner is taken seriously, then the dangers of unregulated, promiscuous breeding and of venereal disease extend beyond personal tragedy to generalised social threat. This sense of moral mission, combined with the simplistic, pre-genetic notion of transmission of characteristics (physical, psychological, moral, even economic, all jumbled together) on which eugenic theories were based, led many contemporary feminists to support the idea of state control of, or intervention in, fertility.

In all this discussion, women became central; but the effect of the emphasis on motherhood, which seems at times to have taken on all the reverence of a religious cult, was to make synonymous women and ('fit') mothers, and hence to confirm their traditional roles. Women's rights were to be 'balanced' by duties, and both were to be discovered by careful attention to physiology and to evolutionary possibilities. Pearson again puts the argument:

> We have first to settle what is the physical capacity of woman, what would be the effect of her emancipation on her function of race-reproduction, before we can talk about her "rights", which are, after all, only a vague description of what may be the fittest position for her, the sphere of her maximum usefulness in the developed society of the future. . . . Feminists must show that the emancipation will tend not only to increase the stability of society and the general happiness of mankind, but will favour the physique and health of both sexes.[34]

The spectre of 'degeneration' – a concept given particular prominence in and after Max Nordau's *Degeneration* (translated in 1895) – was an effective threat to hold over feminists who could not predict with 'scientific' certainty the effects of higher education or the vote upon the physiology of future generations. C. G. Harper (who singles out Hardy for the justice of his portraits of women) claims that

> [N]ature, which never contemplated the production of a learned or a muscular woman, will be revenged upon her offspring, and the New Woman, if a mother at all, will be the mother of a New Man, as different, indeed, from the present race as possible, but *how* different the clamorous females of today cannot suspect . . . There is the prospect of peopling the world with stunted and hydrocephalic children.[35]

This kind of sociobiology, with its direct and unmediated connection between zoology and politics, dominated the sexual ideology of the last two decades of the nineteenth century.[36]

The attitudes of feminists to fertility and to contraception varied. Some leading suffragists, such as Millicent Garrett Fawcett, seem to have been unwilling to confront the issue, for fear of jeopardising such widespread acceptance as their aims of political and professional reforms had achieved. Those who discussed it publicly took a variety of positions, from the (temporary) radicalism of Annie Besant to the eccentric position of Frances Swiney, who held that semen was poisonous and accordingly advocated the spacing out of intercourse at two year intervals.[37] Apart from the support for contraception as a method of social engineering, among the Fabians or the

eugenists like Jane Hume Clapperton,[38] some feminists, like
Besant, supported it for libertarian reasons. Feminist opposition to contraception was based on a variety of grounds. Some
felt that it deprived women of their significant, active role in the
sexual relationship, reducing them to the passive objects of
male lust; Elizabeth Blackwell supported Francis Newman in
this line in their pamphlet *The Corruption Now Called Neo-
Malthusianism* (1889). Josephine Butler and other 'Social Purity'
campaigners sometimes combined a demand for male chastity
with a more progressive feminist demand for a woman's right
to defend herself against infection with venereal disease, selfish
or excessive sexual demands, and over-frequent pregnancies.
The medical establishment showed considerable reluctance to
involve itself in recommending, explaining or providing
methods of contraception or abortion; the first English doctor
to do so publicly was Dr H. A. Allbutt, whose manual *The
Wife's Handbook* (1885) eventually led to his being struck off the
Register in 1887. Consequently, they remained largely a para-
medical phenomenon, and as a result often placed women at the
mercy of false information, quacks, and (in the case of abortifacients) blackmailers or legal prosecution. This places in a rather
more rational light the argument, in Carpenter and elsewhere,
that there was a possible danger to women's health in the use of
artificial methods of fertility control, usually on the grounds of
the supposed absorptive ability of the female cells; Frances
Newman quotes Blackwell to the effect that 'Her internal
structure fights against the success of unnatural arts; her tissues
imbibe any poisonous drug, and resent the absence of what is
natural.'[39] The anti-contraception writer Ussher provides
medical 'evidence' from several sources that artificial birth
control will cause hysteria, sterility and still-births. In the light
of such arguments, temperance and self-control were often
recommended, as by Ellis Ethelmer.[40] More helpfully, the use
of the 'safe' period was sometimes advised; Carpenter describes
it as natural and practicable, if not certain.[41] In fact, it was an even
more unreliable method than it is now, since it was generally
thought that conception was most likely to occur immediately
before or after the menstrual period.[42] Other 'natural' methods
delegated to men the responsibility for preventing conception.
Withdrawal seems to have been acceptable even to opponents

of artificial methods, and was practised by W. T. Stead, a
leading purity campaigner.[43] The Oneida Colony's method,
coitus reservatus, was publicised in England by Alice B. Stockham's *Karezza: Ethics of Marriage* (1896) and by the fiction and
essays of George Noyes Miller, who commends it thus:

> It is not only intrinsically pure and innocent, but in teaching self-control and
> true temperance, without asceticism, it powerfully reacts for good on the
> whole character. It is not a merely nugatory device but a splendid stimulus
> to spirituality.[44]

It is, he claims, good for the physical health of both participants:
the woman is spared the undue strains of repeated pregnancies,
and the man gains an increase in 'magnetic, mental and spiritual
force' from the reabsorption of the semen into his blood.[45]
There is also evidence that some women were prepared to take
sole control over their own fertility; several contemporary
advertisements for the less cumbersome female methods of
contraception, pessaries and diaphragm, stressed as a selling
point the fact that they could be used without the husband's
knowledge.

The increased availability and reliability of contraception
gave women a greater chance than before of controlling the
formidable biological *donnée* of their reproductive potential. At
the same time, however, the mutations of sexual ideology
during the last thirty years of the nineteenth century are such
that the authority of Christian morality, which at once provokes and leaves room for opposition on both individualist and
collectivist grounds, gives way to the apparently universal and
incontrovertible authority of biological law. Evolution effec-
tively replaces God as origin and goal of moral behaviour, and
merges together the moral and the 'natural'. Opposition, in this
case, is disarmed or underestimated by the appeal to the 'nature'
of women, fixed by an evolutionary process which defers
possibilities of change into an unforeseeable, far-distant future.
The eugenic movement recuperated some of the energy of the
feminist protest into a long-term strategy for change that was
only another version of the doctrine of female influence exercised through maternal function which had informed the
earlier, predominantly moral ideology of sexual roles. The
sexual ideology of the time cannot be adequately described or
explained by what Foucault calls '*l'hypothèse répressive*';[46] there is

no pre-existing given, 'the sexuality of women', which is suppressed or diverted by an external force. Rather, sexuality is constructed through the identification of female reproductive potentialities and the 'nature' of woman, calling on the woman to subject her body to surveillance and intervention, and making of the female body itself at once the site and the determinant of women's social disabilities.

Of course such changes in sexual ideologies cannot be simply transferred by analogy or homology to an account of female characters in fiction of the same period. Nevertheless, the very fact that female sexuality was so much a matter for discussion, speculation and research, and the accompanying questioning of marriage, would have been enough to make unselfconscious writing involving these subjects almost impossible. The choice of a marriage partner, long a staple element of plot, takes on new resonances. For Hardy, it will continue to be a significant structure, but its power as an organising principle of coherence is evidently unsettled. The centrality of female characters in Hardy's novels brings into prominence the problematic question of the female nature, and of its otherness of the male writer, and these pose new problems for the handling of form and narrative voice. I propose now to look at the productive experimentalism and at the tense and ambivalent writing which mark the development of Hardy's fiction in the period.

NOTES

1 See for instance, J. A. and Olive Banks, *Feminism and Family Planning in Victorian England*, Studies in Sociology (Liverpôol, 1964); Constance Rover, *Love, Morals and the Feminists* (London, 1970); Ronald Pearsall, *The Worm in the Bud: the World of Victorian Sexuality* (London, 1969).

2 Fernando Henriques, *Modern Sexuality*, Vol. III of *Prostitution and Society* (London, 1968), pp. 279–83; cf. Iwan Bloch, *A History of English Sexual Morals*, trans. W. H. Forstern (London, 1936), pp. 188–91.

3 Henriques, *Modern Sexuality*, p. 231.

4 E.g. Steven Marcus, *The Other Victorians: A Study of Sexuality and Pornography in Mid-Nineteenth Century England* (London, 1966); Eric Trudgill, *Madonnas and Magdalens: the Origins and Development of Victorian Sexual Attitudes* (London, 1976).

5 Michel Foucault, *La volonté de savoir*, Vol. I of *Histoire de la sexualité* (Paris, 1976), pp. 31–2.

6 'Ellis Ethelmer' [Elizabeth Wolstenholme-Elmy], *Woman Free* (London, 1893), p. 1.

7 Mrs H. E. Harvey, 'Science as a Moral Guide,' *Westminster Review*, 149 (1898), 192–3.

8 See Robert H. MacDonald, 'The frightful consequences of Onanism: Notes on the History of a Delusion,' *Journal of History of Ideas*, 28 (1967), 423–31; and R. P. Neuman, 'Masturbation, Madness and the Modern Concepts of Childhood and Adolescence,' *Journal of Social History*, 8 (1975), 1–27.

9 See John Hawkins Miller, ' "Temple and Sewer": Childbirth, Prudery and Victoria Regina,' in *The Victorian Family: Structure and Stresses*, ed. Anthony S. Wohl (London, 1978), pp. 23–43.

10 Robert Brudenell Carter, *On the Pathology and Treatment of Hysteria* (London, 1853), p. 69.

11 See, respectively, Gerhart S. Schwartz, 'Devices to Prevent Masturbation,' *Medical Aspects of Human Sexuality*, 7 (1973), 141–53; Patricia Branca, *Silent Sisterhood: Middle-Class Women in the Victorian Home* (London, 1975), pp. 114–42; Angus McLaren, *Birth Control in Nineteenth-Century England* (London, 1978), pp. 78–89.

12 William Acton, *The Functions and Disorders of the Reproductive Organs in Childhood, Youth, Adult Age, and Advanced Life Considered in their Physiological, Social, and Moral Relations* (1857; 3rd ed., London, 1862), pp. 101–2.

13 *London Medical Review*, 3 (1862), 145.

14 'Prostitution,' *Westminster Review*, 53 (1850), 448–506.

15 See Peter T. Cominos, 'Innocent Femina Sensualis in Unconscious Conflict,' in *Suffer and Be Still: Women in the Victorian Age*, ed. Martha Vicinus (London, 1973), pp. 155–72.

16 Charles Darwin, *The Descent of Man, and Selection in Relation to Sex*, 2 vols. (London, 1871), II, 326–7.

17 For a Darwinist account of secondary sexual characteristics using only the method of analogy, see George J. Romanes, 'Mental Differences between Men and Women,' *Nineteenth Century*, 21 (1887), 654–72.

18 Patrick Geddes and J. Arthur Thomson, *The Evolution of Sex* (London, 1889). See also Jill Conway, 'Stereotypes of Femininity in a Theory of Sexual Evolution,' in *Suffer and Be Still*, pp. 140–54.

19 Frederic Harrison, 'The Emancipation of Women,' *Fortnightly Review*, 56 (1891), 443–4.

20 Havelock Ellis, *The New Spirit* (London, 1890), pp. 8–9.

21 Havelock Ellis, *Man and Woman: A Study of Human Secondary Sexual Characters* (London, 1894), pp. 174–6.

22 Eliza Burt Gamble, *The Evolution of Woman: An Inquiry into the Dogma of her Inferiority to Man* (London, 1894), p. 31.

23 *Woman Free*, p. 12.

24 Edward Carpenter, *Love's Coming-of-Age. A Series of Papers on the Relations of the Sexes* (Manchester, 1896), p. 161.

25 Clement Scott, 'An Equal Standard of Morality,' *Humanitarian*, 5 (1894), 353–5.

26 See Keith Thomas, 'The Double Standard,' *Journal of the History of Ideas*, 20 (1959), 195–216.

27 In this account of the eugenics movement, I have drawn on McLaren, *Birth Control in Nineteenth-Century England*; George Halliday, 'Social Darwinism: A Definition,' *Victorian Studies*, 14 (1971), 389–405; and Geoffrey R. Searle, *Eugenics and Politics in Britain 1900–1914*, Science in History No. 3 (Leyden, 1976).

28 Edward Aveling, *Darwinism and Small Families* (London, 1882), p. 3.

29 'Letter to the Malthusian League,' 1894, rpt. in 'Socialistic Malthusians: A Review,' by C. R. Drysdale, *Malthusian*, 21 (1897), 90.

30 Karl Pearson, 'The Woman's Question,' in *The Ethic of Freethought: A Selection of Essays and Lectures* (London, 1888), p. 391.

31 Lady Cook, *A Check on Libertines* (London, [1890]).

32 See Victoria C. Woodhull Martin, *The Rapid Multiplication of the Unfit* (London, 1891); Lady Cook, 'Maternity,' in *Talks and Essays*, 4 vols. (London, 1897), I, 24–38.

33 William Logan, *The Great Social Evil: Its Causes, Extent, Results, and Remedies* (London, 1871), pp. 141–2.

34 'Woman Question,' pp. 371–2.

35 Charles G. Harper, *Revolted Woman: Past, Present, and to Come* (London, 1894), p. 27.

36 For a contemporary view of this trend, see Robert Mackintosh, *From Comte to Benjamin Kidd: The Appeal to Biology or Evolution for Human Guidance* (London, 1899).

37 Frances Swiney, *The Bar of Isis, or the Law of the Mother* (London, 1907).

38 Jane Hume Clapperton, *Scientific Meliorism and the Evolution of Happiness* (London, 1885).

39 Francis William Newman, *The Corruption Now Called Neo-Malthusianism. With Notes by Dr E. Blackwell* (London, 1889), p. 7.

40 *Woman Free*, pp. 173–8.

41 *Love's Coming-of-Age*, p. 150.

42 See Elaine and English Showalter, 'Victorian Women and Menstruation,' in *Suffer and Be Still*, pp. 38–44.

43 J. W. R. Scott, *The Life and Death of a Newspaper* (London, 1952), p. 244.

44 George Noyes Miller, *After the Strike of a Sex or, Zugassent's Discovery* (London, 1896), pp. 15–16.

45 *After the Strike*, p. 23. This idea occurs frequently in anti-masturbation tracts; e.g. 'A Graduate,' *A Lecture to Young Men on the Preservation of Health and the Personal Purity of Life* (London, 1885).

46 *La volonté de savoir*, pp. 23–67.

CHAPTER 2

Hardy's Fiction, 1871–1886

In the Prefatory Note to *Desperate Remedies*, written some twenty years after the novel itself, Hardy describes himself in retrospect as a young author 'feeling his way to a method' (p. 35). And indeed, one of the most notable aspects of his earlier work is the diversity of forms and approaches which he attempts. Each novel emerges as a kind of corrective or a reaction against its predecessor, so that the minimally plotted and consciously archaic *Under the Greenwood Tree* follows the dense plot and contemporary setting of *Desperate Remedies*, and the ironic comedy *The Hand of Ethelberta* is succeeded by the ambitiously tragic *Return of the Native*. Hardy's process of experimentation is unusually overt. Yet throughout this feeling of the way there remains a consistent attempt to accommodate that which is unusual or innovatory to normative popular taste; for Hardy held strong preconceptions about public taste, not necessarily corresponding to the views of his actual or potential readership. With a bitterness in part self-directed, he repeatedly calls attention to this accommodation. His sensitivity to criticism is apparent from the first, and his reaction is commonly defensive rather than defiant, so that instead of writing or re-writing *The Return of the Native* to what he proclaims to be its correct austere ending, he merely adumbrates this alternative conclusion in a footnote; he follows the same procedure with the story 'The Distracted Preacher'; and he continually succumbs, with however bad a grace, to the exigencies of the family serial. He defends what may be controversial in his novels – *The Hand of Ethelberta*, or the end of *The Woodlanders* – by an indictment of public taste or of his failure to judge it correctly: *Ethelberta*, he writes, suffered 'for its quality of unexpectedness in particular', and he remarks in a 1912 addition to this Preface that the book, 'appeared thirty-five years too soon' (pp. 31–2). Hardy's fiction, then, is from first to

all but last shaped by his desire at once to challenge and to keep
within the demands of the dominant form, the three-decker
novel, with its established mode of publication: first as a serial in
periodicals intended for middle-class family reading, then later
in an expensive three-volume format which sold primarily to
lending libraries, whose owners were enabled thereby to
exercise a substantial degree of influence over the publishing
houses.[1] Hardy's difficulties in his unsuccessful attempts to
publish his first novel, *The Poor Man and the Lady*, show how the
evidently radical political content of the work was undermined
by the traditions of realism, allowing Alexander Macmillan to
elide his political objection to Hardy's class-partisanship with
that concern with verisimilitude which the idea of a mimetic
realism invites. He praises the 'admirable' and 'truthful'
account of the working-men's lives, but is scandalised and
frightened by Hardy's presentation of the other characters:

> But it seems to me that your black wash will not be recognised as any-
> thing more than ignorant misrepresentation. Of course, I don't know
> what opportunities you have had of seeing the class you deal with. . . .
> But it is inconceivable to me that any considerable number of human
> beings – God's creatures – should be so bad without going to utter wreck
> in a week.[2]

Hardy's adaptation of the challenging to his sense of the
publicly acceptable takes various forms. One obvious instance
is the sometimes strained emulation of authoritatively artistic
models; his frequently recherché comparisons and heavily
cultural allusions have on occasion been interpreted as the
hallmark of the humourless autodidact, but they surely function rather as a kind of credential of the seriousness of the work,
guaranteeing its attempt to place itself within the traditions of
'fine writing'. Another example is the presentation of sexual
encounters in a manner so metaphorical or symbolic that they
can be recuperated into the family serial: Troy's phallic sword-
play, which leaves Bathsheba feeling 'like one who has sinned a
great sin' (p. 206), still found a place in the novel, while Leslie
Stephen, editor of the *Cornhill* where the serial appeared, raised
gingerly objections to the account of Fanny's illegitimate child
in her coffin. Similarly oblique, though notably less successful,
is the way in which Cytherea Graye's sexual attraction towards
Aeneas Manston, in *Desperate Remedies*, is conveyed through

her stirred response to his virtuosity at the organ in the middle of
a thunderstorm. The explicit – however mild its erotic or
sexual content – was subject to editorial censorship, while the
implicit largely escaped. In Hardy's later works, this was to
reach absurd proportions; so, as has been often remarked, the
serial version of *Tess of the d'Urbervilles* had to show Clare
ridiculously transporting the female dairy-workers through
the puddles in a handy wheelbarrow in order to obviate any
suggestion of direct physical contact, but the imagery of phallic
penetration and the transposed seduction scene in which Alex
persuades the reluctant girl to take a strawberry into her mouth
remained intact. A further, and interestingly ambiguous, form
of this adaption is recurrent: the tawdry equivocations over legal
marriage – Viviette's unconsciously bigamous marriage with
Swithin St Cleeve, or the falsified ceremonies in the manuscript
of *The Return of the Native* and the serial version of *Tess* – are
quite clearly a half-cynical obeisance to convention, which
nevertheless scarcely disguise the illicit sexual nature of the
relationships involved. By exercising this kind of imaginative
pre-censorship of his own, Hardy managed on the whole to
retain the sexual character of such episodes, while at the same
time preserving the decencies of the three-decker. It is in those
novels usually called 'minor' or 'failed' – those which Hardy
himself placed in the categories 'Romances and Fantasies' and
'Novels of Ingenuity' – that the search for a form most evidently revolves upon the problem of the female characters. The
originality and vitality of the central women in these novels
provokes an uncertainty of genre and tone which unsettles the
fictional modes in a disturbing and often productive manner. In
the 'successful' earlier novels, by contrast, Hardy runs closer to
the established genres of pastoral and tragedy.

Under the Greenwood Tree, still often described in such terms
as Irving Howe's 'a masterpiece in miniature',[3] provides an
example. Fancy Day conforms almost exactly to the unfavour-
able literary stereotype of female character in her vanity,
fickleness, whimsical inconsequentiality, and coquetry. She
lacks what this image would have her lack: personal sexual
identity (as opposed to generalised gender identity), genuine
feeling, independence of thought, consideration in the exercise
of her will. Here, it should be noticed, Hardy is clearly

employing the stereotype as such; *Under the Greenwood Tree* is a consciously – even self-consciously – conventional work. Fancy Day is not the only type-figure in the book, for the male characters are just as generically pre-determined, and the patronising narrative tone extends beyond her to include all the 'rustics', as they are commonly – and here perhaps fairly – known. A sense of effort is evident behind this narrative condescension, in the proliferation of quaint names and odd appearances bestowed on these characters.[4] After the cool reception of *Desperate Remedies*, Hardy seems consciously to have aimed at a work with a respectable lineage of genre. In a letter written to Macmillan while the book was on offer to them, he refers at length to reviews of the earlier novel before concluding that 'It seemed that upon the whole a pastoral story would be the *safest* venture.'[5] Congruent with this urge towards the safe and respectable is the superior and yet ingratiating tone of the narrator; the novel's narrative voice is curiously and uncharacteristically masculine, perhaps denoting an overstrenuous effort to insinuate into the confidence of the projected reader. The novel reader may be traditionally female, but the authoritative role of novel-narrator had so far been largely presumed male, as the male pseudonyms and assertively male tone adopted by so many mid-nineteenth-century women writers – the narrator in George Eliot's *Adam Bede* is an obvious example – would suggest.

Through her role in the plot of *Under the Greenwood Tree*, Fancy Day also provides a near paradigm for Hardy's recurring central fable. The novel focuses on her choice among possible lovers, a choice made in relative freedom from the most tangible forms of female dependency, parental control and direct financial pressure. Differences in class and education among the various men accentuate the gap between the Fancy and the husband of her choice, and the later addition of Maybold to the roster of lovers may well have been intended to emphasise this element. These and other factors cause a series of hesitations, misgivings and recantations before the original choice is finally confirmed. What is unusual here is the resolution of the plot in a marriage clearly to be seen as successful, despite the mild threat of Fancy's 'secret she would never tell' (p. 192), which is rather a last irony at her expense than an equivalent to the damaging sexual secrets of Elfride Swancourt or Tess Durbeyfield. This particular resolution is never reproduced in so unequivocal a form by Hardy, though (with the exception of *The Return of the Native*) marriage represents an ending in all but the last novels. The contrast between Fancy's marriage to Dick and the marriage of Ethelberta to Lord Mountclere reveals how uniquely close *Under the Greenwood Tree* runs to the sentimentalised happy ending of much popular fiction.

In the minor early novels, there is not the same authority of genre or confidence of narrative tone. Elements of sensation fiction, pastoral, romance, tragedy and even Meredithian social comedy, are superimposed upon the basis of realism. More significantly, there is a disruptive instability in narrative points of view. Irving Howe has found in Hardy 'a curious power of sexual insinuation, almost as if he were not locked into the limits of masculine perception, but could shuttle between, or for moments yoke together, the responses of the two sexes.'[6] He identifies here the distinctive ambivalence of the earlier novels, a kind of androgynous voice which permits at the same time of aphoristic and dismissive generalisations about women – 'Woman's ruling passion – to fascinate and influence those more powerful than she' (*Blue Eyes*, p. 202) – and of an attempt to make the central female characters the subjects of their own experience, rather than the instruments of the man's. This narrative ambivalence can be seen in regard to Paula Power. Her relative independence in thought (her rejection of the Baptist religion of her father) and in action (her reluctance to marry) is expressed rather negatively, as a refusal (even literally) to take the plunge. In the latter part of the novel she pays for her rebellion, in the excessively protracted pursuit of Somerset by which she is brought to heel.

Similarly, Bathsheba Everdene's resistance to becoming ' "men's property" ' (p. 64) and her sense of marriage as being 'had', that glorying in the idea of her inviolate selfhood which finds expression in her original fierce chastity, and her perception of the fact that ' "language . . . is chiefly made by men to express their feelings" ' (p. 356), are given authority by her experiences in the novel. But at the same time, there is an undercurrent of sexual antagonism towards her, expressed both in the action of the plot and in direct narrative comment.

Far from the Madding Crowd is not only the story of the education of Bathsheba; her moral and emotional growth are parallelled by the breaking of her spirit. Images of taming pursue her. Her relationship with Troy is marked by instruments of violence, begun with the spurs, consummated by the sword, and ended by the gun. The scenes in which Oak jealously nips the ewe he is shearing in the groin, and in which Troy, after their marriage, walks beside her gig, holding reins and whip, lightly lashing the horse's ears as he walks, are a kind of surrogate for the physical punishment of Bathsheba herself. The stress on the humiliation to which she is subjected by Troy culminates in his repudiation of her before the dead bodies of Fanny Robin and her child.

T. S. Eliot wrote of Hardy that 'the author seems to be deliberately relieving some emotion of his own at the expense of the reader. It is a refined form of torture on the part of the writer.'[7] The comment seems almost justified here, but the 'torture' is rather at the expense of Bathsheba than of the reader. Every expression of her independence or strength is opposed by a stress on the 'taming' that she must undergo. The process by which she is made into a fitting wife for Oak involves not only growth, but also loss. Her initial rejection of Oak is partly due to his lack of masterfulness: ' "I want somebody to tame me; I am too independent; and you would never be able to, I know" ' (p. 66). But this feeling is given in relation to the way in which she experiences her sexual identity, and that is primarily as the object of male desire. Richard Carpenter has written of Bathsheba's behaviour as subconscious rape-provocation, betraying her need to be dominated and possessed.[8] And indeed, throughout Hardy's novels, women experience attraction to a man as a feeling of being hypnotised, paralysed, rendered will-less. However, this must be related to the way in which they require the confirmation of a man's desire to authorise their own sexual feeling. Bathsheba's coquetry with Oak and her sending of the Valentine to the previously indifferent Boldwood are both ways of simultaneously taking and concealing the sexual initiative. It is not to rape that she seeks to provoke them, but to desire, which alone will make her visible to them. George Wotton has described this process:

> She becomes the *observed subject* whose very existence is determined by her reactions to the conflicting acts (of sight) of the *perceiving subjects* by which

she is beset. Living in the ideology of femininity, the woman demands to be seen by men. But each of the men by whom she is surrounded demand [sic] that she should be seen only by him and treats her according to his vision of her.[9]

As Hardy's formal experimentation continues it will be through the manipulation of this structure of perceptions – the woman's, the narrator's, the desiring man's, those implied by Biblical or literary parallels or allusions – that the novels throw into question those generalisations and aphorisms which bear the weight of contemporary ideologies of femininity and of the womanly nature. The submission of such ideologies to conflicting and contradictory points of view and narrative voices will test them to their limits, and in doing so will make those limits apparent.

In these earlier novels, Hardy moves towards an attempt to depict the woman as self-perceiving sexual subject, and at the same time give the external or erotic response of the male observer. At the beginning of his career, the text itself is implicated in the process of sexual reification; Fancy Day is presented for much of *Under the Greenwood Tree* only as an object. She enters it as the object – her boot – of communal discussion; she then figures as 'a picture' (p. 53), ironically compared by Michael Mail – the name is surely not idle – to ' "rale wexwork" ' (p. 53); as 'The Vision' (p. 58) to Dick Dewey; as a 'comely . . . prize' (p. 67) at the Christmas dance. The narrator's term for her, 'a bunch of sweets' (p. 124), typifies her role as the object of desire, envy, or rivalry. Here, the woman herself provides no focus of contradiction. She shares in this view of herself, offering Dick a kiss as if handing him a gift: ' "Now that's a treat for you, isn't it?" ' (p. 166).[10] In the light of this continual reduction of Fancy to object-status, there is some irony in the inscription on the card Dick hands to Parson Maybold when announcing his engagement to her: 'Live and Dead Stock, removed to any distance on the shortest notice' (p. 175).

A Laodicean is a novel in part concerned with ambivalence, both as ambiguity of class – the whole complex of meanderings and hesitations between aristocracy and bourgeoisie – and of sex. Dare, as well being the one to ' "exercise paternal authority" ' in his relationship with his father (p. 172), and having no discernible age or nationality, wears his hair 'in a fringe like a girl's' (p. 168). Paula in the gymnasium looks like ' "a lovely young youth and not a girl at all" ' (p. 181), and her friendship with Charlotte de Stancy is described as ' "more like lovers than maid and maid" ' (p. 75). In this context, Paula Power marks a first attempt at what Hardy will later do with Sue Bridehead – to create by the interposition of commentators and interpreters a female character who will resist the appropriation of the narrative voice. The manipulation of points of view, however, lacks the subtlety and assurance of the later work, and Somerset never acts as a mediating consciousness in the way that Jude will do. The retention of the omniscient narrator gives equal authority to the comments on both characters. Consequently, Paula's 'Laodicean' hesitations, instead of conveying the sense of a logic and motivation not available to the narrator, remain emptily enigmatic.

There is, throughout Hardy's fiction, a radical split in women's consciousness between self-perception and perception by others; it is this latter which gives birth to self-consciousness and to that concern with the judgment of others which is common to the female characters: 'as without law there is no sin, without eyes there is no indecorum' (*Crowd*, p. 56). These female characters merge together their identity and that of the objects around them; Hardy repeatedly remarks that women's clothes seem a part of their bodies by virtue of their incorporation into the woman's sexual awareness. Bathsheba in the Corn Exchange seems to have 'eyes in [her] ribbons' for Boldwood's lack of interest in her (*Crowd*, p. 120); and Cytherea Graye experiences a sexual *frisson* at the slight touch of her dress against Manston's coat: 'By the slightest hyperbole it may be said that her dress has sensation. Crease but the very Ultima Thule of fringe or flounce, and it hurts her as much as pinching her. Delicate antennae, or feelers, bristle on every outlying frill' (*Desperate Remedies*, p. 155). Geraldine Allenville, in *An Indiscretion in the Life of an Heiress*, typifies the division. Early in the novel, young and inexperienced, she is nonetheless aware of a conflict in her relationship with Mayne between her dominant class role and the submissive, acquiescent part assigned to her by sex. This conflict leads to her

confused, covert initiatives towards the teacher, and leads him
into an equally bemused state:

> Geraldine had never hinted to him to call her by her Christian name, and
> finding that she did not particularly wish it he did not care to do so. 'Madam'
> was as good a name as any other for her, and by adhering to it and using it at
> the warmest moments it seemed to change its nature from that of a mere title
> to a soft pet sound.[11]

Later, she becomes more conscious of the division between
what Mayne sees as 'the fashionable side' and 'the natural
woman' – though neither fashion nor nature can be adequately
invoked as origins of the conflict of class and sex expectations.
The two 'sides' predominate in turn in Geraldine's emotions,
and she is able to generalise the significance of the 'fashionable
side' to her experience as a woman: ' "To be woven and tied in
with the world by blood, acquaintance, tradition, and external
habit, is to a woman to be utterly at the beck of that world's
customs" ' (p. 93). The conflict is rendered less acute by
Mayne's social rise to a more evenly-matched level – a resolution which the later Hardy will repudiate, preserving the
class-difference in all its sharpness in, for instance, the relation
between Grace Melbury and Giles Winterborne. In *An Indiscretion*, however, the blunting of the dilemma allows Geraldine to
enter into a clandestine marriage with Mayne, in flight from the
fashionably brilliant proposed match with Lord Bretton.

Geraldine Allenville, in a book which shows in relatively
unsophisticated form many of Hardy's characteristic preoccupations and plot-motifs, is the first in a line of women
undermined or destroyed by the conflict between their feelings
and their strongly internalised sense of conventional social
values, a conflict suggested in his repeated use of a quotation
from Browning's 'The Statue and the Bust':

> The world and its ways have a certain worth:
>
> And to press a point while these oppose
> were simple policy; better wait:
> We lose no friends and we gain no foes.[12]

Hardy's women are rendered particularly vulnerable to destruction by such conflict by their entrapment at the point where
individual and physiologically determined experience inter-
act. Hardy, who claimed to have been an early convinced

Darwinist,[13] shows in his fiction the tracks of that biologistic determinism which became dominant in the last quarter of the century. He seems to have shared with Schopenhauer and others a notion that women, by virtue of their physiological organisation and their biological or social role as mothers, were closer to the operative forces of evolution, natural and (more particularly) sexual selection. In *Tess* this will develop into an almost Zolaesque naturalism, when the girl workers at Talbothays are to be found in sultry high summer writhing 'feverishly under the oppressiveness of an emotion thrust on them by cruel Nature's law', their individuality extinguished into 'portion of one organism called sex' (p. 174). In *Jude the Obscure*, he will draw back from such naturalism; writing of Jude's attraction towards Arabella, he replaces his original naturalistic statement – 'in the authorititative operation of a natural law' – with a jocularly masculine militaristic metaphor: 'in commonplace obedience to provocative [?] orders from head quarters' (ms. f. 37). It seems that naturalism, in Hardy and elsewhere, corresponds most satisfactorily to the similarly organicist dominant ideology of femininity, and that its inadequacies become apparent faced with the exploration of male sexuality.

The conflict of feeling and convention is present in Hardy's men also, most notably in Giles Winterborne, but usually in a less destructive form. Women, for Hardy, have an inherent physical weakness which makes them more vulnerable to mental conflict. This susceptibility would probably be explained by Hardy in terms of female nervous organisation, as Grace Melbury suffers because of her combination of 'modern nerves with primitive feelings' (*Woodlanders*, p. 309), and Sue Bridehead because of her 'ethereal, fine-nerved, sensitive' character (*Jude*, p. 235). This was a prevalent presupposition of the medical establishment when dealing with middle-class women; hysteria, neurasthenia, and chlorosis, the three great diseases of the Victorian bourgeois woman, were all commonly diagnosed as 'nervous disorders' arising from some frequently undefined disturbance to the all-determining reproductive system.[14] Such an interdependence of physical and mental processes is the motive force of the plot in, for example, 'An Imaginative Woman', where a sensitive woman conceives a child with her husband, but in the likeness of a young poet for whom she has developed a wholly imaginary passion. Hardy was not alone in believing this a genuine medical possibility, the grounds on which he defends the story in his Preface to *Life's Little Ironies*; it also appears in the famous 'spiritual adultery' in Goethe's *Die Wahlverwandtschaften*. It is clearly related to telegony, a respectable medical phenomenon of the nineteenth century, in which a woman's cells are impregnated in some way by her first lover so that her child by any subsequent sexual partner could resemble the first – an idea important in Ibsen's *The Lady from the Sea*.[15]

So it is that the interaction of dominant, but largely unrecognised, sexual feeling and apparently independent feeling or action creates in Hardy's women a predisposition towards intense physical response to mental or emotional conflict; hence Elfride's feverish illness after Knight defeats her at chess, Mrs Yeobright's limited resistance to fatigue and illness after her estrangement from Clym, Viviette's death from joy at St Cleeve's return, Lucetta's death after the skimmity-ride, and Geraldine Allenville's fatal haemorrhage when she revisits her father after her clandestine marriage. The quasi-scientific nature of such ideas does not disguise, of course, their place in a prescriptive diagnosis of physical weakness and emotional susceptibility for women; similar medical 'facts' were used by opponents of higher education for women and of the suffrage campaign.

Furthermore, as Patricia Stubbs has remarked, there are among Hardy's women *femmes fatales* – 'emotional vampire[s],' she calls them – whose potential for self-destruction and for destroying others arises from their excessively literal application of the idea that women's proper sphere is that of the emotions and, pre-eminently, of romantic love.[16] Work rivals relationships for the attention of the male characters; as Barbara Hardy says in her interesting introduction to *A Laodicean*:

> Hardy's men are generally all too willing to sacrifice intellectual and professional aspirations to . . . sexual appetite . . . , but Hardy's women reflect the limited conditions of their time and place in having nothing to do except choose a husband.[17]

The working-class women are rendered vulnerable to direct economic exploitation in conjunction with their sexual oppression, but are shown as less dependent on the vagaries of emotion. Even Tess Durbeyfield, who is at the point of conjuncture of economic and sexual exploitation, can withstand the deprivations and pressures of her working life until she is threatened be a more distinctively sexual pressure from Clare and d'Urberville. The difference is remarked after the departure of Alec from Farmer Groby's field:

> . . . the farmer continued his reprimand, which Tess took with the greatest coolness, that sort of attack being independent of sex. To have as a master this man of stone, who would have cuffed her if he had dared, was almost a relief after her former experiences (p. 343).

For most of Hardy's middle-class women, by contrast, work is a dilettantish thing, like Elfride's romance-writing, or a means of filling in the time until marriage, like Fancy's teaching. In *The Return of the Native*, both Mrs Yeobright and Eustacia Vye are able to confer significance on their lives only through the roles they adopt in relation to men. Mrs Yeobright and Clym enact a struggle of reciprocal oppression through emotional dependence and guilt; Eustacia can conceive of no fulfilment other than an extravagantly romanticised passionate love which will confirm her sense of herself as a ' "splendid woman" ' (p. 357). It should be noticed that in neither case is there a simple dichotomy between man as oppressor and woman as victim; these situations are mutually destructive for mother and son, mistress and lover. Yet the sexual and social power which lies behind the personal strength of the men gives them at least a wider range of alternatives. Emotional struggles do not place their whole existence at stake; Clym, however debilitated by his experiences, will survive with a residual sense of purpose and possibility. For the women a life outside the closed circle of personal relationships is all but unimaginable, as Clym's unlikely plan for Eustacia's future career – to become matron of a boy's boarding-school – suggests; from this confinement to the womanly sphere there results a distinctively feminine vulnerability. Even when women possess social advantage or economic power, it is so closely bound to this circumscribing sphere of the emotions that it is frequently exercised in a fashion that appears damagingly capricious: Bathsheba dismisses Oak from his employment in pique at an imagined slight to her feelings, and Geraldine Allenville is

prepared to have an old man evicted from his cottage because
she has been kissed by his nephew.

It is here that the originality of Hardy's use of his 'Poor Man
and the Lady' motif is most striking: while the class-relation –
taking most often the form of disparity – between lovers is
always important, it never takes on a primacy that would make
of the sexual relationships merely a symbol, or a displacement,
of class relations. Rather, and more interestingly, the variations
on the theme of class-difference permit a searching examination
of the articulation of class and gender. For there is one notable
and significant oddity common to many of Hardy's bourgeois
women: their lack of a father. In some cases the absence of the
father is never really remarked – Tamsin Yeobright, for example, or Bathsheba Everdene – while in others, he disappears,
once with extraodinary violence, at the point where the women
accedes to marriageability – Paula Power, for instance, or
Cytherea Graye, whose father plunges to his death before her
eyes. Geraldine Allenville and Grace Melbury are the only
conventionally fathered daughters in the novels. The result is to
liberate these characters into an illusion of free subjectivity. It
has been written of Charlotte Brontë's similarly orphaned
female characters that:

> the devised absence of the father represents a triple evasion of . . . class
> structure, kinship structure and Oedipal socialisation. Its consequences are
> that there is no father from whom the bourgeois woman can inherit
> property, no father to exchange her in marriage, and no father to create the
> conditions for typical Oedipal socialisation.[18]

While Hardy's women often do inherit property (Bathsheba
Everdene's farm, Paula Power's mediaeval castle and modern
wealth), the other two paternal absences remain crucial. These
women are freed to negotiate their own re-entry into the family
through their choice of a marital or sexual partner – a choice
which equally marks their re-assimilation into class-structure.
The effect of this is to highlight the modes of oppression specific
to their gender; all the privileges of economic power are
undercut by the marginality of women to the processes of
production. The only freedom granted them by the absence of
the father is the freedom to choose a man; it is only by a
voluntary re-subjection to the patriarchal structures of kin that
women find any point of anchorage in the social structure at all.

As Melbury will remark in *The Woodlanders*, ' "a woman takes her colour from the man she's walking with" ' (p. 114). So it is, for example, that Paula Power – whose very name draws ironic attention to the significance of this theme – is relieved of all the outward appearances of dependence in a way that serves primarily to emphasise the sterility of her 'freedom'. Her money, her property, and her education all serve solely to enhance her value as a marriage-partner.[19] Similarly, Viviette Constantine, despite the extra latitude granted her by her maturity and her supposedly widowed status, can only benefit vicariously from her wealth and leisure by making St Cleeve's career her own vocation.

But while the father himself is largely absent, the patriarchal law that he embodies is frequently displaced on to a pseudo-father, usually a male relative – Viviette's brother, Elizabeth-Jane's step-father, Sophy Twycott's son, even Sue Bridehead's elderly husband. So it is not merely the tie of blood that confers authority upon the father: paternal (patriarchal) power is diffused, but this does nothing to limit its effectivity. Yet while it may not be escaped, it may be evaded; and this is the case of Ethelberta Chickerel, who, paradoxically, has not only a present father, but also several brothers. Ethelberta usurps the authority of the father in order to become the regulator of her own exchange: she takes on the paternal role in the family by supporting her mother and sisters, and also acts as her own 'father' by investigating the financial suitability of her suitors and ensuring that she does not sell her sexual commodity below market price. *The Hand of Ethelberta*, which is among the most experimental of Hardy's earlier novels, interestingly fore-shadows Meredith's *Diana of the Crossways* in its creation of a structure of comment and observation (discussion among her friends, interpretation by her family, public gossip, newspaper reviews, the generalisations of the narrator) that prevents her rebellion from becoming a Utopian fantasy of social transcendence.[20] Ethelberta, like Meredith's Diana, is a writer of sorts, and this too is important. It bestows upon her 'The charter to move abroad unchaperoned, which society for good reasons grants only to women of three sorts – the famous, the ministering, and the improper. . .' (p. 241). It also gives a congruence to her creation of her own best, if least plausible,

story – the romance of free choice and action. She tells her sister
' "But don't you go believing in sayings, Picotee: they are all
made by men, for their own advantages. Women who use
public proverbs as a guide through events are those who have
not ingenuity enough to make private ones as each event
occurs" ' (p. 153). Faith Julian and the other women who
rebuke Ethelberta's lack of womanliness speak the public
proverbs that consolidate male advantage, while Ethelberta's
story-telling is a unique case of the private saying made into a
spectacle. She takes speech for herself, and in doing so trans-
gresses all the determinations of class and kin. And yet it is
evident from the first that her power of free choice is confined
within limits that cannot forever be evaded. The free subject is a
fairy-tale, which takes on a most ironic inflection when her
chosen suitor proves more frog than prince. An elderly aristocrat with a resident mistress in tow, Lord Mountclere is an
almost parodically exaggerated instance of the patriarchal
male. It is a mark of the subversiveness of Ethelberta's case –
and, equally, of Hardy's experimental blend of romance and
social comedy – that Ethelberta is able to repeat her act of
usurpation within a marriage which allows her to become
' "my lord and my lady both" ' (p. 387). The drying-up of her
story-telling power proves to be only a hiccup in her prolonged
act of speech; marriage does not silence her, for at the end of the
novel she is writing an epic poem. The power of her dispassionate female sexuality escapes the entanglements of womanliness
and subverts the authority of the patriarch by exploiting his
dotage of desire.

For the 'Poor Man and the Lady', the articulation of dominance in gender and class frequently takes the form of contradiction, but in the inverted relationship (the 'Gentleman and the
Poor Girl' theme, perhaps) the sexual dominance of the man is
reinforced by his economic power. There is often a pre-existing
relation of employer and worker in such couples, which clearly
shapes the sexual relationship: Mr Twycott, the vicar in 'The
Son's Veto', marries his parlourmaid Sophy largely because she
is 'a kitten-like, flexuous, tender creature . . . the only one of
the servants with whom he came into immediate and continuous relation' (*Life's Little Ironies*, p. 36), and she in turn
accepts his proposal out of 'a respect for him which almost

amounted to veneration . . . she hardly dared refuse a person-
age so reverend and august in her eyes' (p. 37). In such a case, the
otherness of the woman's class-experience provides a focus for
the man's emotional fantasies or needs. This is clear in *Tess of the
d'Urbervilles*, where the desire of the two men for Tess crystallises their relation to her class. Alec, idly living on the profits of
his capital, slips into the role of local squire, superimposing
upon his origins in urban manufacturing capitalism his local
situation as mock-aristocrat. He is crassly exploitative, alter-
nating an acquisitive greed with an unthinking open-
handedness. Angel Clare, in his fantasy of Tess as the unspoilt
and incorruptible country girl, adopts a romanticising patronage which clearly reveals his class-situation. He, as much as
Clym or Jude, is a study in the difficulty of class-mobility; the
simple abjuration of economic advantage cannot in itself bring
about a change in consciousness. He may question religious
orthodoxy (though doubt, as opposed to disbelief, had itself by
this time acquired a certain respectability as the mark of
intellectual integrity), but the sexual ethic so closely related to it
remains firmly rooted in his consciousness. That he exploits
Tess as much as Alec does, and in much the same way, is stressed
in their momentary transposition of roles in the middle of the
book, when Alec takes up a particularly virulent form of
dissenting religion, and Clare first unthinkingly invites the
devoted Izz to go to Brazil with him, and then as thoughtlessly
changes his mind.

Class-disparate couples are commonly shown caught up in
unhappy and mutually destructive relationships. Sophy Twycott lives out a wretched widowhood, despised by her public
schoolboy son, forbidden by him to marry her former lover, a
market-gardener. Tess is ultimately destroyed by the complementary forms of exploitation of her two lovers. Giles
Winterborne dies for decorum's sake, and Grace returns to an
unsatisfactory marriage. The exceptions – Bathsheba and
Oak's practical *camaraderie*, Fancy and Dick's idyll under the
greenwood tree, Ethelberta's unconventional but prosperous
union with Lord Mountclere – are all in novels whose genre
enforces a happy – or at least a non-tragic – ending. This could
be seen as the mark of a deep conservatism, a glorified version of
knowing your place and sticking to it, but this is surely to

misread Hardy. It suggests, rather, a complex understanding of class differences that sees further than simple variations in manners or grammar – the boiled slug in Grace's salad, or Sophy Twycott's 'confused ideas on the use of "was" and "were"' (p. 37). The distrust of sexuality shown by Clare and by Knight is not the product of some temperamental vagary, but an integral part of their situation as bourgeois intellectuals. Clym Yeobright's attempt to change the face of Egdon through doctrineless preaching is a futile attempt to alter consciousness while leaving untouched material conditions – an act of pure idealism which the heath-dwellers at once see through.

But the class content of relationships cannot be isolated from the contemporary ideology of sex differentiation which exerts a significant pressure on their form. The relative passivity of some of Hardy's heroes – of Oak, for instance, or of John Loveday – has sometimes been 'explained' by speculation over Hardy's own sexual pathology. It serves, rather, to point up the entanglement of the women characters in an ideology of romantic love that calls upon them to experience their sexuality rather in being desired than in desiring, and this is obviously related to their confusion of sexual passion and aggression – a confusion characteristically echoed by Desmond Hawkins in his claim that it is 'a fineness of perception', some mystic Lawrentian call of blood to blood, which motivates such choices.[21] Bathsheba's prolonged reluctance to see in Oak more than a capable shepherd contrasts with her rapid seduction by the glamorous military patina and forceful sexuality of Sergeant Troy; similarly, Anne Garland is vulnerable to the cavalier charm of Bob Loveday and unresponsive to the quiet worth of his brother. In both cases, the point is underlined by the introduction of a second female character, the comic Matilda Johnson in *A Trumpet-Major*, and the pathetic Fanny Robin in *Far from the Madding Crowd*. Troy is the prototype, for Hardy, of the sexual adventurer. While Fanny is obviously and straightforwardly a victim, the situation is rendered more complex by the counterpointing of her life with Bathsheba's, explicitly remarked in the novel,[22] which leads eventually to a temporary reversal of their status. Bathsheba, the legitimate wife, is spurned and deserted, and becomes the outcast, however briefly, during the night spent in her personal slough of despond. Fanny's physical sufferings are balanced against Bathsheba's grief as she gradually realises the truth about her husband. Fanny dies in misery, but is translated after her death into a kind of triumph, while Bathsheba is eclipsed. The chapter in which she discovers the truth is called 'Fanny's Revenge', and represents a formal acknowledgement of the crossing of the curves of their fortunes:

> The one feat alone – that of dying – by which a mean condition could be resolved into a grand one, Fanny had achieved. And to that had destiny subjoined this rencounter tonight, which had, in Bathsheba's wild imagining, turned her companion's failure to success, her humiliation to triumph, her lucklessness to ascendancy; it had thrown over herself a garish light of mockery, and set upon all things about her an ironical smile (p. 306).

Bathsheba's tending of Fanny's grave represents at once an atonement and a tribute. The two women are made equal in their exploitation and humiliation by Troy.

However, it is not only the adventurer, his exploits endorsed in the name of virility, who proves destructive, as the idealising Angel Clare will illustrate. Clare is prefigured by Henry Knight in *A Pair of Blue Eyes*, who adopts the official mid-Victorian view of women as creatures of effortless sexual immaculacy. In contrast to Clare's relatively crude application of the double standard in the later novel, Knight takes chastity as a principle to which he adheres equally in his own conduct. His prudish over-prizing of his virginity contrasts with Elfride's franker and more impulsive sexuality. This overthrow of convention is part of an interesting series of role-reversals in the novel, at once evoking and ironically undermining the romance paradigm; for example, Elfride – author, it must be remembered, of a pseudo-mediaeval romance – rescues her Virgin Knight in distress from the Cliff without a Name by means of a rope of knotted underclothes. The rigidity of Knight's moral standards, and his fastidious distrust of sexuality, lead him to a repudiation of Elfride which again prefigures Angel Clare, but which employs a wholly different narrative tone. While the scene in *Tess* is replete with tragic ironies, Knight's rejection is most decisively conveyed in the disturbingly literal, curiously humourous, image of detumescence as the 'strong tower' crashes to the ground (p. 311). The whole suggests the inadequacy of the figure of the Virgin Knight, and of his chivalrous ethic of chastity, to the complexities of sexual relationship.

This exploration of the destructive power of contemporary ideologies of sex difference and sex roles presses the novels increasingly towards an analysis of relationships in breakdown, where a wedding in the last chapter cannot adequately resolve the tensions and contradictions set up in the course of the novel. This, in turn, will lead Hardy away from irony and pastoral towards two modes of writing whose problematic articulation is to become the chief formal characteristic of the late major novels: that is, towards tragedy and realism. *The Return of the Native* is the first of Hardy's attempts to bring the 'fine writing' of tragedy to bear upon the sexual realism of his material, and I propose now to examine the novel from that point of view.

NOTES

1 See Guinevere L. Griest, *Mudie's Circulating Library and the Victorian Novel* (London, 1970); and J. A. Sutherland, *Victorian Novelists and Publishers* (London, 1976).

2 Charles L. Graves, *Life and Letters of Alexander Macmillan* (London, 1910), pp. 289–92.

3 Irving Howe, *Thomas Hardy* (London, 1968), p. 46; cf. Richard Carpenter, *Thomas Hardy* (London, 1976), pp. 42–8.

4 Cf. Robert Draffan, 'Hardy's *Under the Greenwood Tree*,' *English*, 22 (1973), 55–60.

5 'To Malcolm Macmillan,' 7 August 1871, *Collected Letters of Thomas Hardy; Vol. 1: 1840–1892*, ed. Richard Little Purdy and Michael Millgate (Oxford, 1978), p. 12.

6 Howe, *Thomas Hardy*, p. 109.

7 T. S. Eliot, *After Strange Gods: A Primer of Modern Heresy* (London, 1934), p. 56.

8 Richard Carpenter, 'The Mirror and the Sword: Imagery in *Far from the Madding Crowd*,' *Nineteenth Century Fiction*, 18 (1964), 331–45.

9 George E. Wotton, 'Ideology and Vision in the Novels of Thomas Hardy,' D.Phil. Oxford, 1980, p. 227.

10 Desmond Hawkins accurately comments that this is precisely the kind of dialogue that Hardy's later novels will render impossible: *Thomas Hardy* (London, 1950), pp. 31–2.

11 *An Indiscretion in the Life of an Heiress*, ed. Terry Coleman (London, 1976), p. 70.

12 The Statue and the Bust,' ll. 138–41, quoted at varying length and with varying degrees of accuracy in *An Indiscretion*, p. 72; *Desperate Remedies*, p. 257; 'The Waiting Supper,' *A Changed Man*, p. 232; *Jude the Obscure*, p. 368.

13 *Early Life*, p. 198.
14 See Lorna Duffin, 'The Conspicuous Consumptive: Woman as an Invalid,' in *The Nineteenth-Century Woman: Her Cultural and Physical World* (London, 1978), pp. 26–56; and Karl Figlio, 'Chlorosis and Chronic Disease in Nineteenth-Century Britain: the Social Constitution of Somatic Illness in a Capitalist Society,' *Social History*, 3 (1978), 167–97.
15 See Frank Finn, 'Some Facts of Telegony,' *Natural Science*, 3 (1893), 436–40; and Edward Carpenter, *Love's Coming-of-Age* (Manchester, 1896), p. 22.
16 Patricia Stubbs, *Women and Fiction: Feminism and the Novel 1880–1920* (Brighton, 1979), pp. 58–87.
17 Barbara Hardy, Introduction, *A Laodicean* (New Wessex ed., London, 1975), p. 15.
18 Marxist-Feminist Literature Collective, 'Women's Writing: *Jane Eyre, Shirley, Villette, Aurora Leigh*,' in *1848: The Sociology of Literature.* Proceedings of the Essex Conference on the Sociology of Literature July 1977, ed. Francis Barker and others (Essex, 1978), p. 188.
19 Cf. Barbara Hardy, pp. 17–18.
20 See John Goode, 'Woman and the Literary Text,' in *The Rights and Wrongs of Women*, ed. Juliet Mitchell and Ann Oakley (Harmondsworth, 1976), pp. 241–7.
21 Hawkins, *Thomas Hardy*, p. 77.
22 E.g. on pp. 217 and 303.

CHAPTER 3

The Return of the Native (1878)

The Return of the Native is the first of Hardy's novels to deal with marriage, not simply by employing marriage, more or less ironically, as a plot resolution, but by presenting the relationship itself as a continuing, lived process; and in this it foreshadows the later novels, from The Woodlanders to Jude the Obscure. It takes on a subject, sexual discord and marital breakdown, which has previously only hovered impendingly on the periphery of Hardy's fiction. It continues his explorative experimentation with genre and mode: the novel has been seen as an attempt to unite prose romance, dramatic form, and psychological or social theory; as an exercise in mock-heroic, replete with parodic allusions to the conventions of courtly love; as a direct descendant of the ballad tradition; and as a modified pastoral.[1] The breadth and variety of such critical allusions point up the major structural characteristics of this novel: the attempt to cast sexual material which leads towards realism on the rigidly formalised model of Greek tragedy; the conception of the three main female characters in terms of three different modes; and, a related problem, the disjunction between an overt and ambitious mythological scheme and the realism of the narrative.

It is important to notice that Hardy's first attempt to write a tragedy is a double tragedy, and that it turns upon marriage. A pattern emerges for the first time that will be repeated in the later novels: the man's tragedy is primarily intellectual, the woman's sexual. This distinction will be more subtly handled in the later novels. In Tess of the d'Urbervilles, Angel lives out the intellectual dimension of his own tragedy, while its sexual component is split off and acted out through Alec d'Urberville. In Jude the Obscure, both Jude's and Sue's tragedies will involve intellect and sexuality; indeed, the novel will focus upon their interaction and apparent mutual hostility. In The Return of the Native, however, the polarisation is relatively crude, and the sexual ideology reinforcing the split is quite evident. Clym's dilemma is conceived as an intellectual and moral choice. It involves testing his personal wishes and ambitions against social forces; his problem is therefore in part one of his class and community, and is historically located by Hardy. His very appearance characterises him as 'a modern type' marking the transition from the 'zest for existence' of an earlier age to the sense of 'life as a thing to be put up with' which, according to the narrator, will come to predominate in later generations (p. 185). His ideas and his wish to 'raise the class at the expense of individuals rather than individuals at the expense of the class' (p. 190) are shown as topical and, indeed, advanced, connected with the French ethical systems of the time (which, in the 1840s when the novel is set, is likely to mean those of Saint Simon and Comte) and certainly implying a continuing 'dialogue' with Matthew Arnold.[2] Clym's tragedy, then, is given a certain historical typicality. Eustacia's sexual tragedy, however, is evoked as a consequence of her 'nature'; it is removed from history by a dual process, being at once naturalised and mythologised. From the first, she is 'the raw material of a divinity' (p. 89), while Clym's mythological assimilation to Oedipus becomes dominant only after the events of his tragedy. Hardy, in fact, is writing another version of the Ruskinian polarity of man as culture, woman as nature. This disparity makes the attempted fusion of the two tragedies in the marital breakdown particularly difficult. It represents the culmination of the disjunction between the sexual realism of the material and the self-consciously imitative writing. The scene of Eustacia and Clym's argument and subsequent separation is obviously theatrical in conception, the dialogue interrupted only by actions described in a way that, except for the tense, reads very like stage directions:

> "Then I'll find it myself." His eye had fallen upon a small desk that stood near, on which she was accustomed to write her letters. He went to it. It was locked.
> "Unlock this!"
> "You have no right to say it. That's mine."
> Without another word he seized the desk and dashed it to the floor. The hinge burst open, and a number of letters tumbled out.
> "Stay!" said Eustacia, stepping before him with more excitement than she had hitherto shown.

"Come, come! Stand away! I must see them."
She looked at the letters as they lay, checked her feeling, and moved indifferently aside; when he gathered them up and examined them (p. 332).

Hardy clearly feels that a 'high style' is necessary at a point of such intense feeling, and looks, as elsewhere in the novel, to tragic models. Here, however, the language and style seem to come not from Greek drama, but from Elizabethan or Jacobean tragedy. Clym, in particular, adopts an archaic and rhetorical mode of speech, addressing his wife as ' "my lady" ' and ' "mistress" ', and falling into Websterian turns of phrase such as ' "what a finished and full-blown adept in a certain trade my lady is" ' (p. 332). The text is disrupted by the imposition of a model, and by the attempt to force a spurious tragic grandeur on the reader's attention; but the model itself draws attention to the dominance of the sexual – which, I shall argue, has been displaced throughout the relationship – in this scene. Jacobean tragedy, and that of Webster in particular, is dominated by a concept of sexuality in which it functions as a corrupting disease or as an inexpiable crime. Similarly, in *The Return of the Native*, it is the very *fact* of her sexuality which from the first dooms Eustacia, as it will Hardy's later *femmes fatales*, such as Lucetta Templeman or Felice Charmond. Wildeve's signal to Eustacia after her marriage to Clym is a moth, which flies once or twice around the candle and then straight into the flame; it is a common enough image of a 'fatal attraction', but it is nevertheless appropriate.[3] Eustacia's sexuality leads her to destruction with a certainty which in this novel seems almost as instinctual as the moth's flight.

The three women of the novel act as a kind of working-out of the various modes within which Hardy has been writing, or will write. Thomasin Yeobright is a pastoral survival; Eustacia Vye is both an expression and a critical placing of Hardy's anxious relationship to Romanticism; Mrs Yeobright belongs unequivocally to realism. The literary derivation of the first two is clear and explicit. Tamsin seems 'to belong rightly to a madrigal' (p. 64), and the end of the book is hers, with its maypole-dancing, the transformed, infatuated Venn, and its reassertion of the pastoral convention of 'The Inevitable Movement Onward' (p. 381) through the cycle of marriage and reproduction. After the narrative of disruptive sexuality and illicit relationships, Tamsin is evoked to close the novel in a coda of cosy domesticity with husband and child.

The Return of the Native is much concerned with frustration, with ill-matched couples, incoherent aspiration, and a restless dissatisfaction with the material conditions of life as it presents itself on Egdon. Mrs Yeobright's sense of higher social possibilities – both retrospectively in her own life and marriage 'beneath' her, and prospectively, in her son's potential rise to wealth – permeates all her actions, and revisions for the 1895 Osgood, McIlvaine edition of the novel intensify Mrs Yeobright's insistence on wealth, rather than status, in her attempts to dissuade Clym from his course.[4] Wildeve is a figure of wasted talents and missed opportunities, benefitting gratuitously from the labour of the two previous owners of his land, who have worn themselves out in the effort to wrest some fruitfulness from it. Clym's unanswered question, ' "what is doing well?" ' (p. 193), resounds throughout the book, preoccupying all the central characters. For Clym himself, the dilemma presents itself as an intellectual challenge, as a choice among work possibilities. His change of occupation, from diamond merchant (or, originally, jeweller's assistant) to worker on the land, finds a distinct echo in Shelley's notes on *Queen Mab*:

> No greater evidence is afforded of the wide extended and radical mistakes of civilized man than this fact: those arts which are essential to his very being are held in the greatest contempt; employments are lucrative in an inverse ratio to their usefulness: the jeweller, the toyman, the actor gains fame and wealth by the exercise of his useless and ridiculous art; whilst the cultivator of the earth, he without whom society must cease to subsist, struggles through contempt and penury, and perishes by that famine which but for his unceasing exertions would annihilate the rest of mankind.[5]

For Eustacia, however, the problem takes only the form of choosing – or rather finding, in an environment where 'coldest and meanest kisses were at famine prices' (p. 92) – a lover adequate to her longing.

For Tasmin, who, rather like Elizabeth-Jane Newson, early learns that adaptation to the expectations and possibilities of her society which characterises the pastoral, 'doing well' is entirely a question of marrying well; she is truly one for whom 'doing means marrying, and the commonwealth is one of hearts and hands' (pp. 93–4). She early graduates from romantic fantasy, as Eustacia never does:

> "Here am I asking you to marry me; when by rights you ought to be on your knees imploring me, your cruel mistress, not to refuse you, and saying it would break your heart if I did. I used to think it would be pretty and sweet like that; but how different!" (pp. 69–70).

Even dignity must if necessary be sacrificed to propriety. She is compromised by her trip to Anglebury with Wildeve. Indeed, according to Paterson, she was originally to have been more deeply compromised; she and Wildeve were to have returned only after a week in Anglebury, to find later that the ceremony had not been legal (possibly by Wildeve's prior arrangement, foreshadowing the similar situation in the serial version of *Tess of the d'Urbervilles*).[6] So she pursues her self-ordained course firmly, eventually marrying Wildeve whatever the state of her feelings towards him, braiding her hair in sevens on her wedding day because 'Years ago she had said that when she married she would braid it in sevens' (p. 175). Tamsin's behaviour is at once governed and sustained by an awareness of the judgement of others. After the first, unsuccessful attempt at a wedding, she is terrified of skimmity-riding (p. 71); she is spurred on to the second, successful attempt by Clym's comments in a letter; and after Wildeve's death and her period of mourning, she is still restrained from following her inclination to marry Venn by the invocation of Mrs Yeobright's posthumous disapproval. Her life is public, lived in the eye of the community; even the relationship of her inner consciousness to her outward appearance is without concealment: 'An ingenuous, transparent life was disclosed; as if the flow of her existence could be seen passing within her' (p. 64). Adrian Poole has drawn attention to the way in which marriage, in the (pre-1880) Victorian novel, functions as the socially ratified culmination of just this progressive adaptation of the experience of the individual to the 'reality' of restrictive social forms:

> The centrality of the notion of marriage to any analysis of the assumptions underlying the Victorian novel cannot be over-estimated. Marriage is the point of intersection of the infinite desire with the temporal reality, the confirming sanction of the reciprocity between experience in its most secret and private aspect, and the public, visible, declared social forms.[7]

In Tamsin this reciprocity is unproblematic; her experience, precisely at its most 'private', is visibly shaped by the declared social forms of marriage.

For Eustacia, however, the 'infinite desire' and the social forms remain irreconcilable. In contrast to Tasmin, she is, throughout the novel, physically and socially, marginal to the Egdon community. She is literally foreign to it, being the daughter of a Corfiote (or, in an earlier version, Belgian) father. Her physical isolation from the community is reinforced by a mutual awareness of her difference. She regards the local girls with something like contempt. Her alienness, in turn, is perceived by the Egdon inhabitants as a threat, which Susan Nunsuch attempts to exorcise by the long-standing methods of protection against witches. The witch is traditionally supposed to have supernatural powers which allow her to alter the material circumstances of her world to fit her own desires, and this indeed corresponds to Eustacia's image of herself and of fulfilment; she sees herself, for instance, as having somehow materialised Wildeve into existence, rather than having simply summoned him by a pre-arranged signal. Eustacia, furthermore, poses a particular threat to the women of the community, being disruptive by virtue of her unfocused sexuality. She is not the innocent, pre-sexual maiden, nor is she bound by legal, or even emotional, ties to an one sexual partner. In an interesting passage deleted in revision for the first edition, Hardy draws attention to this state of, so to speak, sexual suspension:

> Eustacia was weary of too many things, unless she could have been weary of more; she knew too much, unless she could have known all. It was a dangerous rock to be tossed on at her age. She had done with the dreams and interests of young maidhood; the dreams and interests of wifedom she had never begun, and we see her in a strange interspace of isolation.[8]

Her individualism leaves her on the feared and misunderstood margins of society. It is interesting to notice that her marriage to Clym does not assimilate her into the community, but rather marginalises him. Their isolation in their home removes Clym from the society of his family; his ambition to teach is replaced by his entirely solitary furze-cutting; and by the last Book of the novel, he is quite clearly placed outside the social forms of marriage. He has become an onlooker, as the scene of Tamsin's wedding makes clear. He has removed himself from his society without even leaving a perceptible gap:

> "Do any of them seem to care about my not being there?" Clym asked.
> "No, not a bit in the world. Now they are all holding up their glasses and drinking somebody's health."
> "I wonder if it is mine?"
> "No, 'tis Mr and Mrs Venn's, because he is making a hearty sort of speech. There – now Mrs Venn has got up, and is going away to put on her things, I think."
> "Well, they haven't concerned themselves about me, and it is quite right they should not" (p. 403).

It is almost a critical commonplace to say that Eustacia Vye is a divided figure.[9] The contradictions are partly the result of the hesitation between mythologising and irony: Eustacia as Queen of Night is trivialised by her desire to see the Paris boulevards (and still more by her desire, in earlier texts, to see the Budmouth esplanades), while Eustacia as a restless, intelligent woman trapped in a limiting environment is made ridiculous by the Bourbon roses, Lotus-eaters and other paraphernalia of Romantic mythology which which she is sporadically encumbered.[10] The irony and the mythology remain, on the whole, separate – there is seldom the irruption of the one into the other that could justify a description of mock-heroic. A further inner division results from the ambivalence, expressed through the figure of Eustacia, of Hardy's evocation of Romanticism. In part, she represents a kind of Romantic ideal; as Deen says, 'She is a romantic (she is a whole history of romanticism) seen romantically.'[11] Some of her characteristics are those of the Romantic hero – a solitary status in opposition to the group, a sense of the validity of individual experience and of self-generated ethical values. As always in Hardy, there are quotations from, and reminiscences of, Romantic poets, particularly from Wordsworth and Shelley.[12] Yet, equally, her own Romantic reading (her 'chief priest' is Byron, in an ms. insertion)[13] is partly responsible for the extravagance of her concepts of love and value, and her Romantic qualities prove, ultimately, self-destructive. The novel increasingly takes its distance from her in this respect, moving away from the self-indulgently Romantic writing of the 'Queen of Night' chapter. Both she and Clym are sometimes assimilated to the supreme Romantic hero, Prometheus.[14] Eustacia is, however, an interestingly 'feminised' version of Prometheus: her boundless desire is to be boundlessly desired. Her sense of her own identity constantly seeks reaffirmation, not through action, but through that confirmation of value which is the desire of another. Preoccupied as she is with love, she still displaces her active feelings in a way which I have argued is distinctively female in a male-dominated society. Her aspiration sets up a circle of desire: 'To be loved to madness – such was her great desire' (p. 92). The extreme egotism of her individualism is also the mark of her extreme dependence on the man whose sexual recognition alone confirms her sense of herself as ' "a splendid woman" ' (p. 357). When she is doubly disguised in her mumming costume, she experiences the interdependence of her sexuality and her identity: 'The power of her face all lost, the charm of her emotions all disguised, the fascinations of her coquetry denied existence, nothing but a voice left to her: she had a sense of the doom of Echo' (p. 161). The reference to Echo is apt; although in its immediate context it implies merely the reduction of her identity to a voice, it also evokes her dependence on the utterance of a male other, and relates her quite differently to the narcissism which might on occasion appear to be her mode of relation to her lovers.[15] Deen argues that this mumming episode shows Eustacia's rejection of her femaleness:

> As Hardy is careful to emphasize, in becoming a mummer Eustacia 'changes sex', and the whole episode is an adventure on the outer limits of respectability. What is suggested elsewhere in the novel is clearly revealed here. Eustacia in the mumming assumes the heroic masculine role to which she is always aspiring. She wants to alter her essential human condition, to change her sex. A dissatisfaction so thoroughgoing amounts to a denial of life itself.[16]

But it constitutes rather an exploration of the limits of her gender, a confrontation of the immanence of sexuality in her experience of her identity.

The fragility and vicariousness of her self-esteem make Eustacia vulnerable in a way that relates her to the literary lineage of the destructive and self-destructive *femme fatale*, which takes much of its impetus from Flaubert's Emma Bovary, and culminates in Ibsen's Hedda Gabler. Eustacia's lack of occupation is commented upon more than once, and she herself recognises – though not without some self-aggrandisement – that ' "want of an object to live for – that's all is the matter with me" ' (p. 145). Her emotions develop in a vacuum, cultivated for their own sake – she is 'an epicure' in emotions (p. 116) – because they are the only kind of experience that she has. In the same way, Emma Bovary finds no occupation for her time or her energies outside sexual relationships. Both women look for a man great enough to be worthy of the strength of their emotion, and both are disillusioned. Emma's suicide when she finds herself trapped by her material circumstances and without emotional sustenance parallels Hedda Gabler's suicide and Eustacia's death, although Hardy veils this in an ambiguity similar to that which surrounds the rape or seduction of Tess, and presumably for the same reason – to evade those questions of free choice, and individual moral responsibility that a tradition of moralistic criticism might otherwise press upon the text. Hardy's Notebooks reveal that he was reading about suicide during the composition of *The Return*, at the same time as he was reading a translation of Aeschylus's *Prometheus Chained*,[17] and it may be a sign that, for him, Promethean boundless aspiration was connected with self-destruction.[18]

Like Hedda Gabler, Eustacia finds her potential for effective activity cripplingly limited, and for both women, emotional power over other individuals is the only kind of influence they can exercise. Eustacia's attraction towards Wildeve is partly determined by the eroticism of the power which his relative passivity allows her to imagine that she holds over him:

> "[I] thought I would get a little excitement by calling you up and triumphing over you as the Witch of Endor called up Samuel. I determined you should come; and you have come! I have shown my power. A mile and a half hither, and a mile and a half back again to your home – three miles in the dark for me. Have I not shown my power?" (p. 87).

But this fantasy of power is only a thin concealment for powerless dependence, as Wildeve at once reminds her: ' "I think I drew out you before you drew out me" ' (p. 88). And indeed, she has been waiting for some hours on the heath for this moment of triumph.

Again, Eustacia's conviction that she can persuade Clym, once they are married, to return to Paris, despite his open reluctance to do so, is an attempt to exercise the only power available to her, the power of her own sexuality; it is paralleled by Hedda Gabler's action in tempting Loevberg to break his vow not to drink alcohol. Gabler's temptation seems rather perverse, however, in that it offers no possibility of fulfilment or pleasure for herself, while Eustacia's Paris – like Jude's Christminster, at once an aspiration and a fantasy, although, unlike Jude, she is given no chance to test the one by the other – at least seems to offer some personal satisfaction.

Mrs Yeobright has a less obviously literary derivation, but her literary descendants – principally Lawrence's Mrs Morel – can be more easily traced. In terms of the modes of Hardy's writing, she looks forward to the later novels, rather than back. She is a character belonging to the tradition of realism, a mode which fairly successfully obscures its literariness, and which is dependent upon references to the 'text' of common sense and of received codes of interpreting our experience. She is characterised in part by the use of statements of the category 'one of those . . . who/which', a basic strategy of the realist text,[19] which assign their subject to a class, and hence appeal to a shared code of narrator and reader. Mrs Yeobright is described, for example, as having 'well-formed features of the type usually found where perspicacity is the chief quality enthroned within' (p. 58); her manner shows 'that reticence which results from the conscience of superior communicative power' (p. 59); and her power of understanding is discussed in these somewhat obscure terms: 'She had a singular insight into life, considering that she had never mixed with it. There are instances of persons who, without clear ideas of the things they criticise, have yet had clear ideas of the relations of those things' (p. 205). In every case, the effect is to make the reader 'recognise' Mrs Yeobright as if she were already known to him. It is no coincidence that she is the only main character unencumbered by a mythological prototype, although one is projected back upon her through her association with Clym's increasingly overt assimilation to his prototype, Oedipus. In this respect, she is the focus of the troubling disjunction in the novel between realistic and mythological modes of narrative.

Further, her relationship with Clym crystallises one of the novel's structural problems. The mother–son relationship is at the centre of the novel, particularly in its difficulty interaction with Clym's alternative emotional allegiance, his marriage with Eustacia. Yet both relationships present themselves in the text as a curious vacancy. The novel is unique in Hardy in the intensity and detail with which it confronts the relationships of parents and children; many of his characters, as I have already remarked, are orphaned. When parents appear, they usually bring with them a complex of emotions – possessiveness, guilt, resentment – more commonly evoked in love-relationships. Fathers – at least, present fathers – play only a limited role in Hardy's fiction. Mothers appear rather more often, usually in a relation to their children of mutual dependence and mutual guilt. Joan Durbeyfield, for instance, is the person to whom Tess turns for advice, and also for whom she feels the greatest responsibility. Mrs Yeobright's relationship with Clym, however, is unparalleled in the fiction in the inextricable intertwining of their lives and emotions. She lives vicariously through her son, and this gives her behaviour towards him a curious blend of dependence and dominance. Clym has a life and will of his own beyond this one relationship, yet remains strongly bound to his mother for emotional approval and support. However, there is a uncertainty in the writing about the relationship, possibly because of the implicit sexuality with which it is invested. Its nature is discussed as that which cannot be discussed, shown as that which cannot be shown; their love has 'a profundity in which all exhibition of itself is painful' (p. 205), and their communication takes place through 'a magnetism which was as superior to words as words are to yells' (p. 205). The allusions to the Oedipus legend – the precise Freudian significance of which was, of course, unavailable to Hardy at this time[20] – convey something of the significance of the relationship, but serve no structuring purpose. They simply take their place in a whole cluster of references which continually enforce the model of classical drama upon the novel. The subject-matter, the analysis of intricate psychological and emotional complexities in their relation to social forces, seems to demand a realism which is as yet only sporadic in Hardy's writing. The pressure is relieved with Mrs Yeobright's death, when the clash of realism and mythology is resolved in favour of the latter. Dead, she can play Jocasta without danger.

This formal disjunction at the crucial point of the mother-son relationship is matched by the absence in the text of the breakdown of Clym and Eustacia's marriage. The history of the pre-marital relationship is given in a manner characteristic of Hardy, through the evocation of Eustacia's pre-disposition to love (conveyed in part by her 'knight in shining armour' dream) and by the imagery of 'irradiation' – a favourite word of Hardy's – which suggests the illusory or self-deceiving nature of the relationship. There is a reference to 'the first blinding halo kindled about him by love and beauty' (p. 216); and the early marriage encloses them in 'a sort of luminous mist, which hid from them surroundings of any inharmonious colour and gave to all things the character of light' (p. 251).[21] Their first significant meeting comes when Eustacia is disguised; in a reversal of her dream, it is now she who is the romantic knight-figure, and Clym who is engaged in dancing. The growth of the relationship seems almost pre-determined. It is at the point where it becomes a marriage that it begins to present difficulties which are unresolved in the text. Just as in Eustacia's dream, the moment of consummation gives way to emptiness: ' "It must be here," said the voice by her side, and blushingly looking up she saw him removing his casque to kiss her. At that moment, there was a cracking noise, and his figure fell into fragments like a pack of cards' (p. 137).

The sexuality of the relationship is entirely displaced into allusion and implication. In the scenes of frustration and argument which represent the breakdown of the marriage, there is a stress on Eustacia's sense of social impoverishment which is scarcely justified by her former style of life and which is clearly concealing or obstructing the expression of more intense emotional and sexual disappointments. It is surely not simply a case of censorship, since the sexuality of Eustacia's relationship with Wildeve is apparent even in the serial version of the novel, surviving the careful stress there on the plantonic nature of Wildeve's final offer of assistance. It is also noticeably that the marriage is not followed rapidly by pregnancy, as Tasmin's is, and indeed as Emma Bovary's is. Pregnancy and

motherhood are a major element in the representation of female
characters in nineteenth-century fiction, and in the 'Woman
Question' novels of the 1880s and 1890s will be the index of
recuperation into the prescribed female role – a kind of salva-
tion through motherhood – or of irrecuperability. In *The
Return of the Native*, it is quite simply no part of Eustacia's
experience. After Clym takes to furze-cutting, the bitterness of
Eustacia's response is again far in excess of the expression of
failed social aspiration. She comes upon him singing, as he
works, a song focusing on sexual love and its intensity:

> "Le point du jour
> Cause parfois, cause douleur extrême;
> Que l'espace des nuits est court
> Pour le berger brûlant d'amour,
> Forcé de quitter ce qu'il aime
> Au point du jour!" (p. 263)

Her reaction – 'It was bitterly plain to Eustacia that he did
not care much about social failure' (p. 263) – is obviously inad-
equate to the point of irrelevance. In the argument that ensues,
the sexual disappointment is for once made explicit:

> "And how madly we loved two months ago! You were never tired of
> contemplating me, nor I of contemplating you. Who would have thought
> then that by this time my eyes would not seem so very bright to yours, nor
> your lips so very sweet to mine? Two months – is it possible?" (p. 264).

This is obviously not the language of social ambition thwarted.
Clym admits to jealousy when she wishes to go along to a dance
in a neighbouring village; and indeed, in Hardy, dancing is
often at the same time an expression and a focus of unrestrained
sexuality. Eustacia's dance with Wildeve is described in
language that exactly echoes the language of her earlier dream,
and is contrasted, in its 'tropical sensations' with the 'arctic
frigidity' of her life otherwise (p. 271). This last phrase is surely
not idle; the implication is that her sexuality is unaroused, or
unsatisfied, by her marriage to Clym. The dance attacks their
'sense of social order' (p. 272), and is obviously leading towards
an adulterous relationship; whether the failure of the relationship to take this form is the result of Eustacia's scruples or of
Hardy's pre-censorship is unclear. The way in which all this
sexual material is marginalised and left unstated leaves a

complex of disproportionate emotions focused on the issue of the return to Paris.

It is significant that Hardy's first attempt at a tragedy should revolve upon sexual disharmony and marital breakdown, subjects which will come to occupy a central place in his fiction. But the marital breakdown is not permitted to be the instrument of Eustacia's sexual tragedy; both are displaced by the increasingly rigid imposition on the text of the would-be unifying model of classical tragedy. As the sexual sub-text becomes more pressingly significant, it erupts back into the novel through allusion and implication. Literary and philosophical allusions are to remain part of Hardy's writing – he is always conscious of the interdependence of texts – but here, together with the mythologising, they become increasingly prominent as they become a kind of refuge from the disruptions of the text. The attempted conjunction of literary modes, of tragedy and realism, takes the form of a collision; but it is in the attempt that *The Return of the Native* most valuably prefigures the last novels.

NOTES

1 See, respectively, Louis Crompton, 'The Sunburnt God: Ritual and Tragic Myth in *The Return of the Native*,' *Boston University Studies in English*, 4 (1960), 229–40; David Eggenschwiler, 'Eustacia Vye, Queen of Night and Courtly Pretender,' *Nineteenth-Century Fiction*, 21 (1971), 444–54; Douglas Brown, *Thomas Hardy*, Men and Books Series (London, 1954), pp. 55–63; and Michael Millgate, *Thomas Hardy: His Career as a Novelist* (London, 1971), pp. 130–54.

2 See David J. de Laura, ' "The Ache of Modernism" in Hardy's Later Novels,' *ELH*, 34 (1967), 380–99.

3 In *The Woodlanders*, on p. 224, a similar image accompanies the adulterous liaison of Fitzpiers and Felice Charmond in the form of a quotation from *Epipsychidion*.

4 John Paterson, *The Making of 'The Return of the Native'*, University of California English Studies, No. 19 (Berkeley, 1960), pp. 105–6.

5 *The Complete Poetical Works of Percy Bysshe Shelley*, I, *1802–1813*, ed. Neville Rogers (Oxford, 1972), p. 299.

6 *The Making of 'The Return'*, pp. 10–17.

7 Adrian Poole, *Gissing in Context* (London, 1975), p. 8.

8 *Belgravia*, 34 (1877–8), 507.

9 Robert Evans, for instance, divides her into 'Eustacia Regina' and 'The

Other Eustacia', in 'The Other Eustacia,' *Novel*, 1 (1968), 251–9; see also Eggenschwiler, 'Queen of Night and Courtly Pretender.'

10 The passage is even more extravagantly romantic in the serial version of the 'Queen of Night' chapter, where 'Her presence brought memories of Bourbon roses, jacinths and rubies, a tropical midnight, an eclipse of the sun, a portent; her moods recalled lotus-eaters, the march in *Athalie*, the Commination Service; her motions, the ebb and flow of the sea; her voice, the viola': *Belgravia*, 34 (1877–8), 503.

11 Leonard W. Deen, 'Heroism and Pathos in Hardy's *The Return of the Native*,' *Nineteenth-Century Fiction*, 15 (1960), 211.

12 See Peter J. Casagrande, 'Hardy's Wordsworth: A Record and a Commentary,' *English Literature in Transition*, 20 (1977), 210–37, for an account of borrowings and reminiscences of Wordsworth.

13 *The Making of 'The Return'*, p. 82.

14 Her bonfire, like those of the other inhabitants, is a sign of 'spontaneous, Promethean rebelliousness' (p. 45), and Clym talks of rebelling 'in high Promethean fashion' as she does (p. 265).

15 For a comment on the place of Echo in the Freudian understanding of Narcissism, see Juliet Mitchell, *Psychoanalysis and Feminism* (Harmondsworth, 1974), pp. 30–41.

16 'Heroism and Pathos,' p. 211.

17 *The Literary Notes of Thomas Hardy*, ed. Lennart A. Björk (Goteborg, 1974), I. *Text*, pp. 48–50, entries 463–76, and I. *Notes*, pp. 268–71.

18 C. Heywood, in '*The Return of the Native* and Miss Braddon's *The Doctor's Wife*: A Probable Source,' *Nineteenth-Century Fiction*, 18 (1963), 91–4, has suggested that Braddon's novel was an interposing source for Hardy's novel, but the parallels are not such as to suggest influence, and, in any case, Flaubert's novel was already widely known in England.

19 Roland Barthes, *s/z* (Paris, 1970), pp. 24–5 and 210–12.

20 Though Irving Howe has a relevant comment: 'Hardy is trying to say through the workings of chance what later writers will try to say through the vocabulary of the unconscious': *Thomas Hardy*, p. 66.

21 Taken in conjunction with the later reference to the abrupt departure from Wildeve of 'the glory and the dream' (p. 121), these images suggest a further reminiscence of Wordsworth, and particularly of his concern with the 'light that never was' of the imagination in its interplay with the objects of perception.

CHAPTER 4

Women and the New
Fiction 1880–1900

The last twenty years of the nineteenth century witnessed a quite unprecedented proliferation of women novelists – a phenomenon that did not go unnoticed in its time; a writer complains in 1894 that 'the society lady, dazzled by the brilliancy of her own conversation, and the serious-minded spinster, bitten by some sociological theory, still decide . . . that fiction is the obvious medium through which to astonish or improve the world.'[1] I do not know whether solid statistical evidence could be adduced for the contemporary sense that women dominated the novel, if only numerically; but it is undeniable that they achieved a considerably higher representation in the ranks of professional authors than in any previous period. Nor were they all unknown or unrecognised minor talents: many women writers who are now forgotten were in their time widely read and discussed. Sarah Grand's novel *The Heavenly Twins* sold forty thousand copies within a few weeks of its publication in 1893;[2] George Egerton's first volume of short stories, *Keynotes* (1893), gave its name to a whole series of books published by John Lane, known as 'Petticoat' Lane partly for that reason; and a *Punch* parody of the same book, thinly disguised as 'She-Notes' by Borgia Smudgiton,[3] follows the original in such detail as to suggest that all the magazine's potential readers could reasonably be expected to know it.

But the significance of such women writers was not restricted to their numerical strength or their commercial success. They were perceived, and to some extent regarded themselves, as constituting by virtue of their sex alone a school or class of writers. They often claim to be writing with female readers in mind, and to be making a political or moral statement on behalf of their sex; Ella Hepworth Dixon, for example, wrote to Stead that her novel *The Story of a Modern Woman* (1894) was intended as 'a plea for a kind of moral and social trades-unionism among women.'[4] The example of the trades union probably underlies the recurrent suggestion, in the 'New Women' fiction, that women must and will combine, either against men or against specific abuses. The solidarity of wife and mistress, or of virgin and whore, is often recognised as a crucial element in the struggle against the double standard of sexual morality, as, for example, in Lucas Malet's *The Wages of Sin* (1891) or Annie Holdsworth's *Joanna Trail, Spinster* (1894). In this situation, writing came, to a degree, to be regarded as in itself a political act of sexual solidarity. It is not surprising, then, that reviewers saw in the proliferation of women writers the marks of an organised school. W. T. Stead, reviewing a rather miscellaneous collection of novels and stories by women in 1894, unites them with this dizzying definition: 'The Modern Woman novel is not merely a novel written by a woman, or a novel written about women, but it is a novel written by a woman about women from the standpoint of Woman.'[5] The last phrase isolates the factor which unifies in differentiation – the tendency for the central female characters, either individually or as a group, to be the centres of consciousness in the novel, rather than merely objects encountered by male subjectivity. In fact, this tendency is by no means confined to books by women, as the evidence of Meredith or Gissing indicates; indeed, Carolyn Heilbrun has named the whole *fin de siècle* period that of the 'Woman as Hero'.[6] Nevertheless, the experiencing heroine was felt by many writers and readers to be the distinctive quality of women's writing, and this sense pervades much contemporary discussion.

One manifestation of the centrality of female characters was the introduction of a whole range of hitherto marginalised or suppressed subject-matter into the novel. The exploration of the experience of female characters involved a confrontation of sexual and marital relationships which had long lain on the unspoken and unspeakable periphery of fiction. Issues such as prostitution, rape, contraception, adultery, and divorce[7] appear with increasing frequency and some explicitness, often provoking outrage and disgust in the critics. Arthur Waugh, in the somewhat unlikely setting of that citadel of decadence, *The*

Yellow Book, blames women writers for the prominence of sexual themes:

> It was said of a great poet by a little critic that he wheeled his nuptial couch into the area; but these small poets and smaller novelists bring out their sick into the thoroughfare and stop the traffic while they give us a clinical lecture upon their sufferings. We are told that this is part of the revolt of woman, and certainly our women-writers are chiefly to blame. It is out of date, no doubt, to clamour for modesty; but the woman who describes the sensations of childbirth does so, it is to be presumed – not as the writer of advice to a wife – but as an artist producing literature for art's sake. And so one may fairly ask her: How is art served by all this? What has she told us that we did not all know, or could not learn from medical manuals? and what impression has she left us over and above the memory of her unpalatable details?[8]

This criterion of teaching something 'that we did not all know' is one which does not seem to have been applied to the works of male authors.

In a sense, all this was undoubtedly exhilarating for female writers and readers, for it allowed them to take speech for themselves; one writer comments in 1896 that 'It is only during the last twenty years or so that the voice of woman has really been heard in literature.'[9] Further, it opened up a far greater play of possibilities in both narrative and form, of which many women joyously availed themselves. Ethel Voynich's Gemma Bolla, for example, is a political activist in Italy (as is Mark Rutherford's Clara Hopgood).[10] A particularly rich instance is the eponymous heroine of Lady Florence Dixie's *Gloriana; or the Revolution of 1900* (1890), who passes for a man in order to prove her abilities – which she undeniably does, becoming in turn headboy at Eton, champion Hunt Steeplechase jockey, Commander-in-Chief of para-military women's 'volunteer companies', sponsor of a successful Woman Suffrage Bill, founder of a Hall of Liberty where women students, athletes, and brass bands live and perform, and, perhaps inevitably, Prime Minister; ultimately, revealed as a woman, she finds love and marriage, sparks off a feminist revolution and is secularly canonised by succeeding generations. (This book, incidentally, has the distinction of what must surely be one of the earliest examples of a now familiar phrase, in its disclaimer of any antagonism towards men: 'The Author's best and truest friends . . . have been and are men.'[11])

Gloriana's feminist Utopia – albeit, for much of the book, a transvestite one – is only one instance of the profusion of alternative fictional forms in this liberation of experiment. Short stories, fantasies, dream-stories, essay fiction, and im-pressionistic sketches are all forms largely, though not of course exclusively, developed or re-worked by women writers in the period. So, Jane Hume Clapperton's *Margaret Dunmore: or, A Socialist Home* (1888), a dreary tale of eugenic 'socialism', mixes epistolary form, drama, and omniscient narration; Olive Schreiner's *The Story of an African Farm* (1883) breaks its narrative with lengthy allegories; and many novels include brief or long passages of verse. The leisurely and particularised realist narrative is displaced by the fragmentary and unparti-cularised short story, by fantasy, by mixed modes of prose and poetry, and so on: but the period's challenge to the dominant fictional mode of realism took only in part the form of such experimentalism in genre. More than this, the characteristic narrative voice of the realist novel, that of the omniscient commentator who circumscribes and thus ironises the con-sciousness of the hero, is disturbed by the appearance of other kinds of voice which throw into question this distance between author and character. The 'New Woman' novel was often perceived as a work of propaganda or a disguised tract for precisely this reason: not because its ideological project is any more visible or determining than in other kinds of fiction, but because of the sporadic punctuation of the narrative by medita-tion, harangue or lyric, by an informing commitment which constantly threatens the circumscribing narrative voice.

Now I do not wish here to suggest – with the concomitant risk of reinforcing a sexual stereotype – that the 'New Woman' fiction is marked by its adjustment to a characteristically feminine subjectivity (an interpretation sometimes made at the time, as I shall show). It is rather that the pose of the 'objective' narrator – the anonymous, balanced reporter who can author-itatively interpret the behaviour and states of mind of the characters – is unsettled by the tension between this male voice (it is not an accident that so many female writers take male pseudonyms) and the periodic dissolution of the boundaries between author and character. It is as if at moments there is no mediating narrator; the writing of the fiction becomes for a time its own action, its own plot, enacting as well as articulating the protest of the text.[12] *The Story of an African Farm* holds in tension the dispassionate Emersonian pose of the objective narrator, that 'Ralph Iron' who intervenes between author and text, and the commitment to a passionate vision – Lyndall's and Schreiner's – which is allowed only one articulate eruption into the narrative, but which informs and troubles the structure both before and after the chapter that bears Lyndall's name. In works by male writers, too, the realist narrative mode is frequently unsettled. The example of Hardy comes to mind: the abrupt and disturbing shifts in point of view in *Tess of the d'Urbervilles* enact the threatened dominance of the distanced narrator. In this respect, the 'New Woman' fiction is at the opposite pole from the naturalist novel, which preserves a scrupulously 'scientific' distance from the paticularities of its text; the difference between *Tess* and George Moore's *Esther Waters* (1894) resides partly in this question of the maintenance and manipulation of points of view.

The formal experimentation of the New Fiction, together with its openly sexual character, posed a significant challenge to the power of the editors of periodicals and the proprietors of the circulating libraries; so it is that this period sees the demise of the previously dominant mode of publication, the family serial and the three-decker.[13] As early as 1885, Gissing was able to announce this change, and also to declare his enthusiasm for the modifications in narrative mode and voice which accompanied it:

> It is fine to see how the old three volume tradition is being broken through. One volume is becoming commonest of all. It is the new school, due to continental influence. Thackeray and Dickens wrote at enorr ous length, and with precision of detail; their plan is to tell everything, and leave nothing to be divined. Far more artistic, I think, is the later method, of merely suggesting; of dealing with episodes, instead of writing biographies. The old novelist is omniscient; I think it is better to tell a story precisely as one does in real life, surmising, telling in detail what can so be told and no more. In fact, it approximates to the dramatic mode of presentment.[14]

It is interesting to note that Gissing welcomes the new forms primarily as a new and more thoroughgoing kind of realism. New journals, such as *The Yellow Book* and its imitator *The*

Savoy, sprang up to accommodate poems, short stories, and even fragments – Victoria Cross's 'Theodora. A Fragment' was one of the more notorious examples of the New Woman in action.[15] Publishing houses were quick to open their lists to new writers whose work (sometimes enormously successful on the market) dealt with women or sex, as John Lane's 'Keynotes' series and Heinemann's 'Pioneer' series testify. The New Fiction had an enormous impact, not only on publishers, but on readers and critics too. Reviewers, especially those who wrote in the more long-established periodicals, reacted on the whole with shocked incomprehension. The vocabulary of realism, itself seen comparatively recently as outrageous, was rapidly pressed into service to accuse these new writers of disproportion in their emphasis on the sexual:

> The new fiction of sexuality presents to us a series of pictures painted from reflections in convex mirrors, the colossal nose which dominates the face being represented by one colossal appetite which dominates life . . . everywhere it is a flagrant violation of the obvious proportion of life.[16]

After the initial modified praise of the novelty and freshness of the New Fiction, the figure of the New Woman exploring her own womanhood came fairly rapidly to be perceived as a tired cliché, fit matter for parody.[17] In fact, satire or parody of the New Woman became for a time a sub-genre of its own, taking in such works as Sydney Grundy's play *The New Woman* (1894) and Kenneth Grahame's role-reversal satire *The Headswoman* (1898). The opponents or reformers of marriage were particularly popular targets; this passage is from William Barry's novel *The Two Standards* (1898):

> Some, as, for instance, Miss Vane Vere, the well-known professor of Rational Dress and Dancing, spoke of "terminable annuities", by which it is suspected that they meant engagements lasting for a year and a day, but then to be dissolved at the pleasure – or, more likely, the displeasure – of either contracting party. Others – and among these Mrs. Oneida Leyden was far the most advanced – talked of "perfection". . . . Thus to be perfect and to be married – at least always to the same partner – did not seem in accordance with the Higher Law. Mrs. Leyden was thought to have obeyed the Higher Law. Into this remarkable scheme a lady from the Turkish frontier, speaking many languages, and known by her eloquent books on the subject of woman's freedom, had brought fresh complications by recommending the Oriental household as a pattern for progessive people. But . . . this very Frau von Engelmacher had boldly announced

that superfluous babies should be handed over to the chemist, and was known to take a strong view in favour of vivisection.[18]

Nordau's tireless and massively influential castigation of degeneracy in his *Entartung* (1892; translated into English from the second edition in 1895) gave the critical hostility to the New Fiction a fresh impetus. Diagnosed in a reassuringly medical way as 'erotomania' or 'sex-mania',[19] it was variously condemned for squalor, morbidity, pessimism and decadence, attributed with varying degrees of accuracy to the influence of French poetry, Scandinavian problem-literature, Thomas Hardy, and Oscar Wilde.[20] (Shaw, in the 1905 Preface to his previously unpublished 1880 novel *The Irrational Knot*, was to ridicule such attributions and argue that 'the revolt of the Life Force against readymade morality in the nineteenth century was not the work of a Norwegian microbe, but would have worked itself into expression in English literature had Norway never existed'.)[21] The rhetoric of attacks on the New Fiction becomes highly physical, reflecting perhaps the 'physiological realism' it condemns:

> Instead of walking on the mountain tops, breathing the pure high atmosphere of imagination freely playing around the truths of life and of love, they force us down into the stifling charnel-house, where animal decay, with its swarms of loathsome activities, meets us at every turn.[22]

But even in the censuring of decadence, the difference of sex comes into play. A distinction was sometimes drawn between the varieties of degeneracy practised by male and female writers. As well as those books by men which openly took up the 'woman question' – such as the pro- or anti-free union novels of Grant Allen, William Barry and Frank Frankfort Moore – there were within the New Fiction a number of formally experimental works which dealt with sexual themes from a male point of view. William Platt's *Women, Love, and Life* (1895) mixes poetry, short stories, allegory and essays, and makes use of subject-matter including necrophilia and masochism. In his story 'A Passion', a woman experiences the greatest happiness she has never known through dying during a caesarean, refusing anaesthetics; she makes her husband swear always to wear a girdle made of her flesh. 'The Child of Love and Death' is yet more extraordinary in synopsis: a woman conceives a child while giving her virginity to her newly-killed lover, in a vain attempt to revive him; after a fifteen-month pregnancy, she opens herself with a knife to release the child; she survives until the child is weaned; he devotes his life to preaching purity (carefully distinguished from chastity), and is beheaded by the king, who then orders a prostitute to have sex with his dead body; she, recognising the dead man's holiness, kills the king instead, addresses words of love to the headless corpse, and commits suicide. The sexual grotesquerie of Platt's volume (described by Hardy as 'mere sexuality without any counterpoise'),[23] and the rapturously breathless style of his prose, can both be seen in this description by a woman of the consummation of a love affair:

> "He staggered up to me and the veins on his forehead stood big – he took me in his arms with no word but kissed me with red hot lips till the crisped skin of them crumbled on to my chin. No word passed – but – I would say it proudly and without shame were I standing now at the judgment seat of God! – the act of love passed between us."[24]

Less extravagantly, Henry Murray's *A Man of Genius* (1895) and Francis Adams' *A Child of the Age* (1894; a reworking of his 1884 *Leicester: An Autobiography*) both exploit the same central situation: a struggling 'decadent' artist with a strong sense of his own abilities, living unmarried with a working-class girl whom he feels to be holding him back from the fame and fortune rightfully his. Both novels offer in passing somewhat cold-blooded reflections upon the nature of these relationships. Adams' curiously modern novel, a fragmentary dream-like first-person narrative, has the artist meditating upon his Rosy:

> Then, when I was in bed, I considered what was the real condition of my feelings towards her. Without doubt, they were those of complete callousness and, perhaps, something more. . . . It seemed to me to be something little short of folly to stay here and be troubled with her. I ought to go out into the world and see its ways, so as to prepare myself for my work.[25]

In Murray's more conventional work, a prominent motif is women's attraction towards force and glamour: 'Women are like nations, they admire and love most deeply the tyrant who most completely dominates them.'[26] Again, George Street's stories in *Episodes* (1895) and his novel *The Wise and the Wayward* (1896) adopt a man-of-the-worldly tone of aristocratic boredom in incidents such as a wife's revealing to her sister-in-law that her feeling for her husband is ' "merely sensual. . . . It is simply because he is handsome and big and strong" ',[27] or a husband's laconic reaction to his wife's adultery with his best friend:

> "You see," he continued, "you place me in a very tiresome dilemma. I must either divorce you and quarrel with a man with whom I am not in the least angry – he's one of my oldest friends and has only acted as I have acted many times – or I must put myself in the ridiculous position of the forgiving husband and allow him to laugh at me. Think! I must either quarrel with a man who was my chum at school, or appear absurd to him. See what you women do!" (*Episodes*, p. 112).

Ignoring 'decadent' books by women like Ella Darcy's *Monochromes* (1895) or Mabel Wotton's *Day-Books* (1896), and 'high-minded' books by men like Grant Allen's *The Woman Who Did* (1895) or William Barry's *The New Antigone* (1887), pre-determined notions of sexual difference allowed the New Fiction to be split along the fault-line of the author's sex. Arthur Waugh sees 'want of restraint' and 'the language of the courtesan' resulting from the 'ennervated sensation' of women's writing, while 'coarse familiarity' and the language of 'the bargee' follow 'a certain brutal virility' in men's.[28] A pamphlet, *The New Fiction*, published in 1885, distinguishes a 'revolting woman' novel and a 'defiant man' novel:

> On the man's side it is cynical as well as nasty; it assumes that there is no world except Piccadilly after dark, or perhaps the coulisses of some disreputable music-hall . . . On the woman's side it seems at least to be in deadly earnest, but many of the assumptions are the same, *mutatis mutandis*, and the expression of them is even less veiled.[29]

Still more disturbing to the sensibilities of this truculently self-proclaimed 'Philistine', it should be noted, is that fiction of the 'morbid and lurid classes' which does not at once reveal the sex of its writer.

Not only tone and language, but also the form of the fiction, could be derived from the sex of the author through the idea of a distinct and inherent female temperament. The German critic Laura Marholm Hansson writes in 1896 that:

> Woman is the most subjective of all creatures; she can only write about her own feelings, and her expression of them is her most valuable contribution to literature. Formerly women's writings were, for the most part, either

directly or indirectly, the expression of a great falsehood. They were so overpoweringly impersonal, it was quite comic to see the way in which they imitated men's models, both in form and contents. Now that woman is conscious of her individuality as a woman, she needs an artistic mode of expression, she flings aside the old forms, and seeks for new.[30]

But if the woman writer's mind was ceaselessly returned to her sex, her body was often denied it. In the general attacks on the New Fiction, women writers above all were subjected to a great deal of personal abuse and innuendo about their sexual inclinations. Stead – a relatively sympathetic reviewer – concludes from *Keynotes* that its author is a hermaphrodite, and generalises that the Novel of the Modern Woman is often written by 'creatures who have been unkindly denied by nature the instincts of their sex', who have not 'had the advantage of personal experience of marriage and of motherhood.'[31] Again, C. E. Raimond's novel *George Mandeville's Husband* (1894) takes as what is clearly meant to be a representative case a woman novelist (the 'George' of the title), whose ruthless devotion to her own mediocre talent demands the sacrifice first of her husband's artistic career, and then of her only child's life. There can be no mistake about the kind of novelist George Mandeville is:

> His wife was not long in realising that she had found her mission. Yes, she had "oracles to deliver". She would be not only a novelist, but a teacher and leader of men. She would champion the cause of Progress, she would hold high the banner of Woman's Emancipation. She would not consent, however, to be criticised by the narrow standards applied in these evil days to woman's work. She was assured she had a powerful and original mind – she would not allow the soft veil of her sex to hide her merit from the public eye. She would call herself "George Mandeville".[32]

Mocked as a 'large, uncorseted woman' (p. 9) whose size and coarseness make her sexual demands repellent, she moves in a circle composed entirely of 'effeminate' actors and ugly, fanatical, 'advanced' women. Her husband is devoted to their daughter, from whom he extracts a promise that she will never write or paint, because women's artistic productions are tainted with the vices of amateurism and mediocrity which corrupt taste and lower standards. This is the height of his paternal ambition for her: 'Rosina should never struggle and toil; she should be no more than a dignified looker-on at this new Dance

of Death. . . . Rosina should *be*; the less she "did", the better'
(p. 114). Rosina, neglected by her mother, dies of brain-fever. It
would be naive, and worse, to be surprised that this novel is the
work of a woman; but it is perhaps allowable to be surprised that
the pseudonym 'C. E. Raimond' conceals Elizabeth Robins,
friend of Wilde, pioneer actress in Ibsen's plays, and later author
of the suffragist play *Votes for Women* (1905). (Nor, it must be
said, does the novel lend itself to an interpretation as parody, as a
brilliant and strategic adoption of the male narrative voice,
skillfully undermined by the manipulation of point of view.)
Stead's 'phallic criticism', to borrow Mary Ellmann's phrase,[33]
and Raimond's account of the woman novelist, lead to the heart
of the double-bind: the trouble with women writers is that they
are women – or else that they are writers.

The representative role of the woman writers, and the
frequency with which such terms as 'the woman question', 'the
problem novel', and 'tract' or 'propaganda' recur in contemporary discussion of the New Fiction, draw attention to the
form taken by this irruption of the feminine into the novel.
Women, as writers or as characters, are identified as at once the
source and the focus of a 'problem', the precise terms of which
may vary between, say, the fate of the 'surplus' women when
men are outnumbered in the population, and the levelling out of
the double standard. The woman writer and the New Woman
alike are invariably called upon as spokeswomen: they represent, and are represented by, their sex – or, more accurately,
their sex as it is bounded by their class-situation. The symbolic
names of many such heroines reveal this – names like 'Ideala',
'Speranza', 'Angelica', 'Newman', and 'Eve'.[34] Despite the
historical component implicit in the name '*New* Woman', it is
the typicality of sex which is dominant. The woman is continually returned to her sex, identified, analysed, and made to
explain herself on the basis of her difference, her divergence
from the male norm (there is, after all, no 'Man Question').[35]
This determining typicality of sex marks a shift in the ideological project of novels about women during the *fin de siècle*
period, away from the immediately preceding concern with
womanliness, and toward the elaboration of a concept of
womanhood – a distinction which I shall try to make clear.

'Womanliness', as John Goode has shown,[36] signifies that

which is womanly, or like a woman: it is womanly to be like a woman, and a woman is one who behaves in a womanly fashion – the evident circularity of the definition makes more or less overt its reference to a socially-constructed concept. Womanliness is in this sense recognisably a political concept, proposing an external standard of judgement – it is possible, and indeed common, for a woman to be unwomanly – rather than an inherent disposition. It may (especially in the hands of women writers) hold out a promise of satisfaction to the womanly woman, but its aim is clearly the imposition and maintenance of sharply differentiated sexual roles. Dinah Craik's *The Woman's Kingdom*, first published in 1869, but evidently still popular enough to be reprinting in the 1890s, is structurally paradigmatic for the novel of womanliness: the contrasted fatherless or orphaned sisters can be traced back to Jane Austen. The novel's Ruskinian title, and its epigraph from 'Of Queen's Gardens', betray its frame of reference, that all-powerful but indirect 'influence' which every woman must choose to exert, but which she must never wield. The two sisters here are a teacher, plain, but intelligent and generous, and a convalescent, beautiful, but selfish and petty. They meet two precisely complementary brothers – a doctor, not handsome, but full of character and strength, and a sickly artist, handsome and charming, but weak and unstable. The exact symmetry of character, profession, age and appearance is striking. The frivolous couple drift into equivocal relations, almost marry, but do not; he wastes his talents and becomes a vagabond, while she makes a wealthy but empty marriage and has only a single daughter to show for it. The good pair, however, form a strong and stable relationship – this is the quality of it:

> She watched him coming, a tall figure, strong and active, walking firmly, without pauses or hesitation . . . There he was, the ruler of her life, her friend, her lover, some day to be her husband. He was coming to assume his rights, to assert his sovereignty. A momentary vague terror smote her, a fear as to the unknown future, a tender regret for the peaceful maidenly, solitary days left behind, and then her heart recognised its master and went forth to meet him; not gleefully, with timbrels and dances, but veiled and gentle, grave and meek; contented and ready to obey him, "even as Sara obeyed Abraham, calling him lord." [37]

He comes, she waits; he asserts, she assents. The two marry, live on a small income but in great happiness and mutual respect, the doctor's integrity sustained by his wife's influence. Her womanly virtues are rewarded with a family of sons. The connection between the acceptance of the womanly role and the successful marriage is so overt that the novel's religious rhetoric barely conceals the underlying economism.

But perhaps the major exponent of the fiction of womanliness is Eliza Lynn Linton, who reinforced her essays on *The Girl of the Period* (collected in 1883) with a helpfully schematic exposition of the concept in novels such as *The Rebel of the Family* (1880). Here there are three sisters, all of marriageable age and slender financial resources, to be contrasted. The eldest has every appearance of being an exemplary woman: quietly elegant, unassuming, she seemingly aims only to please:

> When she heard a new-comer say in a loud whisper to his neighbour: "What a charming smile Miss Winstanley has!" or: "What wonderful style there is about her!" or: "What a graceful person she is, and how delightfully well-mannered!" then her soul was satisfied because her existence was justified. She had done her duty to herself, her mother, her future and the family fortunes. She had therefore earned her her right to be well-dressed and taken out into society, as fairly as a workman, who has laid his tale of bricks, has earned his pint of beer and his stipulated week's wages.[38]

But the incongruously clear-sighted economic metaphor should alert the reader to the trap, for Thomasin's exemplary behaviour is vitiated by her excessive awareness of its value as a commodity. Her motivation is too self-consciously directing her behaviour, and so her discretion and modesty are transmuted into 'this quiet immorality, this cynical good sense, this apotheosis of worldly wisdom' (III, 203). The figure of Thomasin, with her 'masculine' name, reveals something of the contradiction inherent in Linton's situation as a woman writer serving the ideology of womanliness: the novel's project is to show that womanliness is the only guarantee of success on the marriage-market, and yet to propose as a naturally womanly quality a selflessness which would necessitate ignorance of that fact. The womanliness of the project is undercut by Linton's unwomanly awareness of its fictionality, and this, as I shall argue, necessitates a certain dexterity in the manipulation of point of view.

If Thomasin is one of the figures from Linton's essays, the self-seeking girl of the period, then the youngest sister is another – the pleasure seeker. She is a kind of early Dickens heroine – blonde, blue-eyed, flower-like, lisping. But her sweetness and charm are undermined by her frivolity and lack of solid moral principle. Here again, though, that principle shows itself to be largely a matter of making the best use of her commodity-status. She fails the womanly ideal in the opposite direction, by failing to realise the full marketability of her charms: she is, literally and metaphorically, cheap. Her sisters only narrowly save her from 'falling' – a possibility telegraphed from the first in her name, Eva.

The middle sister, Perdita, represents the middle way – a way which, again as the name suggests, is temporarily lost. Her combination of an intelligent mind and a generous heart causes her to be ruthlessly sacrificed by her sisters, but also gives rise to a certain questioning rebelliousness in her. She realises that her abilities are stifled by her narrow life, and longs for the change of sex which alone seems to offer a way out of the problem:

> The heart and soul of all poor Perdita's lamentations and day-dreams was always this wish – that she had been born a boy and could go out into the world to make a name for herself and a fortune for her family! . . . The *Sturm and Drang* period with her was severe; and, seeing how the current of modern thought goes, it was an even chance whether it would end in some fatal absurdity or work through its present turbulence into clearness of purpose and reasonableness of action (I, 31).

The 'fatal absurdity' which threatens Perdita takes the form of a third of Linton's Girl of the Period cast of characters: one of the 'Shrieking Sisterhood', the New Woman Bell Blount, who, 'hardened', 'unsexed', 'ungraceful', 'mannish' and 'monstrous' (I, 282–3), lectures on women's suffrage to an audience of 'mannish' women and 'weedy' men. She also poses a more direct sexual threat to Perdita's womanliness, for she lives as the 'male' partner in a lesbian relationship which exactly reproduces the structures of power and dependence of a heterosexual marriage. (This relation of feminism to lesbianism also appears in other contemporary novels, such as James' *The Bostonians* and George Moore's *A Drama in Muslin* (both 1886).) Perdita, though repelled by the coarse talk and advanced manners, finds herself fascinated by the purposefulness of Blount's life. Her moral worthlessness is finally exposed, however, in her betrayal of Perdita's secret love for a local chemist – a betrayal which, although motivated exclusively by sexual jealousy, also serves to discredit her public role as a suffragist. Thus delivered from the dual threat of suffragism and lesbianism, Perdita finds the way that was lost in the prospect of a marriage which is given a certain spuriously radical air by its social 'unsuitability'. But, though her 'rebellion' (stressed in the novel's title) consists in marrying for love rather than for money, the true reward for her womanliness comes in her acquiring both: her chemist makes good and rescues her family from financial ruin. Her accession to womanliness is dependent upon her at once knowing that it will serve her well (in contrast to Eva) and not knowing it (in contrast to Thomasin); the difficulty of effecting a coherent reconciliation between the two means that the narrative voice must, at a certain point, abandon its privileged insight into Perdita's consciousness, and distance her by interposing a mediating interpreter. And so it is that, by the end of the novel, she has resigned the right to speech, and it is her husband who gives the final placing of her experience for the reader – that she has found ' "a woman's duties higher than her rights; the quiet restrictions of home more precious than the excitement of liberty, the blare of publicity" ' III, 287). *The Rebel of the Family* is a parable of the woman's voluntary subjection of herself to a standard of womanliness which, though it is perceived as personally restrictive and unjust, nevertheless constitutes her only means of survival.

Many of the New Woman novels rebel against the limitations and uniformity imposed by this concept. The novels of liberal feminism have as their project, to quote John Goode, 'the possible freedom of woman conceived as a rational application of the social contract';[39] they tend either to be programmatic, embodying a future resolution of the woman question – and hence to take non-realist forms like fantasy – or to concentrate on the symptoms of the contemporary oppression of women, and so to take the form of a realist novel revolving upon the woman in society rather than in a single love-relationship. The characteristic structuring device of the novel of womanliness, the contrasting sisters, gives way to that of the brother and sister: the disparity between their respective abilities and fates

gives focus to the liberal feminist programme of 'equality' with
men in education, professional opportunities, sexual morality,
and marital rights and responsibilities. (The precursor in this
case is rather George Eliot than Jane Austen). So, for example,
Gertrude Dix's *The Girl from the Farm* (1895) shows a classics
graduate forced to postpone her career in order to look after her
father, while her weak and selfish brother passes his time in the
seduction of local servants; Lady Florence Dixie's *Redeemed in
Blood* (1889) is concerned with equal rights of primogeniture for
its sibling aristocrats; and Sarah Grand's *The Heavenly Twins*
(1893) are a boy and a girl, inseparable in childhood, but
subsequently forced apart by the differing expectations of their
parents and teachers. Waldo and Lyndall, in Schreiner's *The
Story of an African Farm*, are quite different, however, in part
because Waldo is not in any degree complicit in the sexual
oppression of Lyndall, but is rather her male counterpart,
outcast and misunderstood; the submerged parallel between
woman as bearer of children and male artist surfaces in the fact
that Waldo's two major projects, his sheep-shearing machine
and his carved stick, each take him nine months to bring to
fruition.[40] Nevertheless, Lyndall's long speech draws an explicit contrast between the lives marked out for them by their
difference of sex:

> "We all enter the world little plastic beings, with so much natural force
> perhaps, but for the rest – blank; and the world tells us what we are to be,
> and shapes us by the ends it sets before us. To you it says – *Work*; and to us it
> says – *Seem* . . . To us it says – Strength shall not help you, nor know-
> ledge, nor labour. You shall gain what men gain, but by other means.
>
> Then the curse begins to act on us. It finishes its work when we are grown
> women, who no more look out wistfully at a more healthy life; we are
> contended. We fit our sphere as a Chinese woman's foot fits her shoe
> exactly, as though God had made both – and yet He knows nothing of
> either. In some of us the shaping to our end has been quite completed. The
> parts we are not to use have been quite atrophied, and have even dropped
> off; but in others, and we are not less to be pitied, they have been weakened
> and left. We wear the bandages, but our limbs have not grown to them; we
> know that we are compressed, and chafe against them" (II, 39–42).

This intensely physicalised sense of chafing against cramping
limitation pervades the feminist novels; the analogy between
the Chinese practice of footbinding and the constraints upon
the growing middle-class girl recurs.[41] But Lyndall's percep-

tion that she is actually *shaped* by what is inscribed upon the 'blank' infant is unusual; more common is the image of a compression that, released, will allow the 'natural' form to reassert itself. Correspondingly, the women of these novels *undergo* their experience, restlessly rubbing against its restrictions. Interestingly, a considerable bitterness is often directed toward the figure of the mother, bearer of the vestiges of womanliness. The womanly woman is a kind of impending threat, to be killed or maimed in self defence, rather as Virginia Woolf talks of needing to murder the hovering Angel of the House before she could write her fiction.[42] The experiencing heroine is polarised: she is all certainty, aspiration, desire, while her doubts and contradictions are split off and embodied in the Mother who binds her about with prejudice and custom. Tant' Sannie, the mother-figure in Schreiner's novel, is a grotesque caricature of the womanly woman, hugely fat and endlessly receptive, consuming dried apricots and dessicated husbands with the same indifferent rapacity:

> "marriage is the finest thing in the world. I've been at it three times, and if it pleased God to take this husband from me I should have another.

> Some men are fat, and some men are thin; some men drink brandy, and some men drink gin; but it all comes to the same thing in the end; it's all one. A man's a man, you know" (II, 297–9).

Perhaps the clearest case of such a polarisation occurs in Mona Caird's two novels, *The Wing of Azrael* (1889) and *The Daughters of Danaus* (1894); in both, the mother is the focus of a curious mixture of guilt, resentment and pity. Every mother, for Caird, is one more link in a long chain binding women to renunciation and sacrifice, and every mother demands vicarious restitution. The mother in both books is at once disabling and disabled, a tyrannical invalid whose very helplessness adds force to her demands:

> She realized now, with agonising vividness, the sadness of her mother's life, the long stagnation, the slow decay of disused faculties, and the ache that accompanies all processes of decay, physical or moral. Not only the strong appeal of old affection, entwined with the earliest associations, was at work, but the appeal of womanhood itself: – the grey, sad story of a woman's life, bare and dumb and pathetic in its irony and pain: the injury from without, and then the self-injury, its direct offspring; unnecessary, yet inevitable; the unconscious thirst for the sacrifice of others, the hungry

claims of a nature unfulfilled, the groping instinct to bring the balance of renunciation to the level, and indemnify oneself for the loss suffered and the spirit offered up. And that propitiation had to be made.[43]

The resignation of that final sentence finds an echo in many of the feminist novels of failed rebellion. Netta Syrett's *Nobody's Fault* (London, 1896) ends rather similarly, with the woman's renunciation of her lover for the sake of her widowed mother: ' "It isn't a question of duty, inclination, religion, or *anything*, but just the one overwhelming necessity of not breaking the tie of blood" ' (pp. 251–2). It is the 'tie of blood' that binds fastest of all in the attempted revolt, and often plays a crucial role in defeating or subverting the woman's protest. The defeat from without, or the collapse from within, usually follows the same cycle: anger and resentment finding expression in violence, suppressed or actual; then a total, self-imposed submissiveness of behaviour combined with the attempt to preserve some inner space of protest; rebellion, sparked off by the prospect of a desired lover, marriage, or career; and a grim final result. Caird's *The Wing of Azrael* (1889) – a novel which, she claims in her Preface, aims 'not to contest or to argue, but to represent'[44] – is paradigmatic: Viola Sedley, child of a self-martyring mother and a domineering father, is tormented by the cynically clever Philip Dendraith. She pushes him over a cliff, and, although he is not seriously hurt, is so horrified and frightened by her own anger that she falls into a submissive and numbing religious fatalism. Later they marry, and he is exasperated by her passivity:

> If she had been a haughty, rebellious woman, giving him insult for insult, sneer for sneer, he might have understood it; but she professed the most complete wifely submission, obeyed him in every detail, and when he reviled her she answered not again; yet behind all this apparent yielding he knew that there was something he could not touch – the real woman who withdrew herself from him inexorably and for ever. (II. pp. 111–12).

Viola endures his humiliating and sadistic treatment out of a sense of duty towards her mother, even when she realises that she loves someone else. Her mother's death offers a glimmer of hope, and Viola arranges to elope with her lover. Trapped at the last minute by her husband, whose sexual interest in her is re-aroused by this sign of rebellion, she stabs him, flees from the momentary horror in her lover's eyes, and jumps over the cliff to her death. (The combination of desperate resignation and anger erupting into violence prefigures Hardy's Tess.) Other equally bleak resolutions occur – death, breakdown into convention, or the renunciation of personal desire and the acceptance of a joyless future.

'Happy endings' are usually to be found only in works which permit of a clearly-defined programme for the liberation of women – works which eschew realism for fantasy or prophesy. I have already mentioned the feminist Utopia of *Gloriana*; into the same category falls Jane Hume Clapperton's *Margaret Dunmore: or, A Socialist Home* (London, 1888), which shows the trials and tribulations of 'a Provincial Communistic group – ladies and gentlemen who intend to live, rather than preach, Socialism; and who hope to rear children of a purely Socialistic type' (p. 23). After both practical and emotional vicissitudes – chapped hands from large-scale potato-peeling, and a potentially adulterous affection – a satisfactory régime is established on the basis of communal domestic labour for the women, meetings of self- and group-criticism, and a eugenic meliorism derived from the works of Patrick Geddes. A lecture hall is then set up to pass on the benefits of the community's experience to the working class.

The programmatic fantasy is a form taken up by several of the male feminist-sympathisers. George Noyes Miller's novel *The Strike of a Sex* ([1895]) is a dream-vision, in which women successfully withdraw their labour – the pun, intentional or not, provides the novel's structuring metaphor – in order to get an unconditional guarantee from the male 'management' that ' "no woman from this time forth and forever, shall be subjected to the woes of maternity without her free and specific consent in all cases" ' (p. 51). This is to be effected by the implementation of 'Zugassent's Discovery'. The novel's form rather curiously mimics its subject in that it constantly approaches the point of defining this discovery, but repeatedly breaks off before the climactic revelation is made. Readers of Miller's pamphlet *After the Strike of a Sex* (1896) – or those who understood the significance of the phrase 'Member of the Oneida Community' that appears on the title page below the author's name – were to find out that it is *coitus reservatus*.

Without doubt the oddest of the fantasy solutions to the

'problem' of women can be found in Henry Dalton's *Lesbia Newman* (1889), a work whose chief distinction lies in its containing characters named The Rev Spinosa Bristley and Fidgfumblasquidiot Grewel. A politico-religious prophecy, it moves somewhat bewilderingly from the mild unconventionalities of Lesbia's membership of a bicycle club and a Reformed Dress Society, to events of rather wider significance: the Tsar is assassinated by ' "two Nihilists, ladies in the Empress' suite" ' (p. 171), Ireland throws off the yoke of the English only to put itself under the voluntary tutelage of the United States, world revolution breaks out in Cork harbour, the twenty-four-hour clock is introduced (a matter of equal importance, it appears), the Catholic church returns to the true faith as the Church of our Divine Lady and appoints women priests and vestals, and women – disdaining the intermediary of the morally inferior male – acquire the ability to secrete the 'zoosperm' and procreate by parthogenesis.

Most liberal feminist novels, however, content themselves with seeking rather humbler reforms; paramount amongst them is the reform of the concept and practice of marriage. The 'Anti-Marriage League', of which Margaret Oliphant writes in her review of *Jude the Obscure* and of works by Grant Allen,[45] begins rather earlier, with the female *Bildungsroman* of the 1880s in which marriage and sex are the crucial educational structures. The difficulty of establishing a satisfactory relationship between an anti-stereotype heroine, capable and independent, and a situation for her adequate to her sense of oppression often leads to the punctuation of realism by melodrama. Few marriages, for instance, are simply boring, or mutally irksome; 'bad' husbands and wives must be alcoholic, syphilitic, cruelly selfish or monstrously violent. Shaw remarks humorously on this tendency in his Preface to *The Irrational Knot*: 'I had made a morally original study of a marriage myself, and made it, too, without any melodramatic forgeries, spinal diseases, and suicides, though I had to confess to a study of dipsomania' (p. xxv). The melodrama is intensified by the desire to make representative the experience of the female characters, and the shift away from a single focal heroine to a number of female characters sometimes lends a note of extravagence to the marital abuses evoked. Sensitive and intelligent women are almost invariably married to violent, boorish, or venereally-diseased husbands with a string of past or present mistresses and illegitimate children in tow. *The Heavenly Twins* offers two complementary cases of the spectre of hereditary syphilis and the possibilities of eugenic feminism, one an example, and the other a warning. Evadne refuses to live with her 'moral leper' of a husband until prevailed upon by parental pressure and the threat of the law. Even then they live, at her insistence and at some cost to her health, on terms of celibacy, despite his attempts to seduce her by leaving 'salacious' advanced litera-ture – Zola, Sand, Daudet, Spencer – where he hopes she will find and read it. The saintly Edith, on the other hand, marries the depraved Sir Mosley Menteith in ignorance, bears a sickly child, and dies of syphilitic brain-fever. [46]

Some other novels explore, not the experience of marriage, but its institutionalised status, vindicating or challenging conventional legalised marriage through alternative forms of relationship: sexless marriage, parthogenesis, lesbianism, or celibacy, by choice or necessity. [47] But the fiction of marital reform is unquestionably dominated by the 'free union', which, on its own valuation, differs from common-law marriage in that it is contracted as a matter of principle, for the sake of humanity or of moral evolution, and not on the grounds of inclination or pragmatism. It is based on the notion of substituting the sanction of personal feeling for the degrading economic basis of legal marriage: the exchange of financial support by the man for exclusive contractual rights to the woman's sexual activity is redefined as, in Stead's phrase, 'monogamic prostitution.' [48] A character of Shaw's puts the case:

> "Somebody said openly in Parliament the other day that marriage was the true profession of women. So it is a profession; and except that it is a harder bargain for both parties, and that society countenances it, I dont [sic] see how it differs from what we – bless our virtuous indignation! – stigmatize as prostitution." [49]

If marriage is to be re-interpreted as prostitution, then non-marriage is often carefully distinguished from it by the scrupulous avoidance of any taint of sensuality; the heroine is protected from confusion with the pathetic victim of a plausible seducer by being herself the initiator, while the man is reluctant. Here is one such high-minded offer:

"Were I to do as you bid me, to go with you before priest or registrar, I should degrade myself beyond redemption. This, Rupert, is the woman's protest against the old bad order, her martyrdom if you will. It is for man to renounce honours, wealth, glory, the power which involves dominion over the weak, and is founded on their weakness. What can a maiden renounce? I will tell you. Do not shrink if I say it, conscious of the unsullied life I have led and the innocent love that is beating in my heart. Rupert, she can renounce respectability."[50]

This woman, incidentally, backs up her plea in a rather less self-congratulatorily idealistic fashion by threatening to kill herself if Rupert rejects her. But the tone – the pre-ordained martyrdom, the stress upon the 'unsullied' and 'innocent' nature of the woman's life, and the preservation of the female role of loving self-sacrifice – is characteristic, and makes clear the free union's exact reproduction of the ideology of marriage (loving, lasting, monogamous). The 'union' undermines the 'freedom'.

The novel of free union has only two possibilities: for or against, martyrdom or marriage. Of the first kind, the best known example (though neither the earliest nor the best) is Grant Allen's *The Woman who Did* (1895). The novel's project is from the first the martyrdom of Herminia, in the 'feminine' heroism of suffering. All doubt or contradiction is marginalised, as Herminia's boredom in Italy, where Alan has brought her, is rapidly resolved by his death. Herminia's experience leaves her wholly untouched, and her consciousness is so utterly and unironically circumscribed by the narrative voice that the novel can simply ride over the increasingly obvious and necessary compromises of her principles which suggest how little of an 'alternative' the free union is, how futile the martyrdom she has elected. This sub-text was at once visible to its conservative reviewers:

> Those who do not know the author, but who take what I must regard as the saner view of the relations of the sexes, will rejoice that what might have been a potent force for evil has been so strangely over-ruled as to become a reinforcement of the garrison defending the citadel its author desires so ardently to overthrow. For there is no mistaking the fact. From the point of view of the fervent apostle of Free Love, this is a Boomerang of a Book.[51]

For the 'pro-marriage league', these contradictions form the substance of the narrative, allowing of a contrast between 'theory' and the 'reality' of living which is invariably resolved in favour of the latter. There are sacramental defences of marriage,[52] but it is more common to see the free union confronted with, and undermined by, social ostracism, self-doubt, and jealousy. In H. Sidney Warwick's *Dust o' Glamour* (1897), the woman's increasing sense of shame, her insecurity and the social restrictions upon their life together which cause her lover to become bored and cold towards her, are all redeemed by the final marriage. In Frank Frankfort Moore's '*I Forbid the Banns*' (1893), the relationship deteriorates as a result of sexual jealousies and anxieties that are given frankly economic expression:

> He felt, when looking at her, as a man might feel who is in possession of a certain charming property, but who knows that he has no title-deeds, and that, consequently, he may be turned adrift at any moment. What is the noblest property in the world to anyone, so long as the title-deeds are in the possession of someone else?[53]

It was probably this self-mocking urbanity of tone that modified the enthusiasm of the reviewers for its argument:

> On the whole the book is a blow on the right side in the discussion, though it could be wished that the author's standpoint had been rather less that of expediency and more that of principle.[54]

Here again, the relationship is saved by legal marriage, which, dissolving all the contradictions of the preceding narrative, is represented as an unproblematic resolution. In almost every case, 'for' or 'against', the fiction of the free union represents the relationship in a vacuum, unrelated, for the woman at least, to any other area of activity. The concentration upon the woman's role in the relationship, and upon the double standard which presses upon her experience of that role, imparts an air of liberalism which is belied by the unchallenged reproduction of the 'feminine sphere' of home and family.

But under the increasing pressure of those biologistic accounts of sexual difference which I have already outlined, the feminist revolt against the womanly took on a new impetus. Writers like George Egerton, rebelling against the womanly ideal, sought to tear aside the veil of convention and hypocrisy in order to reveal the real woman beneath; but precisely this notion of a 'real' woman marks a falling back onto biological or mystical essentialism. Womanhood, in contrast to womanliness, is not an ideal or an aspiration, but an immanent natural disposition, originating in a pre-determining physiological sexual differentiation. The ideology of womanhood necessarily predicates certain kinds of experience as female, and in doing so it privileges the interiority of the female writer and, in turn, of the female narrative voice. It draws much of its strength from its protest against the existing social oppression of women, but it subverts that protest by an appeal to the 'natural' which reinforces the enclosure of women's experience by their physiological organisation. The political content of the ideology is hidden beneath its elevation of anatomically-specific female skills and abilities, which does not allow for deviation except in the sense of a far more literal 'unsexing' than that implied by the failure of womanliness.

'Womanhood' can be invoked both by those who perceive themselves as feminists – as the mystico-physiological feminism of Ellis Ethelmer witnesses – and by avowed antifeminists like Iota. Her novel *A Yellow Aster* (1894) concerns a young woman, distinctively 'modern' in that she has been cheated out of her womanhood by the rationalistic and scientific upbringing that her well-intentioned parents have given her. The title is also the novel's central symbol: Gwen Waring is the 'yellow aster', a hybrid result of human experiment upon nature. The difficulty occasioned by her education is that the spontaneity of instinct and emotion is dammed up by her constant introspection and self-analysis; the unspoken postulate of a hostile duality of body and mind finds an echo in many contemporary 'woman question' novels.[55] Receiving a proposal of marriage, she is moved to accept by the dim promptings of a so far unidentified ' "something outside me" ',[56] despite her lack of emotion and a positive aversion to the sexual side of marriage.

> She turned away to hide the crimson in her cheeks.
> "Then this one-flesh business, this is a horrid thing."
> She squeezed her hands into her eyes.
> "This is maddening!" she cried, and sprang up and stood looking out of the window.
> "One flesh!" she murmured breathlessly, "One flesh!" (II, 87).

The honeymoon leaves Gwen feeling degraded, possessed, irrevocably altered, and her subsequent pregnancy leads her to send her husband away in revulsion. The ' "something outside me" ' now comes to the fore, in the form of the something inside her – the baby, agent and embodiment of the impersonal force of the maternal instinct. Only after a kind of rebirth (she almost dies during a long and difficult labour) does her impeded womanhood assert its supremacy. She bursts into a grateful rhapsody over wife- and motherhood:

> "I am a woman at last, a full, complete, proper woman, and it is magnificent. No other living woman can feel as I do; other women absorb these feelings as they do their daily bread and butter, and they have to them the same placid everyday taste, they slip into their womanhood; mine has rushed into me with a great torrent – I love my husband, I worship him, I adore him – do you hear, my dear?" (III, 172–73).

This conclusion is successfully reached, however, only through the repression of Gwen's feminist protest; her earlier half-contemptuous envy of the 'full, complete, proper woman' has been given powerful expression in terms that cast an unsettling ambivalence over her final surrender:

> "A very strong woman is docked of half the privileges of her sex. . . . Helplessness is such supreme flattery. . . .
>
> The parasitical, gracious, leaning ways, the touch of pathos and pleading, – those are the things I should look for if I were a man, they charm me infinitely. Then that lovely craving for sympathy, and that delicious feeling of insecurity they float in, which makes the touch of strong hands a Heaven-sent boon to them – those women, you see, strew incense in your path and they get it back in service" (II, 126–27).

And further, the final mark of Gwen's triumph is that she has come to resemble exactly the idealised portrait of her which she has earlier dismissed as ' "pre-ordained to the *rôle* of bride" ' (II, 154), and which has been the occasion of an odd distinction between the 'cold living abstraction' and the 'warm, big-hearted, divinely-natural creature, alive there on the canvas' (III, 26). In order to be 'alive', to become 'divinely-natural' – the phrase conferring upon physiology the power of divinity – Gwen must, paradoxically, become static, fixed, a cultural object. Throughout the novel she has been the centre of consciousness, but at the end she is abruptly presented as a portrait, framed by the window, and perceived through the consciousness of her returning husband. Her accession to womanhood is also the resignation of her right (fully exercised in the rest of the novel) to speech: 'she just sat dumbly on the floor' (III, 204). The trajectory of the novel's project is deflected by the ambivalences that threaten its uncertain grasp of point of view.

The most prominent and able of the writers concerned with womanhood, however, is George Egerton. Her stories – especially those in her first volume, *Keynotes* – unsettle the expectations and responses of the reader in their innovatory alternation of abrupt and enigmatic narrative compression with overflowing linguistic excess, and in the unprecedented candour of their reference to sexual themes. It was probably the combination of this last with a male pseudonym – though 'George' had by now acquired from Eliot and Sand a certain tradition as a woman writer's name – that led the first reader of the stories, T. P. Gill, to express his views on them to the author in a swaggeringly 'one of the boys' tone:

> To put it brutally you would not (however Scandinavian your ideas may be) invite your coachman, or even your bosom friend, to 'assist' while you and your wife were engaged in the sacred mysteries. Why the deuce should you write it all out for them and give it them to read about! . . . For example, take the effect on a young fellow in his student period . . . of a particularly warm description of rounded limbs and the rest. It puts him in a state that he either goes off and has a woman or it is bad for his health (and possibly worse for his morals) if he doesn't.[57]

A second, highly embarrassed letter followed when the author was revealed to be one Mary Clairmonte.

Egerton clearly conceived of herself very much in terms of writing *as* a woman *for* women; her subject-matter ('the *terra incognita* of herself')[58] and her manner of writing are alike felt to be determined – or rather, her own phrase implies, restricted – by her sex alone: 'one is bound to look at life through the eyes of one's sex, to toe the limitations imposed on one by its individual physiological functions.'[59] 'The eyes of one's sex': the phrase is ambivalent, evoking at once a personalised sense of gender-identity, and a sense of what is shared with all other women. It recalls the lack of particularity with which Egerton's stories are invested by the avoidance of names and absence of personal histories for characters identified only by their sex:[60] each woman serves to represent the immanence of her womanhood. The breaking of stereotype reveals a further ideological structure within, for the project of the stories is the nature of woman as essential and universal. The stress on physiology in the quotation above is characteristic and important, for it is by virtue of physiology that woman is bound to her 'nature'. The stories foreground the exclusion of women in society, but in a way that allows that protest to be recuperated into the ideology of womanhood. For what is repressed in male-dominated society is represented as something disruptive of the very terms of that society: the 'natural' – woman, instinctive, intuitive, enigmatic, wild:

> [Men] have all overlooked the eternal wildness, the untamed primitive savage temperament that lurks in the mildest, best woman. Deep in through ages of convention this primeval trait burns, an untameable quality that may be concealed but is never eradicated by culture – the keynote of woman's witchcraft and woman's strength.[61]

In this terminology, with its implied analogy between sexual difference and the polarisation of nature and culture, there dwells an unexpected echo of Ruskin. Certainly, Egerton's glorying in the subversive amorality of her women is wholly foreign to Ruskin, but the shared analogy serves to draw out the implications of such a representation. The insistence, in Egerton's stories, upon certain common qualities in women and upon certain images of them – witch, elf, gypsy, sphinx – locate them, as if constitutionally, outside the social framework, and shift the site of their oppression into the realm of nature.

Nor does Egerton's noble female savage mark the irruption of repressed female desire into the male order, for it is the distinctive feature of the ideology of womanhood that it recuperates desire into instinct – here, ' "the deep, underlying generic instinct, the 'mutterdrang', that lifts her above and beyond all animalism, and fosters the sublimest qualities of unselfishness and devotion." '[62] The unresolved contradiction between the 'instinct' and the transcendence of 'animalism' marks the spiritualising of the woman's sexuality through reproduction; motherhood is made not merely an anatomical potentiality common to most women, but, to take up Egerton's own word, the 'keynote' of womanhood. Physiology becomes at once the ground and the expression of women's moral qualities:

"the *only divine* fibre in a woman is her maternal instinct. Every good quality she has is consequent or co-existent with that. Suppress it, and it turns to a fibroid, sapping all that is healthful and good in her nature" (*Discords*, p. 100).

The equipoise of 'healthful' and 'good', and the only half-figurative 'fibroid', reveal a moral organicism invoking nature as the ratification of that morality of vicariousness prescribed for women by womanliness and womanhood alike.

A strength of Egerton's writing is the space it makes for female anger and protest. But, as Elaine Showalter has remarked,[63] the anger and violence are constantly directed towards other women or towards children: the woman in 'Wedlock' murders her step-children to avenge her husband's callous rejection of her own illegitimate child; and the wife in 'Virgin Soil' holds her mother responsible for the abhorrence she feels for sex with her husband. Showalter argues that the anger is deflected from its true, justified target – the husband in each case – and that the 'real' struggle between husbands and wives is thus concealed. It is true that there is an absence of confrontation, but that absence is necessitated by the primacy of enigma in Egerton's account of the nature of woman; her women are incomprehensible, inexplicable, to men, and so confrontation gives way to juxtaposition. The typical Egerton woman – small, slight, pale, full of quivering nervous strength and neurotic changes of mood – attracts male characters and narrator by her eroticised difference from the male. In this feminist ideology of womanhood, that difference confers a strength which the men try to wrest from her by a mixture of threat and cajolement:

"You wait on me, ay, no slave better, and yet – I can't get at you, near you; that little soul of yours is as free as if I hadn't bought you, as if I didn't own you, as if you were not my chattel, my thing to do what I please with; do you hear"(with fury) "to degrade, to – to treat as *I please*?. . . [Yet] you pity me with all that great heart of yours because I am just a great, weak, helpless, drunken beast, a poor wreck" (*Keynotes*, p. 145).

Husbands are brutal, drunken, and weakly dependent (as in 'A Shadow's Slant') or else well meaning, but coarse, simple, and limited in understanding (as in 'An Empty Frame'). In neither case can they satisfy the complex needs of their wives. The women are bound by ' "that crowning disability of my sex" ' affection (*Keynotes*, p. 127), or by the emotional dependence of the man, or by their children; they treat the bullying child-man they have married with a vaguely contemptuous pitying affection:

> "There, it's all right, boy! Don't mind me, I have a bit of a complex nature; you couldn't understand me if you tried to; you'd better not try!"
> She has slipped, whilst speaking, her warm bare foot out of her slipper, and is rubbing it gently over his chilled ones.
> "You are cold, better go back to bed, I shall go too!" (*Keynotes*, p. 123).

The recurrent imagery of hunting – traps, cages, fishing, wounded birds – powerfully conveys the sense of inturned violence in these claustrophobic marriages.

Enigma, dominant 'keynote' of womanhood, structures many of the stories. In her retrospective note on *Keynotes*, Egerton describes the task of the woman writer as 'to give herself away'.[64] Something of this idea of self-surrender is caught in the frequency with which her stories take the form of a woman telling her story for herself, in direct speech, to a listener who is most often also a woman, though sometimes a man. But this woman's story is not co-extensive with the text; rather, it is framed and delineated by an 'objective' or first-person narrator who represents the woman to the reader as enigma, erotic or otherwise. The embedded narrative does not carry all the immediacy and authority of the framing narrative which situates it as partial; narrator and teller of the woman's story never coincide. The woman appears to the narrator from the first as the embodiment of a question (often, when the narrator is implied to be male, an erotic question) or a mystery. The sense of something tantalisingly withheld colours the objectivity of the external description of her actions:

> Free to follow the beck of one's spirit, a-ah to dream of it, and the red light glows in her eyes again; they have an inward look; what visions do they see? The small thin face is transformed, the lips are softer, one quick emotion chases the other across it, the eyes glisten and darken deeply, and the copper threads shine on her swart hair. What is she going to do, what resolve is she making? . . . Again her eyes wander out with an appealing look (to whom do they appeal, to part of herself, to some God of convention?) towards the camp (*Keynotes*, pp. 151–2).

Into this erotic tension established between woman and narrator (and, by extension, reader) breaks the moment of the woman's story, the moment when she 'gives herself away', promising at once the explication of the enigma and the dissipation of the 'woman's strength' which it gives her. Yet, because it is a narrative of direct speech, given by her in response to, and confirmation of, the narrator's question, her self-sufficient inaccessibility is preserved; just as the woman desired is never possessed by the male narrator, her consciousness is never possessed by the narrative voice. The embedded narrative, far from dissolving the enigma, implies a logic and a motivation which remain inaccessible. Even when the narrator has privileged access to the woman's consciousness, that access is partial and abridged. In 'A Cross Line', the narrator makes a very intimate entry into the woman's mind, in the fantasy which dominates the story; but precisely because it is her fantasy, it offers itself only as the possibility of interpretation through a psychoanalytic interrogation which the text will not sustain. It illumines, but it does not explain or circumscribe, the consciousness of the woman. When the woman 'gives herself away', the self-revelation confirms the narrator's erotic gaze.

Against the restriction of the claustrophobic marriages in the majority of the stories is set the notion of the expansion of womanhood – sometimes literally, as when a significant part of the 'freeing' of the woman in the fantasy of liberation 'The Regeneration of Two' is the abjuring of corsets. In that story, the restitution of womanhood, the freeing of nature from the grip of history, is effected by the attacks on contemporary sex-role degeneration of a vagabond poet:

> "I lay my heart on the brown lap of earth, and close my eyes in delicious restfulness. I can feel her respond to me; she gives me peace without taxing me for a return. I sought that in woman, for I thought to find her nature's best product, of all things closest in touch with our common mother. I hoped to find rest on her great mother heart; to return home to her for strength and wise counsel; for it is the primitive, the generic, that makes her sacred, mystic, to the best men. I found her half-man or half-doll" (*Discords*, p. 197).

His spiritual 'rescue' of her is counterpointed by her physical rescue of him, when she nurses him back to health after a near-fatal illness in repayment of his debt: ' "You stung me to analyse myself . . . To see what significance the physical changes in my body had from where the contradictions of my

nature sprang – to find myself"' (*Discords*, p. 241). By now she
has become the 'sacred, mystic' woman he had sought: infi-
nitely restful, endlessly receptive, the 'great mother'. The
expansion of womanhood ends in a confinement. The
woman's restless dissatisfaction is recuperated by a sanctified
nature and its demiurge, physiology, into the maternal role of
'restfulness . . . peace . . . home', bringing the ideology of
womanhood full circle back to the womanly ideal against
which it had defined itself.

All this may seem rather far from the highly plotted,
serialised novels of Thomas Hardy. And yet, the New Fiction
of the 1880s and 1890s in some ways took up the experiments
with genre and narrative voice, revolving upon the central
female characters, that had marked Hardy's writing career
from the beginning. His experimentalism was contextualised
and given a significant contemporaneity by the practices of
many of these lesser-known writers. He was unquestionably
aware of the areas of debate aroused by the fiction of the New
Woman and of the controversy it provoked,[65] and the sense not,
certainly, of belonging to a school, but of participating in a
moment of change in fiction which was recognised as important, seems to have imparted a new boldness to that experiment. It is with *Tess of the d'Urbervilles*, for instance, that he
claims a new significance for his fiction; there is no longer any
question of being merely 'a good hand at a serial', for he makes a
public and unequivocal statement of his views and intentions:

> I will just add that the story is sent out in all sincerity of purpose, as an
> attempt to give artistic form to a true sequence of things; and in respect of
> the book's opinions and sentiments, I would ask any too genteel reader,
> who cannot endure to have said what everybody now thinks and feels, to
> remember a well-worn sentence of St. Jerome's: If an offence come out of
> the truth, better is it that the offence come than that the truth be concealed
> (p. xv).

It is the phrase 'what everybody now thinks and feels' that most
strikingly reveals a new sense of being buoyed up by contemporary opinion. That sense must have been reinforced by
Hardy's awareness of the New Fiction and of the critical debate
around it. Certainly, it is in the novels of the late 1880s and the
1890s – in *The Woodlanders*, *Tess of the d'Urbervilles* and *Jude the
Obscure* – that the sexual and marital themes that have always

been important in Hardy become more overtly and polemically central to his fiction. This in turn will raise new problems in the handling of genre and of narrative voice, turning most particularly upon the articulation of tragedy, realism and polemic. In the chapters that follow, I propose to look at these late novels in the light of such tensions and ambivalences, which are often shared by works of the New Fiction.

NOTES

1 Hubert Crackanthorpe, 'Reticence in Literature: Some Roundabout Remarks,' *Yellow Book*, 2 (1894), 269.

2 Gail Cunningham, *The New Woman and the Victorian Novel* (London, 1978), p. 57.

3 *Punch*, 106 (1894), 109 & 129.

4 W. T. Stead, 'The Novel of the Modern Woman,' *Review of Reviews*, 10 (1894), 71.

5 'Novel of the Modern Woman,' p. 64.

6 Carolyn G. Heilbrun, *Towards Androgyny: Aspects of Male and Female in Literature* (London, 1973), pp. 47–112.

7 Prostitution is central in Annie E. Holdsworth, *Joanna Trail, Spinster* (London, 1894) and Arabella Kenealy, *The Honourable Mrs. Spoor* (London, [1895]); rape in George Moore, *A Mere Accident* (London, 1887) and [Edith Johnstone], *A Sunless Heart*, 2 vols. (London, 1894); adultery in George Slythe Street, *Episodes* (London, 1895) and George Meredith, *One of our Conquerers*, 3 vols. (London, 1891); and divorce in Meredith, *Diana of the Crossways*, 3 vols. (London, 1885) and George Egerton, 'A Little Grey Glove,' in *Keynotes* (London, 1893), pp. 91–114.

8 Arthur Waugh, 'Reticence in Literature,' *Yellow Book*, 1 (1894), 218.

9 H. E. Harvey, 'The Voice of Woman,' *Westminster Review*, 145 (1896), 193.

10 Ethel Voynich, *The Gadfly* (written 1895; published London, 1897); 'Mark Rutherford' [William Hale White], *Clara Hopgood* (London, 1896).

11 Lady Florence Dixie, *Gloriana; or, the Revolution of 1900* (London, 1890), p. ix.

12 Cf. Mary Jacobus, 'The Difference of View,' in *Women Writing and Writing about Women*, ed. Mary Jacobus (London, 1979), pp. 16–17.

13 See Guinevere L. Griest, *Mudie's Circulating Library and the Victorian Novel* (London, 1970).

14 'To Algernon Gissing,' August 1885, *Letters of George Gissing to Members of his Family*, collected and arranged by Algernon and Ellen Gissing (London, 1927), p. 166.

15 'Victoria Cross' [Nivien Corey], 'Theodora. A Fragment,' *Yellow Book*, 4 (1895), 156–88.

16 James Ashcroft Noble, 'The Fiction of Sexuality,' *Contemporary Review*, 67 (1895), 493.

17 E.g. M. Eastwood, 'The New Woman in Fiction and in Fact,' *Humanitarian*, 5 (1894), 375–9; and H. S. Scott and E. B. Hall, 'Character Note. The New Woman,' *Cornhill*, NS 23 (1894), 365–8.

18 Dr William Barry, *The Two Standards* (London, 1898), pp. 345–6.

19 'Erotomania' is used by, among others, Hugh Stutfield, 'Tommyrotics,' *Blackwoods*, 157 (1895), 833–45; and Noble, 'The Fiction of Sexuality.' 'Sex mania' is more common; users include Janet E. Hogarth, 'Literary Degenerates,' *Fortnightly Review*, 63 (1895), 586–98; and Hugh Stutfield, 'The Psychology of Feminism,' *Blackwoods*, 161 (1897), 104–17.

20 In, respectively, Stutfield, 'Tommyrotics;' E. Purcell, '*Degeneration*. By Max Nordau,' *Academy*, 47 (1895), 475–6; William L. Courtney, *The Feminine Note in Fiction* (London, 1904), pp. xxvi–xxvii; and ' "New" Art at the Old Bailey,' *Speaker*, 11 (1895), 403–4.

21 George Bernard Shaw, *The Irrational Knot; Being the Second Novel of his Nonage* (London, 1905), p. xxv.

22 B. A. Crackanthorpe, 'Sex in Modern Literature,' *Nineteenth Century*, No. 218 (1895), p. 614.

23 1 June, 1896, *One Rare Fair Woman: Thomas Hardy's Letters to Florence Henniker 1893–1922*, ed. Evelyn Hardy and F. B. Pinion (London, 1972), p. 52.

24 William Platt, *Women, Love, and Life* (London, 1895), p. 122.

25 Francis Adams, *A Child of the Age* (London, 1894), p. 223.

26 Henry Murray, *A Man of Genius*, 2 vols. (London, 1895), I, 18.

27 George Slythe Street, *Episodes* (London, 1895), p. 30.

28 'Reticence in Literature,' p. 217.

29 'The Philistine' [J. A. Sterry?], *The New Fiction (A Protest against Sex-Mania), and Other Papers* (London, 1895), pp. 83–4.

30 *Modern Women: An English Rendering of Laura Marholm Hansson's 'Das Buch der Frauen'*, by Hermione Ramsden (London, 1896), pp. 78–9.

31 'Novel of the Modern Woman,' p. 74.

32 'C. E. Raimond' [Elizabeth Robins], *George Mandeville's Husband* (London, 1894), p. 7.

33 Mary Ellmann, *Thinking About Women* (1968; rpt. London, 1979), pp. 27–54.

34 These names appear in, respectively, 'Sarah Grand' [Francis Elizabeth McFall], *Ideala* (London, 1888); Dixie, *Gloriana*; Grand, *The Heavenly Twins*, 3 vols. (London, 1893); Henry Robert S. Dalton, *Lesbia Newman* (London, 1889); and Arabella Kenealy, *Dr Janet of Harley Street* (London, [1893]).

35 Except in Laura Marholm, *The Psychology of Woman*, trans. Georgia A. Etchison (London, 1899), pp. 235–53, where it appears in the context of a Nordau-inspired lament for the decline of sharply-differentiated sex-roles.

36 John Goode, 'Woman and the Literary Text,' in *The Rights and Wrongs of Woman*, ed. Juliet Mitchell and Ann Oakley (Harmondsworth, 1976), pp. 217–55.

37 Dinah Maria Mulock Craik, *The Woman's Kingdom. A Love Story*, 3 vols. (London, 1869), II, 18–19.

38 Eliza Lynn Linton, *The Rebel of the Family*, 3 vols. (London, 1880), I, 6.

39 'Woman and the Literary Text,' p. 238.

40 'Ralph Iron' [Olive Schreiner], *The Story of an African Farm*, 2 vols. (London, 1883), I., 175 and I, 288.

41 E.g. in Grant Allen, *The British Barbarians, A Hill-Top Novel* (London, 1895), pp. 93–4.

42 Virginia Woolf, 'Professions for Women,' *Collected Essays* II, ed. Leonard Woolf (London, 1966), pp. 284–9.

43 Mona Caird, *The Daughters of Danaus* (London, 1894), pp. 362–3.

44 Mona Caird, *The Wing of Azrael*, 3 vols. (London, 1889), p. xi.

45 Margaret O. W. Oliphant, 'The Anti-Marriage League,' *Blackwoods*, 159 (1896), pp. 135–49.

46 Also relevant here is Ménie Muriel Dowie, *Gallia* (London, 1895).

47 See, respectively, 'Lucas Cleeve' [Adelina G. I. Kingscote], *The Woman Who Wouldn't* (London, 1895), and John Smith, *Platonic Affections* (London, 1896); Dalton, *Lesbia Newman*; George Moore, *A Drama in Muslin: A Realistic Novel* (London, 1886); and Holdsworth, *Joanna Trail, Spinster*, George Gissing, *The Odd Women*, 3 vols. (London, 1893), and Emma Frances Brooke, *A Superfluous Woman*, 3 vols. (London, 1894).

48 'Novel of the Modern Woman,' p. 65.

49 *The Irrational Knot*, pp. 121–2.

50 Rev. William Barry, *The New Antigone: A Romance*, 3 vols. (London, 1887), II, 148.

51 W. T. Stead, 'The Book of the Month. "The Woman Who Did." By Grant Allen,' *Review of Reviews*, 11 (1895), 177; cf. 'Recent Novels,' *Spectator*, No. 3, 483 (1895), 431–3; Percy Addleshaw, rev. of *The Woman Who Did*, by Grant Allen, *Academy*, 47 (1895); and Millicent Garrett Fawcett, 'The Woman Who Did,' *Contemporary Review*, 67 (1895), 625–31.

52 E.g. Victoria Crosse, *The Woman Who Didn't* (London, 1895), and Barry, *New Antigone*.

53 Frank Frankfort Moore, 'I Forbid the Banns,' *The Story of a Comedy which was Played Seriously*, 3 vols. (London, 1893), p. 23.

54 Elizabeth R. Chapman, *Marriage Questions in Modern Fiction, and Other Essays on Kindred Subjects* (London, 1897), p. 23.

55 In anti-feminist works, it takes most often the form of a mental or physical collapse occasioned by an attempt to develop intellectual or artistic abilities lying outside the 'natural' feminine sphere; see, e.g. Jessica Morgan in George Gissing's *In the Year of Jubilee*, 3 vols. (London, 1894); Alma Frothingham in his *The Whirlpool* (London, 1897); and Phyllis Eve in Kenealy's *Dr Janet of Harley Street*.

56 'Iota' [Kathleen Mannington Caffyn], *A Yellow Aster*, 3 vols. (London, 1894), II, 51.

57 Quoted in *A Leaf from the Yellow Book: The Correspondence of George Egerton*, ed. Terence de Vere White (London, 1958), p. 23.

58 'George Egerton' [Mary Chavelita Dunne Golding Bright,] 'A Keynote

to "Keynotes",' in *Ten Contemporaries: Notes Toward their Definitive Bibliography*, ed. 'John Gawsworth' [Terence Armstrong] (London, 1932), p. 58.

59 'A Keynote to "Keynotes",' p. 58.

60 Cf. Wendell V. Harris, 'Egerton: Forgotten Realist,' *Victorian Newsletter*, No. 33 (1968), 31–5.

61 *Keynotes* (London, 1893), p. 22.

62 *Discords* (London, 1894), p. 101.

63 *A Literature of their Own*, pp. 213–14.

64 'A Keynote to "Keynotes",' p. 58.

65 See Chapter 7 below.

CHAPTER 5

The Woodlanders (1887)

It is difficult to say what kind of a novel *The Woodlanders* is; it draws on genres so widely disparate as to be at times incompatible. Further, the word 'transitional' – which, it must be said, has been applied to almost all of Hardy's novels – is perhaps more apposite here than in many cases. It is possible to isolate elements of practically any earlier Hardy novel within the text, and its reminiscences of *Far from the Madding Crown* and *The Return of the Native*, in particular, are quite evident. At first sight, it might seem that such reminiscences could be dismissed as backward glances or tired repetitions, particularly in the light of Hardy's statement that the 'woodland story . . . (which later took shape in *The Woodlanders*)' was originally conceived, but soon abandoned, as the immediate successor to *Far from the Madding Crown* (*Early Life*, p. 135). Although there have been some attempts to reconstruct a putative Ur-novel,[1] there is really no evidence that any of the extant text dates from the period of this earliest intention. Nevertheless, the novel certainly recalls that earlier work, not least in the apparent recrudescence of the pastoral mode which is invoked by the patterning of the seasonal cycle, the fertility-rites and fertility-deities, and the underlying myth of Eden and Fall that is evoked by the pervasive apple tree motif. At the same time, the central plot – the returned native faced with a choice between lovers, that also serves to focus a choice between possible allegiances of class and lifestyle – clearly recapitulates that of *The Return of the Native*, and, indeed, that of *Under the Greenwood Tree*.[2] Yet the new and challenging centrality of the sexual and marital themes in *The Woodlanders* marks also its pivotal role in the career of its author. As Gregor has remarked, 'the significance of Grace [lies] in the fact that she provides Hardy with an opportunity to do a first sketch for Sue Bridehead.'[3] Her dilemma, caught between Giles Winterborne and Fitzpiers, her repudiation and

ultimate re-acceptance of the first marital partner, the 'Daphnean instinct' (p. 310) that impels her to flee the returning
Fitzpiers and the superficial pieties of her readings in the Bible
and the prayer book, foreshadow Sue Bridehead's agonised
hesitations between Jude and Phillotson, her leap from Phillotson's bedroom window and her violent espousal of religious
orthodoxy: Grace's gentle lapse into a concern with propriety
rehearses in miniature the desolating 'breakdown' of Sue
Bridehead.

Such disparate formal elements point to the novel's major
characteristic, the uncertainties of genre, rapid substitutions of
points of view and abrupt shifts of tone that make it unsettling to
read. Several critics, both contemporary and modern, share an
unease arising from the 'cynicism' (a recurring word), not
merely of the obdurate primacy of plot manipulation which
insists on reinstating an unrepentant Fitzpiers to his conjugal
Grace, but also, more or less vaguely, of the novel's tone.[4] It is
not difficult, I think, to see what is meant. *The Woodlanders* (and
particularly, as I shall go on to argue, the second half of it) shares
with *The Well-Beloved*, and with no other work of its author, a
self-consciousness that verges at times upon self-parody. References to literary models are almost obtrusively in evidence;
Melbury, for example, falls at once into the cadence and
rhetoric of Old Testament narrative in his appeal to Felice
Charmond:

> "I am an old man," said Melbury, "that, somewhat late in life, God thought
> fit to bless with one child, and she a daughter. Her mother was a very dear
> wife to me; but she was taken away from us when the child was young; and
> the child became precious as the apple of my eye to me, for she was all I had
> left to love" (p. 249).

The overtness of the novel's 'dialogue' with other texts and
genres marks the degree of its self-reflexivity. Certainly,
frequent literary allusions are in themselves nothing new in
Hardy, but whereas that reference has hitherto – say, in *The
Return of the Native* – served primarily to bestow significance
and gravity upon the text by invoking the authority of conse-
crated literary models, the allusiveness of *The Woodlanders* is
often more ironic and oblique, undercutting rather than
reinforcing its own aspirations to tragic status. The elements of
tragedy which allow the narrator to claim for his narrative 'a

grandeur and unity truly Sophoclean' (p. 40) disconcertingly
adjoin elements of pastoral, melodrama, and even farce. There
is, for instance, a curious and disturbing blend of melodrama
and farce in the scene in which the three lovers of Fitzpiers stare
in genuine grief at his empty nightshirt, or, again, in the
self-mockingly obvious metaphorical quality of the man-trap
in which Grace loses her skirt.[5] The various Spinozan and
Shelleyan pretensions of Fitzpiers at once invoke and uncere-
moniously parody the Romantic egotism that had undergone a
more tragic scrutiny in *The Return of the Native*, and the parodic
component is strengthened in the successive revisions that
make flippant insincerity and selfishness more prominent in his
character.[6] The brooding Romantic discontent of his early
morning soliloquy (' "Ah, Edred . . . to clip your own wings
when you were free to soar!" ' (p. 237)) inclines, again, towards
parody in the overwritten quality which it shares with Grace's
late conversion to melodrama: ' "O, Edred, there has been an
Eye watching over us to-night . . .!" ' (p. 366).

The Woodlanders, then, is characterised by its interrogative
awareness of the literary modes within which it is working.
That interrogation is crystallised in the figure of Grace Melbury, who is at the centre of its shifts in tone and point of view.
For it is not possible to represent Grace satisfactorily throughout as a realist heroine: rather, she migrates unsettlingly
between pastoral survival, tragic protagonist, realist centre of
consciousness, and melodramatic heroine. The very fluidity of
her narrative role and function makes of her at times an almost
nebulous figure. The narrator is able to offer summaries of
other characters, guaranteeing their authoritative quality by
reference to 'fact'. Of Fitzpiers, for example, he writes this:

> But, as need hardly be said, Miss Melbury's view of the doctor as a
> merciless, unwavering, irresistible scientist was not quite in accordance
> with *fact*. The *real* Dr. Fitzpiers was a man of too many hobbies to show
> likelihood of rising to any great eminence in the profession he had
> chosen. . . . *In justice to him* it must be stated that he took such studies as
> were immediately related to his own profession in turn with the rest (p. 148;
> my italics).

The 'truth' of his account of Grace, on the other hand, rests in
its denial of the possibility of giving a fixed and authoritative
summary:

> What people therefore saw of her in a cursory view was very little; in truth, mainly something that was not she. The woman herself was a conjectural creature who had little to do with the outlines presented to Sherton eyes; a shape in the gloom, whose true quality could only be approximated by putting together a movement now and a glance then, in that patient attention which nothing but watchful loving-kindness ever troubles itself to give (p. 69).

It is only by a sustained act of attention that she becomes more than 'conjectural', taking on more than 'outlines' and 'shape'. The tentative and deferential tone of the narrator's comments is notable.

In view of this, it is not surprising that Grace seems at times empty, passive, a mere reflector or register of the other characters, as she is to Melbury at once the object and the vehicle of his social ambition. Even her sexual attraction towards Fitzpiers seems, at their first meeting, simply to reflect back the unknowing gaze of desire which she intercepts in the mirror. Yet it is the very insubstantiality of her characterisation in this sense that allows her sexuality to become the central point upon which the novel's formal disjunctions revolve. A closer examination of the fluctuating presentations of Grace in the narrative will show how sexuality and marriage figure for the first time in Hardy as the explicit concern of the fiction.

Elements of pastoral, and particularly of pastoral elergy, contribute significantly to both the structure and the tone of *The Woodlanders* in a way that will not be repeated in Hardy. Jacobus has drawn attention to the way in which the novel draws upon a traditional structuring device of the pastoral, the cycle of the seasons. Here, though, it floats free from its conventional significations (the 'life-cycle' of fruition, decay, death, and rebirth) and attaches itself ironically to the frustrating and inconclusive relationships of the human characters.[7] Again, the elegiac tone is in excess of its ostensible focus in the plot, the death of Giles Winterborne, and the ironic counter-pointing of the changing seasons at once invokes and under-mines the implied regeneration which concludes the pastoral elegy. The community of *The Woodlanders* is not merely depleted by the loss of Giles, but radically devitalised. This is a use of pastoral that presses beyond the simply ironic; in the elegiac excess, there dwells almost a sense of mourning for its

own loss, the mark of the text's recognition of the final
inadequacy of the pastoral mode.

Nevertheless, critical readings of *The Woodlanders* have often
emphasised the novel's elements of pastoral at the expense of all
its other modes of writing. Dataller's is a particularly explicit
pastoral account:

> [*The Woodlanders*] is rather a personification of the eternal struggle between
> Town and Country. The town represents the sophisticated, the artificial,
> the meretricious element of the story; the country, the deeply seated,
> instinctive, and forthright habit of living. The townees rejoice in every
> attribute, but lack virtue. The country-folk lack many things, the graces of
> intellect, the advantage of riches, but are sustained by their innate
> well-being.[8]

There are a number of objections that could be raised to this
construction of a scenario opposing the simple and traditional
life of those who live in harmony with 'nature' (Giles Winterborne and Marty South) to the corrupting sophistication of the
demonic urban intruders (Fitzpiers and Felice Charmond) who
invade and destroy it.[9] First, in reducing Grace's hesitations
between her two lovers to a mere symbolic transposition of
some timeless and genderless choice between rusticity and
urbanity, it quite simply supresses the importance of the sexual
choice, travestying the complex specificities of her dilemma
into some allegorical quirk of temperament. Secondly, it
would appear at least naive to enforce upon the text a pastoral
reading which is not only made, but also resisted, within it. It is
Grace, separated by her education from the society she
observes, who sees in Giles' seasonal cider-making work the
image of 'Autumn's very brother' (p. 225), as is made clear
when she later notices a change in him: 'Was [his face] not
thinner, less rich in hue, less like that of ripe Autumn's brother
to whom she had formerly compared him?' (p. 320). Such
pastoralising patronage has already been bitterly repudiated by
Giles: Grace calls down to him from the balcony where she sits
musing in Keatsian and Chattertonian vein upon the beauties of
'the margin of Pomona's plain' (p. 197), but Giles declines to be
subsumed into the landscape, and reminds her sharply that he is
'"moiling and muddling for [his] daily bread"' (p. 199). In an
analogous episode, Fitzpiers, coming to read in the woods,
chances upon a group of labourers stripping the bark from

felled trees; he is charmed by 'the scene and the actors' of 'this sylvan life' (p. 159), but the Arcadian quality is undercut (even if not for him) by Marty's matter-of-fact recall of its economic realities by which she, as a woman worker, is doubly oppressed:

> "You seem to have a better instrument than they, Marty," said Fitzpiers.
> "No, sir," she said, holding up the tool, a horse's leg-bone fitted into a handle and filed to an edge; " 'tis only that they've less patience with the twigs, because their time is worth more than mine." (p. 159).

Such collisions between pastoral and realism throw the pastoral reading into question so overtly as to make its inadequacy as a critical analysis wholly evident.

But perhaps the most significant objection is that to read *The Woodlanders* simply as pastoral, whether 'classical', 'traditional', or 'grotesque',[10] is to make an ideological resolution of the competing views of nature which inhabit the text and are played out upon the figure of Grace. Alongside the pastoral nature, there runs a quite incompatible vein of the Spencerian-Darwinian representation of nature as the site of a struggle for survival in which mere physical proximity is certain to produce conflict and involuntary violence, as the woodland trees are 'disfigured with wounds resulting from their mutual rubbings and blows' (p. 323), or as Melbury and Grace drive off in their carriage 'silently crushing delicate-patterned mosses, hyacinths, primroses, lords-and-ladies, and other strange and common plants, and cracking up little sticks that lay across the track' (p. 162). The Spencerian component of such a view resides, of course, in the consecration of the evolutionary struggle as an apt, and even inevitable, metaphor for human society, so that 'the Unfulfilled Intention' (p. 82) is expressed alike in the distortions and stuntings of the woodland growths and in the deflected and frustrated plans and desires of the novel's protagonists.[11] This stress, all but unique in Hardy, upon the continuity of human and non-human modes of existence is mediated in part through what has been called ' "naturalistic" imagery (imagery bestowing vegetal and human qualities upon humans)'[12], a variety of imagery that co-exists in the novel with the use of a 'pathetic' imagery more often evoking a Romantic view of nature. The organicism of such imagery, the emphasis upon the determinations of environment on physical and mental development alike (Marty's hands that 'might have skilfully guided the pencil or swept the string, had they only been set to do it in good time' (p. 43) or the 'wildly imaginative' inferences drawn from 'narrow premises' (pp. 39–40), at least in part because of the isolation of Little Hintock), and the importance of the group and its interaction at the expense of the single, dominating protagonist: all of these mark the novel's closeness at times to French naturalism, prominent in England at this period rather as the subject of a fierce critical controversy than as a model of literary practice.[13] This irruption of naturalism, as I shall go on to argue, partially determines the form taken by the novel's treatment of its sexual themes.

Nevertheless, the pastoral polarisation of rusticity and urbanity as equivalents to innocence and sophistication unquestionably takes its point of departure in *The Woodlanders* from Grace's position as an educated country-woman; what may be called 'nature' (doubly constituted by her gender and her rural origins) reconstructed as 'culture' (by the urban education that her father's relative wealth and ambitions have prescribed for her). It is in this sense that her conflicting allegiances towards Giles and Fitzpiers make of her a tragic protagonist. It is true that the novel as a whole cannot be fitted into any current definition of tragedy; Kramer, for example, scrupulously and fruitlessly examines the text for evidence of a single, dominant protagonist (whose absence is the more notable for the novel's chronological placing between *The Mayor of Casterbridge* and *Tess of the d'Urbervilles*), a 'tragic flaw', or the cathartic release of pity and fear, and is obliged to find in it instead a modified tragic genre, the 'tragedy of the group'.[14] But the novel does take up, if only to avert, the form of the double tragedy – that of a woman and of a man, sexual and intellectual – that had already given *The Return of the Native* its structure. In that earlier novel, the tragedies of Clym and Eustacia resolve themselves into a sexually-founded polarity of culture and nature; *The Woodlanders* reproduces that dualism, but within the compass of a single character, Grace Melbury. Her 'veneer of artificiality' and her 'latent early instincts' (p225), her 'modern nerves with primitive feelings' (p. 309), reveal her to be the first of Hardy's female characters to contain

within herself at least the potentialities for a tragic conflict
between sexuality and the intellect. In this, as in much else, she
prefigures Sue Bridehead; but whereas Sue's conflict between
'flesh' and 'spirit' will take on its full sharpness from her
attempts to transcend sexual ideology and her re-implication in
it by marriage (or pseudo-marriage) and motherhood, the
conflict within Grace presents itself as a simple opposition of
mind and body, in the guise of education overlaid upon instinct.
The 'instinctual' body, however, finds expression only in the
mildest of marital transgressions – a single kiss, the chaste
nights in Giles' hut, the quickly retracted retrospective claim to
an adulterous relationship with him – and equally, the 'educated' mind leads her to only the gentlest of interrogations of the
ideology of marriage: 'She wondered whether God really did
join them together' (p. 363). Her breakdown, consequently,
consists in a lapse into a concern with propriety which falls short
of a tragic intensity.

   If we are to accept Rebekah Owen's account, Hardy found
the ending of *The Woodlanders* unsatisfactory (as he did that of
The Return of the Native), and, further, saw that the problem
revolved upon the figure of Grace:

> He said that Grace never interested him much; he was provoked with her all
> along. If she would have done a really self-abandoned, impassioned thing
> (gone off with Giles), he could have made a fine tragic ending to the book,
> but she was too commonplace and straitlaced, and he could not make her.[15]

The difficulty, however, resides not in any conventionality of
Grace's 'character', but rather in the form that the conflict
which she is intended to focus takes on: that of a dualism which
allows itself all too easily to be ideologically dissolved into the
collision of rustic purity and urban corruption. With the death
of Giles, the conflict is simply and definitively resolved by the
removal of one pole, that of the 'natural'; and with that
resolution vanishes the residual tragic potential of Grace's
situation. The fulfilled tragedy of the man in this case obviates
the necessity – and, indeed, withdraws the possibility – of the
completion of the woman's tragedy.

   The vehicle of the tragic component in *The Woodlanders* is a
realist analysis of sexual and marital themes, and once more it
must be said that this is not in itself new in Hardy. For the first

time, however, it is not marital breakdown (as in *The Return of
the Native*) or a mistaken marital commitment to the wrong
partner (as in *Far From the Madding Crowd*) that raises that
prospect of a tragic outcome, but marital commitment *per se*. It
is the first of Hardy's novels to make use of the fictional
possibility of divorce, which had become possible in fact some
thirty years previously, at the time when the novel is set,[16] with
the Matrimonial Causes Act of 1857. It is not by coincidence
that it should also be the first of Hardy's works openly to throw
into question the very basis of the institution of marriage: a
definitive and exclusive sexual commitment to the marital
partner. Hardy himself draws attention to this theme, in a
characteristically *faux naïf* fashion, in his 1895 Preface to the
novel:

> . . . it is tacitly assumed for the purposes of the story that no doubt of the
> depravity of the erratic heart who feels some second person to be better
> suited to his or her tastes than the one with whom he has contracted to live,
> enters the head of reader or writer for a moment (p. 35).

This is misleading, however, and not only in the sense which its
obvious sarcasm signals, for the novel does not show the
unmaking of a 'wrong' commitment in order to replace it by a
second, 'right' commitment to a 'better suited' partner. That
would be rather the pattern of *Far from the Madding Crowd*,
where the violent removal of Troy and Boldwood allows the
interrupted courtship of Bathsheba and Oak to reach its fitting
conclusion at last. Only by a drastic distortion of the tone of *The
Woodlanders* can it be made to correspond to this account: 'Then,
after Fitzpiers' salutary rustic cure and the Socratically placid
death of Winterbourne, begins the quiet Indian-summer re-
wooing of Grace by Fitzpiers, with happy ending.'[17] Grace's
eventual reunion with Fitzpiers is not so much enabled as
enforced by the death of Giles, which puts an abrupt and
decisive end to her emotional vacillations between the two
men. Grace is not alone in such fluctuations; almost every
character in the novel has more than one partner, either actually
(as Felice Charmond has a dead husband, a discarded lover and a
current one), or potentially (as Giles has both Grace and Marty
South). The general multiplicity of involvements, frustrations
and retractions undermines the notion of the exclusivity and
irrevocability of the marriage contract. Marital and non-

marital liaisons alike are formed and broken by the vagaries of inconstant sexual desire, as much in the restrained and 'Daphnean' Grace as in the restlessly passionate Felice, whose strong feeling in itself marks her as doomed. Both these women experience desire as if it were an external compulsion to which they must submit, locating in Fitzpiers the source of an emanation of 'compelling power' which calls forth in Felice a gloomy fatalism and in Grace a somnambulistic passivity:

> She felt like a woman who did not know what she had been doing for the previous hour; but supposed with trepidation that the afternoon's proceedings, though vague, had amounted to an engagement between herself and the handsome, coercive, irresistible Fitzpiers (p. 186).

The 'coercive, irresistible Fitzpiers', however, is himself acting no less under compulsion: he is drawn against his conscious, rational decisions both to marry Grace (of whom he has earlier concluded that ' "Socially we can never be intimate" ' (p. 157)) and, later, to carry on his affair with Felice. Nor is Grace the only sleep-walker; Fitzpiers is asleep at the moment of his first meeting with Grace, and returns from an assignation with Felice asleep on horseback; and Giles absently caresses the flower at Grace's breast 'Almost with the abstraction of a somnambulist' (p. 226). Desire operates in *The Woodlanders* as a kind of mechanism of natural law, and the novel's naturalist impulse is nowhere more evident than in the quasi-scientific accounts of desire (in the shape of 'emotion') which are offered in relation to Grace, Fitzpiers and Felice in turn. Grace, on her return to Little Hintock from school, is 'a vessel of emotion, going to empty itself on she knew not what' (p. 87). The metaphor as used by the doctor has, fittingly, more scientific precision: ' ". . . people living insulated, as I do by the solitude of this place, get charged with emotive fluid like a Leyden jar with electric, for want of some conductor at hand to disperse it" ' (p. 142). The two elements of the phenomenon – the building up of emotion followed by the random discharge – recur in Felice's account: ' "Hintock has the curious effect of bottling up the emotions till one can no longer hold them; I am often obliged to fly away and discharge sentiments somewhere, or I should die outright" ' (p. 210).

There is, of course, an obvious exception to this law, and that is Marty South. It is clear, however, that her passionate singleness of commitment is attained only at the cost of that voluntary abdication of her sexuality which opens the novel and is invoked once more in her 'abstract humanism' (p. 375) at its conclusion.[18] Marty's cutting off of her hair is at once a sexual act, a 'rape' that leaves her 'deflowered' (p. 52), and a sacrifice of her sexuality; it is a self-mutilation that makes her (as her name suggests) androgynous, and thereby, within the novel's Darwinian framework, vows her to stasis and death. The Schopenhauer-influenced reading of Darwin's account of the role of women in the evolutionary process that Hardy was sometimes apt to make surfaces in the novel here: women, by virtue of their reproductive function, are the most active vehicle of the operation of the processes of sexual selection, and Marty's irrelevance to this process has, by the end of the novel, isolated her from its central concerns. It is for related ideological reasons that Felice Charmond dies (at least in volume versions of the text[19]) less from the direct effects of a bullet than from that interdependence of mind and body, postulated at its strongest or at least its most complex in women, that allows pregnancy – 'her personal condition at the time' (p. 344) – to render her particularly vulnerable to shock and fear. Fitzpiers' musings on the union of Nature and the Idea (p. 155) take on a further irony from their appearance in a novel whose representation of sexuality finds its point of departure as close to Zola as to Shelley.

Desire, then, represents an arbitrary but compelling irruption of the irrational into the area of choice and decision, producing in male and female characters alike a response of will-less acquiescence. Set against this is the exploration of marriage, not so much as experience (for the novel displays very little of any marital relationship) as, rather, in its function as a legal and ideological regulator of such lawless impulses, operating quite clearly on a gender differential. It is once more the figure of Grace that provides a narrative centre of consciousness for this investigation; through her, that contemporary sexual ideology which would polarise virtue and vice into wife and mistress is tested and discredited. When she first finds Fitzpiers out in his past and present amours, her response is unconventional, for it is her mistaken passivity in the face of her father's plans for her, rather than any jealousy of her husband's wandering affections, that disturbs her: 'But though possessed by none of the feline wildness which it was her moral duty to experience, she did not fail to suspect that she had made a frightful mistake in her marriage' (p. 229). The irony which here encompasses the 'moral duty' is dispelled, as the narrative progresses, by the emergence of an unexpected and interesting alliance among the women of the novel. It is, for example, Melbury's 'allusion to Grace's former love for her' (p. 250), rather than any of his appeals to conscience or reputation, that most affects Felice. When the two women meet again, despite Grace's initial sick distaste for the encounter, what emerges most clearly is the likeness between them, and not the opposition. Grace looks at Felice 'like a wild animal on first confronting a mirror or other puzzling product of civilisation' (p. 254), and the polarity of nature and civilisation in the image (bringing with it all the pastoralising resonances of rusticity *vs.* urbanity, innocence *vs.* sophistication) can easily obscure the significance of the mirror, whose function, after all, is to reflect the observer – to reproduce similarity and not difference. Grace's generous transcendence of self-pity and self-righteousness – ' "if I have had disappointments, you have had despairs" ' (p. 256) – is followed by a further image of likeness, as the two women, disorientated and following separate paths through the wood, find themselves led back to the same point and to a moment of spontaneous physical supportiveness. (It is surely unnecessary to find any implications of a lesbian attachment in this scene, as Millgate does.[20]) Once more *The Woodlanders* prefigures a later work here: the 'pure' and 'fallen' women who will be encompassed within the single figure of Tess Durbeyfield are here brought together by such juxtaposing imagery, as well as by the careful patterning and repetition that relates the adulterous liaison of Felice to the more decorous extra-marital relationship of Grace. This repetition is explicitly remarked in the novel: Giles tells Grace that he would not have risked his caress of the flower at her breast ' "if I had not seen something like it done elsewhere – at Middleton lately" ' (p. 226), and the narrator compares Grace's nursing of Giles with Felice's of Fitzpiers: 'Six months before this date a scene, almost similar in its mechanical parts, had been enacted at Hintock House' (p. 325).

Later in the novel Suke Damson, too, takes a place within this allying similarity. After Fitzpiers' accident, all three women – wife, past and present mistresses – gather round his bed in distress, and Grace hesitates over the contradictory demands of convention ('Ought she not to order Suke Damson downstairs and out of the house?' (p. 274) and of generosity ('But could she order this genuinely grieved woman away?' (p. 274). Her mixture of 'virtuous sarcasm' and of sympathy for 'these fellow-women whose relations with him were as close as her own' (p. 275) finds its analogue in the disconcerting blend of farce and compassion which marks the narration of the episode. What is crucial in it is the only half-sarcastic description of the women as ' "Wives all" ' (p. 275), for it goes directly to the main impetus of the novel's challenge to marriage: its naturalistic undermining of monogamy.

It would be wrong, however, to construct from this a kind of sexual pastoral in which the 'innocence' of desire is opposed to the 'alien intrusion' of marriage. Grace's dilemma over the choice of a marital partner provides the main realist element of *The Woodlanders*. Her reluctance to make a final commitment to either of her possible husbands results in part from the specificities of gender and class of her situation. Her much-vaunted education has given her some degree of access to the culture (or perhaps more accurately in her case, the manners) of the urban bourgeoisie; for a male character, as for Clym Yeobright, that education can, either in itself or by virtue of its opening up of certain kinds of employment, constitute at once the means and the mark of his class-mobility. Grace, on the other hand, is simply left by it 'as it were in mid-air between two storeys of society' (p. 235) until the new class-position is consolidated by a suitable marriage. Later, during her temporary separation from her husband, she will be left in a similar state of suspension, here sexual, as " 'neither married nor single" ' (p. 309), that marginalises her both literally and figuratively to the community during the period she spends in Giles' isolated hut. Marriage alone has the power to resolve this double ambiguity, of class and of sexual status; as her father puts it, ' "a woman takes her colour from the man she's walking with' " (p. 114). Marriage is the sole recognised index of status for a middle-class woman; in this, Grace differs both from the mock-aristocrat Felice, who is

sustained by her independent wealth – itself, of course, acquired by marriage – and from the labourer Marty, whose
class-position allows of no ambiguity.

In the light of this dependence upon a husband for the
conferral of a social role, it is not surprising that the notion of
propriety comes increasingly to regulate the progress of
Grace's various relationships. The significance of propriety, as
an awareness of potentially judging onlookers, is enacted in the
mode of narration, with its constant shiftings of point of view,
in which the centre of consciousness does not normally coincide
with the protagonist of the action: so, for example, the growth
of the liaison between Felice and Fitzpiers is given largely
through the observation and interpretation of Melbury.[21] It is in
its narration that *The Woodlanders* takes its greatest distance
from the naturalist novel, which normally assumes an authoritative and dispassionate – in short, a 'scientific' – narrative
voice. The lack of such a unifying voice, by contrast, suggests
the partiality of the succeeding points of view – a partiality
enacted in turn by the way that so many events or crucial pieces
of information are observed or overheard, rather than directly
narrated. So, every main character except Giles Winterborne
first appears in the novel as overheard, seen from afar, watched
through a window or glimpsed in a mirror. Further, information obtained by such means is frequently misinterpreted:
Melbury's decision not to 'sacrifice' his daughter in a marriage
to Giles follows a snub by Felice which he attributes to Grace's
presence at Winterborne's inauspicious Christmas party, but
which the narrator attributes to Grace's greater freshness of
beauty; and Tim Tangs sets his man-trap for Fitzpiers in the
mistaken belief that there is a continuing affair between the
doctor and Suke. The effect of this is to distance the narrative
from logic and intention, undercutting the realist notion of the
subject shaping a life in favour of an unpredictable 'great web' of
interactions and effects. Michael Millgate has dismissed all this
as 'little more than a rather literal-minded concern on Hardy's
part of the question of how people know what they know',[22]
but it is surely just this manipulation of point of view that
enforces the significance of propriety as a regulator of sexual
behaviour upon the reader.

With the death of Giles, however, there is a rather abrupt shift in the dominant narrative mode of the novel. Whereas Grace has for some time been the centre of consciousness, during the episodes of her separation from Fitzpiers and her turn towards Giles, there is a sudden withdrawal from such privileged access to her consciousness in this latter part of the novel. A series of increasingly remote observers and commentators are interposed between her and the narrator (Marty, Fitzpiers, Melbury and his employees, the anonymous observers on the Sherton road), rendering her opaque and her behaviour all at once unmotivated. The slightly disconcerting effect is to turn her suddenly into something like a sly coquette in the style of Fancy Day, bargaining the terms of her return to her husband (no more foreign philosophy or French romances) with a most untragic knowingness. This brusque change of tone results from the shift of dominant genre in the novel, as the possibility of a tragic outcome recedes, and the inevitable reconciliation with Fitzpiers shapes up. The so-called 'happy ending' is in fact a most sardonic conclusion, and is brought about by means of a lurch into melodrama that verges at times upon high farce.

Throughout the novel, the most unequivocal focus of its semi-parodic, self-conscious literarity is the relationship of Felice and Fitzpiers.[23] It is evident in Fitzpiers' mediation of his emotions through scraps of Shelley and Spinoza, in Felice's self-image as the author and protagonist of a new *Sentimental Journey*, in the literary quality of a beauty that has reached its '*édition définitive* (p. 248), and in their joint invention of the narrative of their own romance through 'infinite fancies, idle dreams, luxurious melancholies, and pretty, alluring assertions which could neither be proved nor disproved' (p. 214). The relationship begins with a literary cliché, the dropped handkerchief (which is substituted in an 1896 revision for the marginally less trite gloves of earlier texts), and it ends with the superlatively melodramatic gesture of revenge by the betrayed, exotic lover; Hardy emphasises the arbitrary quality of this episode by the excision of a manuscript passage in which the Italianised American launches an earlier passionate attack upon Felice.[24] The eroticism of the affair takes on a peculiarly charged quality from the stylised, theatrical gestures in which it is enacted by *grande dame* and Don Juan:

They looked in each other's faces without uttering a word, an arch yet gloomy smile wreathing her lips. Fitzpiers clasped her hanging hand, and, while she still remained in the same listless attitude, looking volumes into his eyes, he stealthily unbuttoned her glove, and stripped her hand of it by rolling back the gauntlet over her fingers so that it came off inside out. He then raised her hand to his mouth, she still reclining passively, watching him as she might have watched a fly upon her dress (p. 236).

The theatricality is all the more prominent in that the scene is recounted from the point of view of its audience, the watching Melbury.

But for the greater part of the text, the self-parodic, over-written quality of this relationship is counterpointed by the unironic deployment of literary allusions in the narratives of Giles and Marty. The incompatible elements of genre and tone displace one another serially, each allowing another in turn only a brief dominance. Between the death of Giles and Marty's final elegy for him, however, there intervenes the reconciliation of Grace and Fitzpiers in which the increasingly pronounced melodrama and farce culminate in the stagey humour of Grace's encounter with the man-trap. The placing of this ascendancy of the parodic in the narrative throws a subversively ironic light backward and forward upon the faithful lovers Giles and Marty. It also marks a shift in the narrative tone with respect to Grace – a shift away from Marty, her unironised duplicate at the pastoral-cum-tragic 'end' of her spectrum, and towards Felice, the intensely ironised melodramatic-cum-tragic duplicate. In a sense, *The Woodlanders*, like *The Return of the Native* before it, has alternative endings, appropriate to each of its competing genres. Marty's elegy is the pastoral ending, Grace's reunion with her husband the realist ending, and the death of Felice and the intervention of the man-trap are the melodramatic finale. The plethora of conclusions results, paradoxically enough, in irresolution.

The Woodlanders, for all the prominence of the traditional established fictional modes upon which it draws, is one of Hardy's most experimental novels. Its experimentation becomes clear in relation to such earlier works as *The Return of the Native*, where a single genre provides a dominant model that in the end determines the structure of the novel and enforces the eradication of the traces of competing modes. In *The*

Woodlanders, by contrast, there is a continuing multiplicity of generic elements almost to the end(s). The disjunction is most evident in the crucial figure of Grace Melbury, for whom no coherent personality or psyche capable of ordering those elements is constructed. Instead, the full play of ambiguities and tensions is enacted in the shifts and vacancies of her role as narrative centre. It is not by coincidence that Grace is also the focus of Hardy's most radical attempt so far to confront the issues of sexuality and marriage in his fiction; once again it is the problem of finding a satisfactory way of raising those questions in a narrative centred upon a woman that determines the formal characteristics of the work. Within the novel, however, it is possible to trace the emergence of two ways of writing that will come to prominence (though not to cohering dominance) in the central female characters of the two succeeding novels: the attempt, akin to the naturalist project, to give a 'scientifically' authoritative encompassment that will shape the narrative of Tess Durbeyfield, and the deflected and overtly partial mode of narration that will grant to Sue Bridehead an inaccessibility pushing beyond the emptiness of enigma.

NOTES

1 E.G. William H. Matchett, '*The Woodlanders*, or Realism in Sheep's Clothing,' *Nineteenth-Century Fiction*, 9 (1955), 241–61. For a discussion of the novel's early development, see Dale Kramer, 'Revisions and Vision: Thomas Hardy's *The Woodlanders*. Part I,' *Bulletin of New York Public Library*, 75 (1971), 195–230.
2 Cf. Peter J. Casagrande, 'The Shifted "Center of Altruism" in *The Woodlanders*: Thomas Hardy's Third "Return of a Native"', *ELH*, 38 (1971), 104–24.
3 Ian Gregor, *The Great Web: The Form of Hardy's Major Fiction* (London, 1974), p. 156.
4 F. R. Southerington, in *Hardy's Vision of Man* (London, 1971), writes of 'a note of cynicism in the author's treatment of his plot' (p. 119); Albert J. Guerard, *Thomas Hardy: The Novels and Stories* (London, 1949), refers to the 'cynicism' of the ending (p. 52); and Mary Jacobus, 'Tree and Machine: *The Woodlanders*,' in *Critical Approaches to the Fiction of Thomas Hardy*, ed. Dale Kramer (London, 1979), finds a 'cynical determinism' in the latter part of the novel (p. 123).
5 That the symbolic quality of the image is in excess of any single 'meaning' is graphically demonstrated in the array of symbolic interpretations

offered by critics: they include an outdated social and economic *status quo*, Grace's quality as a survivor, entrapment in social class and convention, woman, and sexuality. See, respectively, Gregor, *Great Web*, p. 163; John Holloway, 'Hardy's Major Fiction,' in *The Charted Mirror: Literary and Critical Essays* (London, 1960), p. 100; Mary M. Saunders, 'The Significance of the Man-Trap in *The Woodlanders,' Modern Fiction Studies*, 20 (1974–5), 529–31; Michael Steig, 'Art Versus Philosophy in Hardy: *The Woodlanders,' Mosaic*, 4, No 3 (1971), 109–10 and Geoffrey Thurley, *The Psychology of Hardy's Novels: The Nervous and the Statuesque* (St. Lucia, Queensland, 1975), p. 123.

6 See Dale Kramer, 'Revisions and Vision, Part I,' p. 221, and 'Part II. Years to Maturity,' *Bulletin of New York Public Library*, 75 (1971), 257–8.

7 Jacobus, 'Tree and Machine,' pp. 121–2.

8 'Roger Dataller' [A.A. Eaglestone], *The Plain Man and the Novel*, Discussion Book Series (London, 1940), p. 137.

9 Cf. Merryn Williams, *Thomas Hardy and Rural England* (London, 1972), p. 157.

10 See, respectively, David Lodge, Introduction, *The Woodlanders*, New Wessex Ed. (London, 1975), pp. 13–22; Robert Y. Drake, Jr. '*The Woodlanders* as Traditional Pastoral,' *Modern Fiction Studies*, 6 (1960), 251–7; and Charles E. May, '*Far from the Madding Crowd* and *The Woodlanders*: Hardy's Grotesque Pastorals,' *English Literature in Transition*, 17 (1974), 147–58.

11 Cf. George S. Fayen, Jr., 'Hardy's *The Woodlanders*: Inwardness and Memory,' *Studies in English Literature*, 1, No. 4 (1961), 90–1.

12 Casagrande, 'The Shifted "Center"', p. 114.

13 On contemporary responses to naturalism, see Clarence R. Decker, 'Zola's Literary Reputation in England,' *PMLA*, 49 (1934), 1140–53, and William C. Frierson, 'The English Controversy over Realism in Fiction 1885–1895,' *PMLA*, 43 (1928), 533–50. On Hardy's relation to naturalism, see William B. Newton, 'Hardy and the Naturalists: their Use of Physiology,' *Modern Philology*, 49 (1951), 28–41, and 'Chance as Employed by Hardy and the Naturalists,' *Philological Quarterly*, 30 (1951), 154–75.

14 Dale Kramer, *Thomas Hardy: The Forms of Tragedy* (London, 1975), pp. 92–110.

15 Quoted by Carl J. Weber, 'Hardy and *The Woodlanders*,' *Review of English Studies*, 15 (1939), 332.

16 The year is clearly identified as 1858 by a reference on p. 284 to ' "the new statute, twenty and twenty-one Vic., cap. eighty-five" '.

17 H. C. Duffin, *Thomas Hardy: A Study of the Wessex Novels, The Poems and 'The Dynasts'*, 3rd ed. (1916; rpt. Manchester, 1937), p. 102.

18 This phrase replaces in manuscript the original 'pure animism', which shares the misleading connotation of a philosophical system; see Kramer, 'Revisions and Vision. Part I,' p. 222.

19 The phrase is inserted in revision between the serial version and first edition of the novel; see Kramer, 'Revisions and Vision. Part II,' p. 256.

20 Michael Millgate, *Thomas Hardy: His Career as a Novelist* (London, 1971), p. 249.
21 Cf. Dale Kramer, *Forms of Tragedy*, p. 103.
22 Millgate, *Thomas Hardy*, p. 87.
23 Cf. Fayen, 'Inwardness and Memory,' pp. 85–8.
24 See Kramer, 'Revisions and Vision, Part I,' pp. 214–15.

CHAPTER 6

Tess of the D'Urbervilles (1891)

Tess of the d'Urbervilles marks a particularly important moment in Hardy's representations of women in sexual and marital relationships. It takes up many of the concerns and narrative modes of his earlier novels: it picks up the ideological tragic polarities of *The Return of the Native*, for example, and that use of the female body to explore contradictory views of nature that I have already discussed in the case of Grace Melbury. These concerns are developed in a number of new ways, however. No novel of Hardy's – not even *The Mayor of Casterbridge* – focuses more exclusively on its central character; and that character is, of course, a woman. Tess brings together for the first time the 'types' of woman that have frequently been counterposed in the earlier work – the woman compromised and doomed by her own sexuality, either as victim or as *femme fatale* (Fanny Robin, for instance, or Lucetta Le Sueur), and the young woman poised at the moment of marriageability (Paula Power, or Elizabeth-Jane Newson). Gregor has noted this change, particularly in relation to *The Woodlanders*:

> The novel finds a single person capable of revealing the conflict [between a divided human consciousness and its environment] which, in the earlier novel, had been widely dispersed. The temptations of Su[k]e, the endurance of Marty, the troubled consciousness of Grace, come together and find a fresh definition in Tess.[1]

At the same time, the components of Tess's complex class-position (decayed aristocratic lineage, economic membership of the newly-forming rural proletariat, modified by an education that provides her with a degree of access to the culture of the bourgeoisie) enables Hardy at once to evoke and invert his recurring 'Poor Man and the Lady' motif, as Bayley has remarked:

> She was an ideal of the peasant girl, the sort of girl who in his earlier novels would have been regarded sympathetically but without personal senti-

ment, but who has now become the kind of *princesse lointaine* whom the girl
in the grand house once represented. His first conception of Tess stopped
there, but the ingenuity of reverie then provided her with an under-image
of the distinction – even the hauteur – possessed by his early aristocratic
heroines.[2]

Tess, then, has no need of shadowy contrasts or parallels to
point up or ironise its central character: it is structured entirely
by the sexual and marital history of Tess Durbeyfield.

It is also at this period that Hardy's elaborately constructed,
resolutely non-controversial public persona begins to break
down. Repeatedly during his career, Hardy was careful to
distinguish between his private views and those expressed in his
novels, and, indeed, to disclaim any personal views at all on
their more controversial subjects. Indeed, he never ceased to
feel that certain things simply could not be said publicly, such as
that 'Fitzpiers goes on all his life in his bad way, and that in
returning to him Grace meets her retribution "for not sticking
to Giles"'; or that Sue Bridehead wishes throughout their
relationship to restrict herself to only 'occasional' intimacies
with Jude.[3] He was, furthermore, among those who, in 1910,
advocated suppression of a translation of Sudermann's *Das hohe
Lied*, on the grounds that 'its unflinching study of a woman's
character . . . of a somewhat ignoble type' required more in the
way of 'good literary taste' to make it acceptable.[4] Nevertheless, it was during the 1890s that he also began to make more
forthright and challenging statements in his own right. The
essay 'Candour in English Fiction' records with great bitterness
and force the shifts and trimmings to which the 'undescribably
unreal and meretricious' narrative conventions of the family
serial condemned him (or, rather, to which his insistence on
publishing his novels in that form condemned him). Later, he
contributed to a symposium on the need for sex education, and
expressed his progressive views quite emphatically.[5] These are
essays, however, and remain wholly separate from his fiction.
His Preface to *The Woodlanders* uses an oblique and distancing
irony to imply his real views on the subject of divorce, but it is
only with the Explanatory Note to the First Edition of *Tess* that
he makes the unusually straightforward and challenging claim
to have represented in his novel 'what everybody nowadays
thinks and feels' (p. 25). A subsequent Preface will temper this

uncompromising account, claiming that 'the novel was intended to be neither didactic nor aggressive' (p. 27), but the tone
of the original Note helps to explain why it was with *Tess of the
d'Urbervilles* that Hardy came to be thought of as a writer with a
philosophical-cum-moral axe to grind. 'Let the truth be told'
(p. 133) has almost the air of a manifesto.

It has been claimed that '*Tess* immediately preceded the New
Woman fiction',[6] but, as my account of the New Fiction has
shown, novels dealing with sex and the New Woman were
already no longer a novelty. Some of the attacks on *Tess* –
which was greeted with a moral furore and a degree of
partisanship that must have made most of the earlier criticisms
of his work seem trivial – were surely induced by the fact that
Hardy appeared to be lending the weight of his position as a
well-established (if slightly controversial) author to the more
recent developments of the New Fiction. The early reviews
abound in references to French realism (the term being at the
time virtually synonymous with 'naturalism'), to Zola, and to
Ibsen, and the work is repeatedly characterised as a 'novel with a
purpose' or a 'Tendenz-Roman'.[7] What made *Tess* so controversial was not the relatively harmless plot (after all, many
another young girl in fiction had 'fallen' to a man more
powerful and experienced than herself, and either come to a bad
end, like Eliot's Hetty Sorrell, or redeemed herself by a lifetime
of self-sacrifice and maternal devotion, like Gaskell's Ruth),
but this new element of polemic. A number of factors interacted
to ensure that the novel would be read primarily in this light,
whatever Hardy's intentions. There was, first, the context of an
increasing questioning, both in fiction and in public discussion,
of sex roles and of the double standard. There were elements of
the plot: the ambivalence of Tess's feeling for her child, and the
failure of motherhood in itself to determine the subsequent
course of her experience; the fact that sexual and marital
relationships are presented in such direct relation to economic
pressures and to work; Tess's concealment of her past from
Angel; and, of course, that second 'fall' of the more mature and
experienced Tess that so scandalised Margaret Oliphant.[8] But
above all, there were the sense (reinforced by that aggressive
afterthought of a sub-title, 'A Pure Woman') that Hardy was
presuming to offer a moral argument in the shape of a structured

defence of his central character, and the passionate commitment to Tess herself.

Tess presses the problem of what I have earlier called Hardy's urge towards narrative androgyny to the point where a break becomes necessary. John Bayley claims that 'Tess is the most striking embodiment in literature of the woman realised both as object and as consciousness, to herself and to others'.[9] But this even-handed statement of the case smooths out the tension inherent in this androgynous mode of narration, which has as its project to present woman, 'pure woman', as known from within and without, explicated and rendered transparent. In short, she is not merely spoken by the narrator, but also spoken *for*. To realise Tess as consciousness, with all that that entails of representation and display, inevitably renders her all the more the object of gaze and of knowledge for reader and narrator. John Goode has drawn attention to the erotic dimension of this interplay between reader and character:

> Tess is the subject of the novel: that makes her inevitably an object of the reader's consumption (no novel has ever produced so much of what Sontag required in place of hermeneutics, namely, an erotics of art).[10]

And so it is that all the passionate commitment to exhibiting Tess as the subject of her own experience evokes an unusually overt maleness in the narrative voice. The narrator's erotic fantasies of penetration and engulfment enact a pursuit, violation and persecution of Tess in parallel with those she suffers at the hands of her two lovers. Time and again the narrator seeks to enter Tess, through her eyes – 'his [eyes] plumbed the deepness of the ever-varying pupils, with their radiating fibrils of blue, and black, and gray, and violet' (p. 198) – through her mouth – 'he saw the red interior of her mouth as if it had been a snake's' (p. 198) – and through her flesh – 'as the day wears on its feminine smoothness is scarified by the stubble, and bleeds' (p. 117). The phallic imagery of pricking, piercing and penetration which has repeatedly been noted,[11] serves not only to create an image-chain linking Tess's experiences from the death of Prince to her final penetrative act of retaliation, but also to satisfy the narrator's fascination with the interiority of her sexuality, and his desire to take possession of her. Similarly, the repeated evocations of a recumbent or somnolent Tess awaken-

ing to violence, and the continual interweaving of red and
white, blood and flesh, sex and death, provide structuring
images for the violence Tess suffers, but also repeat that
violence. It has even been suggested that the novel takes the
form it does in part because the narrator's jealous inability to
relinquish his sole possession of her causes both the editing out
of her seduction by Alec, and the denial to her of consummated
marriage or lasting relationship.[12]

But this narrative appropriation is resisted by the very thing
that the narrator seeks above all to capture in Tess: her sexuality,
which remains unknowable and unrepresentable. There is a
sense here in which James' comment that 'The pretence of
"sexuality" is only equalled by the absence of it' could be
justified.[13] It is as if Tess's sexuality resides quite literally *within*
her body, and must be wrested from her by violence. The most
telling passage in this respect is Angel Clare's early morning
sight of Tess:

> She had not heard him enter and hardly realised his presence there. She was
> yawning, and he saw the red interior of her mouth as if it had been a snake's.
> She had stretched one arm so high above her coiled-up cable of hair that he
> could see its satin delicacy above the sunburn; her face was flushed with
> sleep, and her eyelids hung heavy over their pupils. The brim-fulness of her
> nature breathed from her. It was a moment when a woman's soul is more
> incarnate than at any other time; when the most spiritual beauty bespeaks
> itself flesh; and sex takes the outside place in the presentation (p. 198).

It is most revealing here that, as Mary Jacobus has remarked, the
language of incarnation is destabilised by the physicality and
interiority of the 'woman's soul', co-extensive with the 'brim-
fulness of her nature', that it seeks to represent. Jacobus has also
significantly noted that 'The incarnate state of Tess's soul
appears to be as close to sleep – to unconsciousness – as is
compatible with going about her work.'[14] Here, as elsewhere,
and particularly at moments of such erotic response, consciousness is all but edited out. Tess is asleep, or in reverie, at almost
every crucial turn of the plot: at Prince's death, at the time of her
seduction by Alec, when the sleep-walking Angel buries his
image of her, at his return to find her at the Herons, and when
the police take her at Stonehenge. Important moments of
speech are absent, too – her wedding-night account of her past
life, for example, or the 'merciless polemical syllogism', learnt

from Angel, with which she transforms Alec from evangelical preacher to sexual suitor once more (p. 345). Tess is most herself – and that is, most woman – at points where she is dumb and semi-conscious. The tragedy of Tess Durbeyfield, like that in *The Return of the Native*, turns upon an ideological basis, projecting a polarity of sex and intellect, body and mind, upon an equally fixed polarity of gender. In this schema, sex and nature are assigned to the female, intellect and culture to the male. That this is so would have been even more clearly the case had Hardy retained the Ur-*Tess* version of the relation between Tess and Angel. The relatively crude feminist point made by Angel's flagrant application of a double standard of sexual morality replaces what might have been a rather subtler counterpointing of the varieties of heterodoxy available to (intellectual) man and (sexual) woman: there is some evidence that his original wedding-night 'confession' was to have been primarily of lost faith.[15] Angel Clare's dilemma is compounded primarily of elements given a historical and social location: the difficulties of class transition, the confrontation of liberal education and Christian faith, the establishment of a standard of morality in the absence of transcendentally ratified principles. Tess's situation, unlike that of Eustacia Vye, calls upon similar elements: her entrapment in mutually reinforcing economic and sexual oppression, for example, and the characteristically Victorian morality of the double standard. But still, the source of what is specifically *tragic* in her story remains at the level of nature. Tess is identified with nature – or, more accurately, constructed as an instance of the natural – in a number of ways. She is, for instance, particularly associated with instinct and intuition, those 'natural' modes of knowledge which Clare too will ascribe to her, and which form part of a collision in the novel between formal and heuristic education. So, the 'invincible instinct towards self-delight' (p. 128) sends her to Talbothays in relatively good heart; her 'instincts' tell her that she must not play hard to get with Angel Clare, 'since it must in its very nature carry with it a suspicion of art' (p. 221); and the 'appetite for joy' moves her to accept Clare's proposal of marriage (p. 218). It is noticeable, too, that Tess is often bound doubly to her sex and to intuition or instinct by a generalising commentary: 'the woman's instinct to hide' (p. 224), 'it would

have denoted deficiency of womanhood if she had not instinc-
tively known what an argument lies in propinquity' (p. 269),
'the intuitive heart of woman knoweth not only its own
bitterness, but its husband's' (p. 269). Then, too, there is her
explicitly remarked continuity with the natural world: she
(again in common with other members of her sex) is 'part and
parcel of outdoor nature . . . a portion of the field' (p. 116);
images of animals and birds, hunting and traps, cluster around
her; and in the latter part of the novel she becomes increasingly
'like . . . a lesser creature than a woman' (p. 418). Kathleen
Rogers has remarked that 'Tess herself is almost less a personality than a beautiful portion of nature violated by human
selfishness and over-intellectualizing. She is the least flawed of
Hardy's protagonists, but also the least human.'[16] But what
might otherwise be simply a process of diminution is modified
by the new degree of consciousness with which Tess's assimilation to nature is evoked. The ideological elision of woman, sex,
and nature remains a structuring element of the tragedy, but at
the same time presses 'the vulgarism of the "natural woman"' [17]
to a point where it becomes disruptively visible. Angel Clare,
who is patently implicated in Hardy's continuing dialogue with
both Shelley and Arnold, is also the bearer of the vestiges of
certain Romantic and Christian views of nature in his responses
to Tess. For him, Tess is 'a mate from unconstrained Nature,
and not from the abodes of Art' (p. 202); during their courtship,
he creates for himself a pastoral in which the farm life is 'bucolic'
and Tess herself 'idyllic' (p. 232); her wedding-night confession
transforms her, for him, from ' "a child of nature" ' (p. 259) to
an instance of 'Nature, in her fantastic trickery' (p. 263). It is
through Clare, through the obvious contradictions and inadequacies of his response to Tess, that the novel throws into
question the ideological bases of its own tragic polarities.

At the same time there is a remarkable shift in the balance of
sympathies since *The Return of the Native*. In *Tess*, the tragic
claims of an ironised intellect are subordinated to those of
sexuality. The intellectual drama of the male is not itself tragic,
but functions rather as a component of the sexual tragedy of
Tess. *Tess of the d'Urbervilles*, as one contemporary reviewer
remarked, is 'peculiarly the Woman's Tragedy'.[18] If Tess can be
said to have a tragic 'flaw', it is her sexuality, which is, in this

novel, her 'nature' as a woman. Her sexuality is above all provocative: she is a temptress to the convert Alec, an Eve to Angel Clare. Such are her sexual attractions that she is obliged to travesty herself into '"a mommet of a maid"' in order to protect herself from 'aggressive admiration' (p. 304). Her sexuality is constructed above all through the erotic response of the narrator, and it was surely this that gave rise to Mowbray Morris' sneering objections:

> Poor Tess's sensual qualifications for the part of heroine are paraded over and over again with a persistence like that of a horse-dealer egging on some wavering customer to a deal, or a slave-dealer appraising his wares to some full-blooded pasha.[19]

Morris had evidently not realised how far he is implicating himself, as a male reader, in that image of the 'wavering customer'. It is interesting to note, by the way, that Edmund Gosse drew a clear distinction between the responses of male and female readers to the novel; he contrasted the 'ape-leading and shrivelled spinster' who had reviewed *Tess* for the *Saturday Review* with the 'serious male public' who appreciated its qualities.[20]

Set against this provocative sexual quality is a lack of calculation, essential if Tess is not to become a posing and self-dramatising *femme fatale* in the style of Felice Charmond. She never declares herself as either virginal or sexually available, and yet her experience is bounded by the power that both these images exercise. Hardy tries to preserve a narrow balance between her awareness of this sexual force (for if she remains wholly unaware, she is merely a passive and stupid victim) and her refusal deliberately to exploit it (for that would involve her too actively as a temptress). The problem becomes acute at the point of her break from Angel:

> Tess's feminine hope – shall we confess it – had been so obstinately recuperative as to revive in her surreptitious visions of a domiciliary intimacy continued long enough to break down his coldness even against his judgment. Though unsophisticated in the usual sense, she was not incomplete; and it would have denoted deficiency of womanhood if she had not instinctively known what an argument lies in propinquity. Nothing else would serve her, she knew, if this failed. It was wrong to hope in what was of the nature of strategy, she said to herself: yet that sort of hope she could not extinguish (p. 269).

The archness of that parenthetical 'shall we confess it' and the elaborately distancing abstract and Latinate vocabulary testify to the difficulty of negotiating this area of a consciousness that must not become too conscious. The shared pronoun ('shall *we* confess it') hovers awkwardly between implying a suddenly female narrator and pulling the implied male reader into a conspiratorial secret (woman and their little ways) that remains concealed from Tess. He is obliged to fall back on the old standby of instinct (and, on the next page, intuition) for an explanation of a knowledge that Tess must have, in order not to be deficient in womanhood, and must not have, in order to avoid falling into anything 'of the nature of strategy'. 'Purity' is, in a sense, enforced upon Tess by the difficulty of representing for her a self-aware mode of sexuality.

For Tess is doomed by her sexuality in a quite different way from Felice Charmond or Eustacia Vye. She does not share their urgency of desire to be desired, nor their restless dissatisfaction with the actual relationships in which that desire is partially satisfied. Both of those women are complicit in the circumscribing of their identity by their sexuality, and of their experience by their relationships with men. Tess, on the other hand, is trapped by a sexuality which seems at times almost irrelevant to her own experience and sense of her own identity. She is doomed by her 'exceptional physical nature' (p. 269) and by the inevitability of an erotic response from men. That response binds her to male images and fantasies: to the pink cheeks and rustic innocence of Angel's patronising pastoralism (p. 264), and to the proud indifference that Alec finds so piquantly challenging. Her sexuality, provocative without intent, seems inherently guilty by virtue of the reactions it arouses in others: 'And there was revived in her the wretched sentiment which had often come to her before, that in inhabiting the fleshly tabernacle with which Nature had endowed her she was somehow doing wrong' (p. 334). 'Liza-Lu, the 'spiritualized image of Tess' (p. 419), is spiritualised by the execution of Tess, expunging the wrong-doing and expiating the guilt of her woman's sexuality. 'Liza-Lu and Angel Clare give an openly fantasy ending to the novel, in a de-eroticized relationship that nevertheless contravenes socially constituted moral law far more clearly than any of Tess's, since a man's marriage with his sister-in-law remained not only illegal but also tainted with the stigma of incest until the passing of the controversial Deceased Wife's Sister Act (after several previous failed attempts), in 1907. The echo of *Paradise Lost* in the last sentence of *Tess* has often been remarked, but it is notable that the novel in fact offers a curiously inverted image of Milton's fallen world. The post-lapsarian world of *Tess* is attenuated ('Liza-Lu is only 'half girl, half woman', and both she and Clare seem to have 'shrunk' facially (p. 419)) by expulsion from sexuality, and not by the loss of a pre-sexual innocence. In *Tess* are imaged both a Paradise of sexuality (abundant, fecund, succulent) and the guilt of knowledge that inheres within it.

For *Tess of the d'Urbervilles* draws an illusion of cohesion from its single-minded concentration on the figure of Tess herself – an illusion that is rapidly dissipated by attention to the detail of the text. The text is divided not into a series of chapters adding up to a more or less continuous narrative, but into discontinuous Phases which repeatedly edit out the most crucial episodes of the plot. Mowbray Morris, in his rejection of *Tess* for *Macmillan's Magazine*, noted accurately enough that 'All the first part therefore is a sort of prologue to the girl's seduction, which is hardly ever and can hardly ever be out of the reader's mind'.[21] It is all the more noticeable, then, that after this build-up, the seduction itself is given only obliquely and by implication. The physical particularities of the incident, as Allan Brick has remarked, are transposed graphically enough on to the episode in which Alec persuades Tess to take into her mouth a strawberry – forced and out of season – that she only half resists.[22] But at the point when access to Tess's consciousness would do most to 'fix' the text into a particular significance, it is abruptly withdrawn. The same can be said of other crucial narrative moments – Tess's account of her past on her wedding night,[23] her return to Alec, and her murder of him. It has frequently been remarked, and usually deplored, that these moments fall into a hiatus between Phases. Stanzel, for example, has argued that such gaps in the reader's knowledge are a kind of pre-censorship whose effect is to prevent the formation of an independent opinion or interpretation that might act against Hardy's vindication of his heroine.[24] But it seems, rather, that they at once sharply indicate the way in which Tess's sexuality eludes the circumscribing narrative voice, and point up the disturbing discontinuities of tone and point of view which undermine the stability of Tess as a focal character and which, John Bayley has argued, give the novel its form.[25]

These discontinuities, incidentally, have enabled a critical dismembering of Tess. For some, concentrating on such scenes as the Lady-Day move and the threshing-machine, she is the representative of an order of rural society threatened by urbanism, mechanisation, and the destruction of stable working communities. Thus, for Kettle, she typifies the proletarianisation of the peasantry; for the agrarian traditionalist Douglas Brown, she embodies 'the agricultural community in its moment of ruin'; for the Weberian Lucille Herbert, she marks the moment of transition from *Gemeinschaft* to *Gesellschaft*; and John Holloway finds in her evidence of Hardy's increasing awareness of flaws within the traditional rural order that has hitherto functioned to establish a moral norm.[26] For all of these, the significance of Tess's womanhood is negligible, except insofar as it provides an appropriate image of passivity and victimisation. Others, seizing on the way in which Tess is singled out from her community, both by her own outstanding qualities and by her aristocratic descent with its encumbering heritage of omens and legends, have followed Lawrence to find in 'the deeper-passioned Tess' (p. 164) who can assert that ' "I am only a peasant by position, not by nature!" ' (p. 258) a natural aristocrat, the suitable subject of a tragedy.[27] Alternatively, by taking up the novel's allusions to, or recapitulations of, Biblical and literary plots (Eden and Fall, *Paradise Lost*, *Pilgrim's Progress*, and so on), or by following through the chains of imagery centring upon altars, druids and sacrifices, it is possible to find in Tess the shadow of innumerable cultural archetypes (Patient Griselda, the scapegoat, the highborn lady in disguise).[28] That each of these views finds its point of departure in the detail of the text indicates how complex and contradictory Tess is, viewed in the light of a critical practice that demands a stable and coherent consolidation of character.

And there is more to the discontinuity than this. The narrator shifts brusquely between dispassionate, long-distance observation (Tess as 'a fly on a billiard-table of indefinite length, and of no more consequence to the surroundings than that fly' (p. 133)) and a lingering closeness of view that particularises the grain of her skin, the texture of her hair. The transparency of her consciousness is punctuated by the distancing reflections of a meditative moralist who can generalise ('women whose chief companions are the forms and forces of outdoor Nature retain in their souls far more of the Pagan fantasy of their remote forefathers than of the systematised religion taught their race at later date' (p. 132)), allude ('But, might some say, where was Tess's guardian angel?. . . Perhaps, like that other god of whom the ironical Tishbite spoke, he was talking, or he was pursuing, or he was in a journey, or he was sleeping and not to be awaked' (p. 101)), and abstract ('But for the world's opinion those experiences would have been simply a liberal education' (p. 127)). Equally, the narrator's analytic omniscience is threatened both by his erotic commitment to Tess, and by the elusiveness of her sexuality. The novel's ideological project, the circumscribing of the consciousness and experience of its heroine by a scientifically dispassionate mode of narration, is undermined by the instability of its 'placing' of Tess through genre and point of view. Structured primarily as tragedy, the novel draws also on a number of other genres and modes of writing: on realism, certainly, but also on a melodrama that itself reaches into balladry, and, of course, on polemic.

The polemic itself also exhibits a series of radical discontinuities. As many of the novel's more recent critics have remarked, what van Ghent has dismissively called the 'bits of philosophic adhesive tape'[29] do not in any sense link together into a consistent or logical argument, and it would be a frustrating and futile exercise to seek in the generalisations and interpretations of the narrator any 'position' on extra-marital sex, or on the question of 'natural' versus 'artificial' morality, that could confidently be ascribed to Hardy as an individual or posited as a structuring imperative of the text. The 'confusion of many standards' of which Paris has written,[30] the overlapping of contradictory and conflictual points of view, probably results in part from Hardy's successive modifications of his manuscript in the face of repeated rejections. The serial bowdlerisations, irritating though they may be, are insignificant compared to the changes which Hardy made in order to secure publication. There was, for example, a major shift of emphasis, which involved superimposing upon a tragedy of the ordinary (in which Tess is representative by virtue of being like many other girls in her position) a mythic tragedy of the exceptional (in which she is marked out from these other girls by a superior sensibility that assimilates her to prototypes in legend and literature).[31] Further, although some of the 'philosophical' comments on Tess's experience are present from the earliest stages of composition, others (including the idea that Tess remains innocent according to natural morality) are added in later revision.[32] The 'argument' that seeks, contradictorily, both to exonerate Tess and to secure forgiveness for her is partly an attempt to rescue her for a conventionally-realised purity; as Jacobus has remarked, 'Tess's purity . . . is "stuck on" in retrospect like the sub-title to meet objections which the novel had encountered even before its publication in 1891.'[33] By a series of modifications, both to the original conception of the story and to those parts of the text that had been written first, Tess is rendered innocent in a revealingly double sense: that is, lacking in knowledge and lacking in guilt. A number of revisions, for example, emphasise chastity and reticence at the expense of passion and spontaneity; so, a passage suggesting that Tess would have been willing to live unmarried with Angel Clare is cancelled in manuscript. There is evidence, too, in the earlier versions of the text, that Tess's relationship with Alec was to have been far more that of equals, and certainly it is only when she must be retrieved from sexual guilt that any suggestion that ' "A little more than persuading had to do wi' the coming o't" ' (p. 118) is added (the phrase being inserted in the 1892 revisions). As Tess is purified, so there is also a far-reaching and wholesale blackening of Alec and Angel that transforms them unequivocally into rake and hypocrite.[34]

The contradictions in the defence of Tess, however, cannot all be ascribed straighforwardly to textual revision. They are also closely related to the diverse and conflicting accounts of nature that inhabit the text. Tess, like Grace Melbury before her, acts as the site for the exploration of a number of ideologies of nature that find their focus in her sexuality. The Darwinist nature of amoral instinct and the 'inherent will to enjoy' (p. 310) runs close to a naturalist version of sexuality, which posits an organicist continuity between the human and the non-human.[35]

The broody hens and farrowing pigs of Talbothays, the 'stir of germination' (p. 127) and the 'hiss of fertilization' (p. 176), give a context of impersonal biological process to the equally impersonal instinct that torments the women dairy-workers:

> The air of the sleeping-chamber seemed to palpitate with the hopeless passion of the girls. They writhed feverishly under the oppressiveness of an emotion thrust on them by cruel Nature's law – an emotion which they had neither expected nor desired. . . . The difference which distinguished them as individuals were abstracted by this passion, and each was but portion of one organism called sex (p. 174).

Yet, even as the 'naturalness' of the sexual instinct is proclaimed, it is simultaneously perceived as 'cruel' and 'oppressive', by virtue of its extinction of difference and its imperviousness to circumstance. Here, almost implicitly, there dwells a hint of the tragic potential of sexuality in this novel: individual consciousness, or consciousness of individuality ('She was not an existence, an experience, a passion, a structure of sensations, to anybody but herself' (p. 119)), in conflict with non-human biological process, instinct.

But, further, Romantic ideologies of nature, themselves divergent, are also invoked through the philosophical commentary. There is a strain of Rousseau-ism, positing nature as moral norm: 'She was ashamed of herself for her gloom of the night, based on nothing more tangible than a sense of condemnation under an arbitrary law of society which had no foundation in Nature' (p. 303). There is also a version of the pathetic fallacy:

> At times her whimsical fancy would intensify natural processes around her till they seemed a part of her own story. Rather they became a part of it; for the world is only a psychological phenomenon, and what they seemed they were.
>
> But this encompassment of her own characterization, based on shreds of convention, peopled by phantoms and voices antipathetic to her, was a sorry and mistaken creation of Tess's fancy – a cloud of moral hobgoblins by which she was terrified without reason. It was they that were out of harmony with the actual world, not she (p. 114).

Here there is a quite openly paradoxical argument, confronting two views (the world as a 'psychological phenomenon' and the 'actual world') which clearly cannot be reconciled. There is, again, an intensely ironised evocation of the benevolent Words-

worthian nature, akin to the Christian providence, which
works out a ' "holy plan" ' through individual lives (p. 49).
Christian nature, 'fallen' along with Tess, is implicit in the
allusions to the *Paradise Lost* motif, and is tellingly drawn upon
in the description of Tess in the rank but fertile garden of her
sexual response to Angel. Clearly, there can be no synthesis into
a philosophically or logically coherent argument of such
contradictory and paradoxical fragments of commentary. It
has been claimed that these 'recognisably limited perspectives –
partial insights', and the multiplicity of 'explanations' offered
for Tess's tragedy, form part of the novel's onslaught on moral
dogma and absolutism, and that they have as their primary
effect to undermine the authority of the whole notion of
explanation.[36] And it is true that they deter the reader from
repeating Alec d'Urberville's act of appropriation or Angel
Clare's moment of repudiation, by highlighting the partiality
of such views. For both of these male characters, Tess is
representative of her sex. For Alec, she says what all women
say, but does what all women do:

> "I didn't understand your meaning till it was too late."
> "That's what every woman says."
> "How can you dare to use such words!" she cried . . .
> "My God! I could knock you out of the gig! Did it never strike your mind
> that what every woman says some women feel?" (p. 106).

For Angel, on the other hand, she represents a spirtualised
version of her sex:

> She was no longer the milkmaid, but a visionary essence of woman – a
> whole sex condensed into one typical form. He called her Artemis,
> Demeter, and other fanciful names half teasingly, which she did not like
> because she did not understand them.
> "Call me Tess," she would say askance; and he did (p. 158).

Tess, it should be noted, resists both of these representative
roles. And, of course, they are not the opposites that they might
at first appear; they are precisely complementary, as is emphasised, not only by Alec's temporary conversion to evangelicism
and Angel's momentary transformation into a rake with Izz,
but also by the similarities between their ways of gaining Tess's
acquiescence. It is not only Alec who is associated with the gigs
and traps that, on occasion, literarlly run away with Tess;[37] it is

during a journey in a wagon driven by Angel that he finally secures Tess's acceptance of his proposal. Equally, the two ride to their wedding in a sinister, funereal carriage, and when Angel makes his proposition to Izz, she is riding in his gig. It is noticeable, too, that during their wagon-ride, Angel feeds Tess with berries that he has pulled from the trees with a whip, recalling the scene at The Slopes when Alec feeds her with strawberries.

Clearly, then the novel's narrative method in a sense enacts the relativism of its structuring argument. But there is more to the discontinuities than this. They also mark Hardy's increasing interrogation of his own modes of narration. The disjunctions in narrative voice, the contradictions of logic, the abrupt shifts of point of view, form what Bayley has called 'a stylisation . . . of the more natural hiatus between plot and person, description and emotion';[38] they disintegrate the stability of character as a cohering force, they threaten the dominance of the dispassionate and omniscient narrator, and so push to its limit the androgynous narrative mode that seeks to represent and explain the woman from within and without. The formal characteristics of *Tess of the d'Urbervilles*, its increasingly overt confrontation of subjectivity and subjection,[39] will enable the radical break in the relation of female character to narrative voice that intervenes between the violated subjectivity of Tess Durbeyfield and the resistant opacity of Sue Bridehead.

NOTES

1 Ian Gregor, *The Great Web: The Form of Hardy's Fiction* (London, 1974), p. 178.
2 John Bayley, *An Essay on Hardy* (Cambridge, 1978), pp. 167–8.
3 See, respectively, Carl J. Weber, 'Hardy and *The Woodlanders*,' *Review of English Studies*, 15 (1939), 332; and *Later Years*, pp. 41–2.
4 Hardy's letter is reprinted in the Publisher's Note of Hermann Sudermann, *The Song of Songs: A New Translation by Beatrice Marshall* (London, 1913), p. x. For an account of the whole affair, see Samuel Hynes, *The Edwardian Turn of Mind* (London, 1968), pp. 273–9.
5 'Candour in English Fiction,' in *Thomas Hardy's Personal Writings*, ed. Harold Orel (London, 1967), p. 130; and 'The Tree of Knowledge,' *New Review*, 10 (1894), 675–90.
6 Gail Cunningham, *The New Woman and the Victorian Novel* (London, 1978), p. 103.

7 French realism is mentioned by, among others, 'Sylvanus Urban,' 'Table Talk,' *Gentleman's Magazine*, NS 49 (1892), 321; [Thomas Nelson Page], 'Editor's Study, I,' *Harper's*, 85 (1892), 152–3; and Richard Le Gallienne, rev. of *Tess*, in *Retrospective Reviews: A Literary Log* (London, 1896), I, 14. Zola is mentioned in 'Mr. Hardy's *Tess of the D'Urbevilles* [sic], '*Review of Reviews*, 5 (1892), 19; and by D. F. Hannigan, 'The Latest Development of English Fiction,' *Westminster Review*, 138 (1892), 657. Hannigan, p. 659, also mentions Ibsen, as does Charles Morton Payne, rev. of *Tess*, *Dial*, 12 (1892), 424. Harriet Waters Preston, in 'Thomas Hardy,' *Century Magazine*, NS 24 (1893), 358, talks of a 'Tendenz-Roman,' while Andrew Lang, in 'At the Sign of the Ship,' *Longman's*, 21 (1892), 106, prefers 'tendenz story'. W. P. Trent, in 'The Novels of Thomas Hardy,' *Sewanee Review*, 1 (1892), 19, describes *Tess* as a 'novel with a purpose'.

8 [Margaret O. W. Oliphant], 'The Old Saloon,' *Blackwood's*, 151 (1892), 474.

9 Bayley, *Essay*, p. 189.

10 John Goode, 'Sue Bridehead and the New Woman,' in *Women Writing and Writing about Women*, ed. Mary Jacobus (London, 1979), p. 102.

11 E.g. by Tony Tanner, 'Colour and Movement in *Tess of the d'Urbervilles*,' *Critical Quarterly*, 10 (1968), 219–39.

12 Bayley, *Essay*, p. 183.

13 'To Robert Louis Stevenson,' 17 February 1893, *Letters of Henry James*, ed. Percy Lubbock (London, 1920), I, 205.

14 Mary Jacobus, 'The Difference of View,' in *Women Writing*, ed. Jacobus, p. 13.

15 See Mary Jacobus, 'Tess: The Making of a Pure Woman,' in *Tearing the Veil: Essays on Femininity*, ed. Susan Lipshitz (London, 1978), p. 87.

16 Kathleen Rogers, 'Women in Thomas Hardy,' *Centennial Review*, 19 (1975), 249–50.

17 Bayley, *Essay*, p. 176.

18 'Mr. Thomas Hardy's New Novel,' *Pall Mall Gazette*, 31 December, 1891, p. 3.

19 Mowbray Morris, 'Culture and Anarchy,' *Quarterly Review*, 174 (1892), 325.

20 'To Thomas Hardy,' 19 January 1892, *Life and Letters of Sir Edmund Gosse*, by Hon. Evan Charteris (London, 1931), p. 226. In his reply, Hardy repudiated the distinction: 'I hardly think the writer in the *Saturday* can be a woman – the sex having caught on with enthusiasm;' 'To Edmund Gosse,' 20 January 1892, *Collected Letters*, p. 255.

21 'To Thomas Hardy,' 25 November 1889, Dorset County Museum. See Michael Millgate, *Thomas Hardy: His Career as a Novelist* (London, 1971), pp. 284–6.

22 Allan Brick, 'Paradise and Consciousness in Hardy's *Tess*,' *Nineteenth-Century Fiction*, 17 (1962), 118.

23 Though two versions of this by Hardy can be found in '*Tess' in the Theatre: Two Dramatizations of 'Tess of the d'Urbervilles' by Thomas Hardy, One by Lorimer Stoddard*, ed. Marguerite Roberts (Toronto, 1950), pp. 49 and 182.

24 Franz Stanzel, 'Thomas Hardy: *Tess of the d'Urbervilles*,' in *Der Moderne*

Englische Roman: Interpretationen, ed. Horst Oppel (Berlin, 1963), pp. 38–40. Cf. Laurence Lerner, *The Truthtellers* (London, 1967), pp. 113–31. For an interesting but sharply contrasting view of this aspect of the novel, see Joseph Hillis Miller, 'Fiction and Repetition: *Tess of the d'Urbervilles*,' in *Forms of Modern British Fiction*, ed. Alan Warren Friedman (London, 1975), pp. 43–71.

25 Bayley, *Essay*, p. 189.

26 See, respectively, Arnold Kettle, Introduction, *Tess*, rpt. in *Twentieth Century Interpretation of 'Tess of the d'Urbervilles*,' ed. Albert J. LaValley (Englewood Cliffs, New Jersey, 1969), pp. 14–29; Douglas Brown, *Thomas Hardy*, Men and Books (London, 1954), p. 91; Lucille Herbert, 'Hardy's Views in *Tess of the d'Urbervilles*,' *ELH*, 37 (1970), 77–94; and John Holloway, 'Hardy's Major Fiction,' in *The Charted Mirror: Literary and Critical Essays* (London, 1960), pp. 94–107.

27 D. H. Lawrence, 'Study of Thomas Hardy,' in *Phoenix: The Posthumous Papers of D. H. Lawrence*, ed. Edward D. McDonald (London, 1936; rpt. 1961), pp. 482–8.

28 Myth critics include Jean Brooks, *Thomas Hardy: The Poetic Structure* (London, 1971), pp. 233–53; Henry Kozicki, 'Myths of Redemption in Hardy's *Tess of the d'Urbervilles*,' *Papers on Language and Literature*, 10 (1974), 150–8; and James Hazen, 'The Tragedy of Tess Durbeyfield,' *Texas Studies in Literature and Language*, 11 (1969), 779–94.

29 Dorothy van Ghent, *The English Novel: Form and Function* (1953; rpt. New York, 1960), p. 196.

30 Bernard J. Paris, ' "A Confusion of Many Standards": Conflicting Value Systems in *Tess of the d'Urbervilles*,' *Nineteenth-Century Fiction*, 24 (1969), 57–79. Cf. David Lodge, 'Tess, Nature, and the Voices of Hardy,' in *Language of Fiction: Essays in Criticism and Verbal Analysis of the English Novel* (London, 1966), pp. 164–88.

31 Cf. Jacobus, 'Pure Woman,' pp. 81–2.

32 According to the invaluable account of textual revision by J. T. Laird, *The Shaping of 'Tess of the d'Urbervilles'* (Oxford, 1975), pp. 190–2.

33 Jacobus, 'Pure Woman,' p. 78.

34 See Jacobus, 'Pure Woman,' pp. 83–4.

35 For a detailed discussion of *Tess*'s relation to Darwinist theory, see Peter R. Morton, '*Tess of the d'Urbervilles*: A Neo-Darwinian Reading,' *Southern Review* (Adelaide), 7 (1974), 38–50; J. R. Ebbatson, 'The Darwinian View of Tess: A Reply,' *Southern Review*, 8 (1975), 247–53; and Morton, '*Tess* and August Weismann: Unholy Alliance?,' *Southern Review*, 8 (1975), 254–6.

36 Robert C. Schweik, 'Moral Perspective in *Tess of the d'Urbervilles*,' *College English*, 24 (1962), 18.

37 See Jacobus, 'Pure Woman,' pp. 82–3.

38 Bayley, *Essay*, p. 189.

39 Cf. John Goode, 'Woman and the Literary Text,' in *The Rights and Wrongs of Woman*, ed. Juliet Mitchell and Ann Oakley (Harmondsworth, 1976), p. 255.

CHAPTER 7

Jude the Obscure (1895)

Hardy comments in his 1912 Preface to *Jude the Obscure* that an unnamed German reviewer had described Sue Bridehead as 'the first delineation in fiction of . . . the woman of the feminist movement – the slight, pale "bachelor" girl – the intellectualized, emancipated bundle of nerves that modern conditions were producing. . . '. He adds, 'Whether this assurance is borne out by dates I cannot say' (p. 30). This is a characteristic piece of obfuscation. It is as well to note, first, that Sue is no way representative of any discernible movement, although organised feminism had already appeared in fiction, for example, in, E. L. Linton's *The Rebel of the Family* (1880), Henry James' *The Bostonians* (1886), and George Gissing's *The Odd Women* (1893), all of which, in any case, predate the publication of *Jude*. Sue belongs not to feminism as such, but to the literary tradition of the New Woman; and here again, she is in no sense a precursor. Hardy certainly knew of at least some of the large number of writers, both new and established, dealing at the same period with just that topic. It is evident from his letters that he was personally acquainted with some of these writers – Sarah Grand and Ménie Muriel Dowie, for instance.[1] He received a letter about *Jude* from George Egerton, and he wrote to the editor of the *Contemporary Review* in 1890 to introduce an article abour marriage by Mona Caird, remarking that he believed there to be 'nothing heterodox in it'.[2] Hardy had read at least some of the works in question: he thought *The Heavenly Twins* over-praised,[3] and copied extracts from Egerton's *Keynotes* into his notebook.[4] In 1892 he wrote at some length to Millicent Garrett Fawcett about the portrayal of sex in contemporary fiction:

> With regard to your idea of a short story showing how the trifling with the physical element in love leads to corruption: I do not see that much more can be done by fiction in that direction than has been done already. You may say

the treatment hitherto has been vague & general only, which is quite true. Possibly on that account nobody has profited greatly by such works. To do the thing well there should be no mincing of matters, & all details should be clear & directly given. This I fear the British public would not stand just now; though, to be sure, we are educating it by degrees.

He adds that he has read a recent novel ostensibly on the subject, Lucas Malet's *The Wages of Sin*, and found it 'not very consequent, as I told the authoress'.[5] He was certainly aware of Grant Allen, probably the most widely read and influential of the 'woman question' writers, whose aspirations to martyrdom and posturings of high moral seriousness led a contemporary to describe him hyperbolically as ' "the Darwinian St. Paul".'[6] Allen's works led to a kind of industry of rebuttal and parody; in the year of the publication of *Jude* alone, his *The Woman Who Did* spawned *The Woman Who Didn't* by 'Victoria Crosse' and *The Woman Who Wouldn't* by 'Lucas Cleeve', while *The British Barbarians. A Hill-Top Novel* provoked H. D. Traill's parody, *The Barbarous Britishers. A Tip-Top Novel*. In *The British Barbarians* Allen refers very favourably to *Tess* as a work ' "of which every young girl and married woman in England ought to be given a copy." '[7] Hardy returned the compliment by sending him a dedicated copy of *Jude The Obscure*.[8] There are few similarities between Allen's fiction and Hardy's, but their attacks on marriage have points in common, such as the Owenite idea that unchastity is sex without love, whether within or outside marriage, and the position that marriage as an institution crushes individuality and makes a legal obligation of ' "what no human heart can be sure of performing" '[9]; further, Grant Allen's 'monopolism', the jealous and exclusive annexation which marks patriotism, property, capitalism and marriage,[10] bears some relation to Hardy's ' "save-your-own-soul-ism" ', the common characteristic of possessive parenthood, class-feeling and patriotism, all ' "a mean exclusiveness at bottom" ' (p. 288).

The New Woman – by no means identical with the feminist, but clearly a relative – had, indeed, become almost a cliché by 1895. One contemporary reviewer remarks of *Jude* that 'If we consider broadly and without prejudice the tone and scope of the book, we cannot but class it with the fiction of Sex and New Woman, so rife of late".[11] Meanwhile, H. G. Wells, in a review in February 1896, is able to assert confidently that 'It is now the better part of a year ago since the collapse of the "New Woman" fiction began.'[12] Far from being a pioneer, Sue Bridehead comes in company with a crowd of 'intellectualized, emancipated bundle[s] of nerves' (p. 30). This is not, of course, to suggest that she is commonplace. I shall be considering Sue Bridehead in some detail later, but there are significant differences which mark her out from the type of the New Woman and which should at once be pointed out. A contemporary account of the 'new convention in heroines' describes the characteristic New Woman:

> The newest is beautiful, of course, in a large and haughty way. She is icily pure. . . . She despises the world, and men, and herself, and is superbly unhappy. In spite of her purity she is not very wholesome; she generally has a mission to solve the problems of existence, and on her erratic path through life she is helped by no sense of humour.[13]

This is a caricature, but those features which are being exaggerated and distorted remain clearly identifiable. Sue Bridehead, with all her hesitations, evasions and tentativeness, has none of this messianic sense of purpose which distinguishes her contemporaries, and in fact she consistently refuses to speak for women as a group, posing herself always as a special case. A further difference is made more evident by this description, from the same source, of the hero with whom the free union is to be contracted:

> He is always a young man of excellent birth, connected with the peerage, and has literary or artistic tastes. He has had a reckless past, but it has done him no harm. . . . He is all passion, and coolness, and experience, and gentlemanly conduct.[14]

As this quotation suggests, the New Woman and the free union are, in 1890s' fiction, firmly rooted in the upper middle class; the social hazards to which these women are exposed are of the nature of being ostracised by the wives of bishops. The marryings and unmarryings of working-class characters are more characteristically seen in the brutal and condescending stories of writers such as Henry Nevinson or Arthur Morrison.[15] *Jude the Obscure* is unique in its siting of Jude and Sue at the conjuncture of class and sexual oppression.

Nevertheless, the novel was certainly perceived by its con-

temporary readers as being part of a trend, and, despite Hardy's
disclaimers of writing about the marriage question,[16] his sense
of participating in a continuing debate is evident in, for
example, the argument of Phillotson and Gillingham over
' "domestic disintegration" ' and the collapse of the family as
the social unit (p. 247), or in this rather didactic interchange
after a discussion of marriage:

> "Still, Sue, it is no worse for the woman than for the man. That's what
> some women fail to see, and instead of protesting against the conditions
> they protest against the man, the other victim . . ."
> "Yes – some are like that, instead of uniting with the man against the
> common enemy, coercion" (pp. 299–300).

It seems that, with the advent of 'Ibsenity' and the problem
play, the marriage question and the New Woman novel, Hardy
was able for the first time in a major work to place the
examination of sexual relationships openly at the centre of his
novel, and to make the tragedy turn on marriage, instead of
displacing it with the more traditional materials of tragedy, as
he had done earlier. Whatever Hardy's account of the genesis
and composition of *Jude*, which he describes in a letter to
Florence Henniker as 'the Sue story',[17] there can surely be no
doubt now that, as Patricia Ingham has shown, Sue Bridehead
and marriage are the very impulse of the novel, not an
afterthought.[18]

Nor is this the only area of *Jude*'s contemporaneity. It can be
seen as attempting to superimpose the sexual and marital
preoccupations of the 1890s upon the intellectual concerns of
the 1860s, Hebraism and Hellenism and Mill's liberal individualism.[19] There is obviously some truth in this, though
Mill's name is not in itself a sign of being fixed in the past; it is a
recurring name on the reading lists of the New Woman, though
more often for his *Subjection of Women* (of which Hardy
somewhat ambiguously remarks in September 1895 that 'I do
not remember ever reading [it]')[20] than for *On Liberty*. At the
same time, the novel is very much abreast of contemporary
currents of thought. The 'deadly war waged between flesh and
spirit' to which Hardy refers in his Preface (p. 27) had taken on a
new significance in the latter part of the century, as the
Darwinian notion of an extremely complex material world in
constant change challenged the hitherto dominant form of the

duality by reversing the priorities. The new dualism – materialist, certainly, but often mechanistic – makes physiological organisation the determinant, with consciousness a kind of subsidiary product – an idea which underlies Hardy's image, recurrent in his poetry, of the mind as an evolutionary mistake. Such a privileging of the biological led easily into a scientificism in social theory – in the positivist investigations of the Fabians, for example, in Social Darwinism, and the associated manifestations of the 'science' of eugenics, claimed alike by reactionaries like Max Nordau (*Degeneration*, published in English translation in 1895), radical feminists like the American Victoria Woodhull Martin (editor of *The Humanitarian* (NY) from 1892), and socialists like Edward Aveling. This is the period in which sexuality moves decisively from the area of moral discourse to that of scientific discourse. The relative downgrading of the mind and, hence, of the intellectual surely enters into the 'simple life' philosophy of Edward Carpenter and his associates, as well as giving apparent support to the irrationalism and pessimism of Schopenhauer, for whom (as sometimes for Hardy) human consciousness and the scientific laws of the universe are inherently at odds. The signs of these ideological currents are easily seen in the dominant literary modes of the period, as the three-decker novel gives way to the fleetingly poised moment of the short story, and as the 'scientific' fictions of naturalism become prominent, with their avowedly organicist aim of dissecting a society as though it were precisely analogous with a human body.

This same sense of the ceaseless shiftings and modifications of the apparently stable material world can be related to the ascendancy of the philosophies of relativism and pragmatism, where the petrified social categories of morality and knowledge are felt to be in contradiction with the intricacies and flexibilities of personal experience. *Jude the Obscure* is heavy with this sense: Sue cannot associate her inner life with the Mrs Richard Phillotson she has outwardly become (p. 223); Phillotson's dilemma over Sue is compounded by his feeling that his 'doctrines' and 'principles' are at odds with his 'instincts' (p. 246); and Jude's '"neat stock of fixed opinions"' is torn away from him by his experience, leaving him ' "in a chaos of principles"' (pp. 336–7). One of the novel's most painful

ironies is the way that the desire for education is undercut by its
inadequacy and irrelevance to the experiences of all the central
characters. The tension between 'private' experience and the
cold, superficial generalisations of the public language which
alone is available to articulate that experience comes to dominate the novel. ' "I can't explain" ' becomes a kind of motto – a
variant on one of the senses of the novel's epigraph, 'the letter
killeth' – and is used by both Sue and Jude, particularly in
relation to sex (Sue's half-hearted attempt to give Little Father
Time the truth about the expected child; Jude's failure to
account to Sue for his casual night with Arabella), highlighting
the irreconcilability of individual sexual experience and its
public discourses, whether scientific or moral. Sue and Jude
take divergent paths with regard to language and the literary
culture. Sue moves into silence; in her two last appearances, she
stops her ears to avoid hearing Jude, and clenches her teeth to
avoid addressing Phillotson. Jude, however, moves into a kind
of sardonic or parodic quotation in which the language of
culture becomes a commentary on his own life in a quite
original way – the anthem 'Truly God is living unto Israel', the
last quotation from Job with its choric, amen-like punctuations
of 'Hurrah!'. The two are caught at the point where their
courses diverge in an exchange which appears only in the serial
text: when they overhear two clergymen discussing the
eastward position for altars Jude exclaims ' "What a satire their
talk is on our importance to the world!" ', and Sue replies,
' "What a satire our experience is on their subject!" '[21] These two
processes of distancing from language and literary culture are
mimicked in the form of the novel and its place in Hardy's
work. The end of *Jude* is a most sardonic imposition of the twin
conventions of novel closures, the happy marriage and the
death of the hero, and offers by way of apparent summing-up
Arabella's reinstatement of the romanticised truisms of a love as
strong as death and the two lovers as halves of a single whole.[22]
Jude is also Hardy's last novel, and so is followed, in this respect,
by silence.

Jude the Obscure is Hardy's final double tragedy. In his
previous versions of the double tragedy of a man and of a
woman, the woman's tragedy has resulted from her sexual
nature, while the man's has been more involved with intel-

lectual ideals and ideological pressures. There has been a polarity of nature and culture which has meant that the protagonists have rivalled one another for the centre of the novel, pulling it in different directions and making it hard for him to use marital or sexual relationship as the crucial point of the divergence. In *Jude*, however, Hardy gives for the first time an intellectual component to the tragedy of the woman – Sue's breakdown from an original, incisive intellect to the compulsive reiteration of the principles of conduct of a mid-Victorian marriage manual – and, to the man's, a sexual component which resides not in simple mismatching, but in the very fact of his sexuality. There is no sense that Jude and Sue inhabit different ideological structures as there is in the cases of Clym and Eustacia, or even Angel and Tess. Indeed, for all the emphasis on the 'enigma' of Sue's logic and motivation, there is an equal stress – and this is something new in Hardy – on her similarity to Jude. The fact of their cousinship, besides contravening the exogamy rule and so adding an incestuous *frisson* to their sense of an impending and hereditary doom, serves to highlight their similarities;[23] there are episodes which quite openly draw attention to this, either by careful counterpointing of plot (Jude, in his distress, spending the night at Sue's lodging, balanced by Sue, in hers, spending a night in Jude's room) or by means of images such as that of Sue's appearance in Jude's clothes as a kind of double. Again, the discussion between the two after Jude's impulsive visit to the hymn-writer turned wine-merchant points up their own sense of sameness between them; and Phillotson justifies his action in letting Sue go partly in terms of ' "the extraordinary sympathy, or similarity, between the pair. He is her cousin, which perhaps accounts for some of it. They seem to be one person split in two!" ' (p. 245). Their lives follow a very similar course. Both make a mistaken marriage as a result of sexual vulnerability, as is evident in an interesting ms. revision: when Jude, on his first outing with Arabella, visits an inn, he sees on the wall a painting of Samson and Delilah, a clear symbol of his male sexuality under threat; but the picture had originally been a painting of Susannah and the Elders, a symbol of female sexuality under threat, which corresponds very closely to the roles of Sue and Phillotson (ms. f. 44). Both Sue and Jude escape these first marriages, become parents, lose their jobs, their children, and their lover. Yet Sue is destroyed, while Jude is even at the end able to talk of dying ' "game" ' (p. 394). Jude offers explanations for this phenomenon – 'The blow of her bereavement seemed to have destroyed her reasoning faculty' (p. 368) – and raises questions about it – ' "What I can't understand in you is your extraordinary blindness now to your old logic. Is it peculiar to you, or is it common to woman? Is a woman a thinking unit at all, or a fraction always wanting its integer?" ' (p. 359). Sue's actions and reactions are constantly faced, whether by Jude, by the narrator, or by Sue herself, with this alternative: either she must be peculiar, or she must be representative of her sex.[24] It is worth noting, in passing, that this alternative is one which certain critical readings continue to enforce upon the text; a recent example can be found in John Lucas' argument that 'we need more in the way of women than the novel actually gives us' in order to judge whether Sue is to be seen as a 'pathological case' or as a 'representative woman'.[25] This apart, it is noticeable that Sue's life follows almost exactly the course of the 'after-years' marked out for the female sex in the earlier and notorious passage about the 'inexorable laws of nature' and the 'penalty of the sex': that is, 'injustice, loneliness, child-bearing, and bereavement' (pp. 160–1). It seems to me that Sue is to be seen as a representative of her sex in this sense alone, that her sexuality is the decisive element in her collapse. It has become a critical reflex to refer to Sue Bridehead as sexless or frigid, whether as an accusation of her, in the Lawrentian tradition, or as an accusation of Hardy, as in Kate Millett.[26] There is much in the literature of the New Woman that appears to support such an assumption: their concern with the double-standard, for instance, takes almost invariably the form of a demand for male chastity, and some of the more successful problem novels, such as Sarah Grand's *The Heavenly Twins*, turn on the terrible injuries wreaked on women by libidinous and venereally-diseased husbands. *Jude* itself provides some evidence for this argument also, in Sue's rather absurd wish ' "that Eve had not fallen, so that. . . some harmless mode of vegetation might have peopled Paradise" ' (p. 241), or in the numerous revisions in which Hardy removes expressions referring to Sue's warmth and spontaneity and substitutes references to her reserve or cool-

ness. In one scene, for instance, her reply to Jude's worries that
he may have offended her reads thus in the serial text: "'Oh, no,
no! You said enough to let me know what had caused it. I have
never had the least doubt of your worthiness, dear, dear Jude!
How glad I am you have come!'". In the first edition, however,
she is considerably less affectionate and spontaneous: "'O, I
have tried not to! You said enough to let me know what had
caused it. I hope I shall never have any doubt of your worthiness, my poor Jude! And I am glad you have come!'". As she
comes to meet Jude, the serial text runs: 'She had come forward
so impulsively that Jude felt sure a moment later that she had
half-unconsciously expected him to kiss her.' The revised text,
on the other hand, reads: 'She had come forward prettily; but
Jude felt that she had hardly expected him to kiss her.'[27]

It is simplistic, however, to equate such changes with a total
absence of sexual feeling, or with frigidity. They should be
seen, rather, as her response to the complexities and difficulties
of her sexuality and its role in her relationships than as a
straightforward denial of it. Hardy subjects Sue's sexuality to
some of the same ironies which undercut Diana Warwick's
sexual self-possession in *Diana of the Crossways*, and for some of
the same reasons. It is intimately connected in both cases with
the woman's sense of selfhood, and the reserve is, to quote John
Goode, 'not a "defect" of "nature", but . . . a necessary stand
against being reduced to the "womanly"'.[28] A refusal of the
sexual dimension of relationships can seem the only rational
response to a dilemma; in revolt against the double bind by
which female-male relationships are invariably interpreted as
sexual and by which, simultaneously, sexuality is controlled
and channelled into a single legalised relationship, Sue is forced
into a confused and confusing situation in which she wishes at
one and the same time to assert her right to a non-sexual love and
her right to a non-marital sexual liaison.[29] It is the conflict of the
two contradictory pressures that makes her behaviour so often
seem like flirtation. Diana Warwick is a victim of the same
dilemma, for her unconventionality and intelligence lead her to
despise the taboo placed on friendships with men, and yet any
and every sexual advance, whatever the state of her feelings
toward the man, is felt as at once an insult, a threat, and an
attack. 'The freedom of one's sex' is a double-edged concept.

In the case of Sue Bridehead, her diagnosis of marriage as constraint implies as its apparent corollary the equation of non-marriage and freedom. The myth of the free individual subject leads her to see her life, provided it lies outside sexual coercion, as an affair of personal choices freely made. Telling Jude of her unhappiness, she does not perceive the irony in his repetition of her phrase:

> "How can a woman be unhappy who has only been married eight weeks to a man she chose freely?"
> "Chose freely!"
> "Why do you repeat it?" (p. 227).

Her tragedy takes in part the form of her gradual confrontation with the fact of her non-freedom, with the knowledge that she is no less constrained and reduced by her denial of her sexuality than by Phillotson's legal or Jude's emotional demands upon it. She must learn that sexuality lies to a large degree outside the control of rationality, will, choice. The serene confidence with which she tells Jude of her sexless liaison with the undergraduate and draws from it the general conclusion that ' "no average man – no man short of a sensual savage – will molest a woman by day or night, at home or abroad, unless she invites him" ' (p. 167), is a fantasy of freedom and control which she will not willingly surrender. Hardy states in a letter to Edmund Gosse what the novel itself also implies, that it is irrevocable sexual commitment which she fears and abhors, and that she has attempted to retain control of her sexuality by a straightforward restriction of her sexual availability:

> "One point illustrating this I could not dwell upon: that, though she has children, her intimacies with Jude have never been more than occasional, even when they were living together . . ., and one of her reasons for fearing the marriage ceremony is that she fears it would be breaking faith with Jude to withhold herself at pleasure, or altogether, after it; though while uncontracted she feels at liberty to yield herself as seldom as she chooses" (*Later Years*, p. 42).

The final, ironic twist is that when she can no longer fail to recognise the limitations upon her freedom – the moment is clearly marked for us in her identification of the three commandments of the ' "something external" ' which ironically mock the Hebraic Ten Commandments (p. 347) – she simply re-makes the equation in reverse, preserving the polar opposition of marriage and non-marriage. In her re-marriage with Phillotson, she subjects herself fully to the legalistic and Hebraic codes of the ideology of marriage.

Sue, then, undergoes an exploration of the limits of a liberationist impulse, the demands of a Millian individualism, not in terms of biological destiny (although, at a time when contraception and abortion were still very limited of access and widely abhorred, the biological 'destiny' of motherhood is a very formidable 'given' indeed), but in terms of the impossibility of the free individual. This is, in a sense, a response to certain feminist and anti-marriage novels of the period, where the conversion of marriage into a civil contract varying in individual circumstances (as in Mona Caird), or the levelling 'up' of the double standard (as in *The Heavenly Twins*), or the replacement of marriage by the free union (as in *The Woman Who Did*), are seen as potential guarantees of the freedom of women; symptoms of the oppression of women are taken for the very structures of that oppression, and a perspective of equal rights is seen as not merely a necessary, but a sufficient programme for liberation.

Nevertheless, there is a very important sense in which Sue is right to equate her refusal of a sexual relationship with her freedom, in that it avoids the surrender to involuntary physiological processes which her pregnancies entail. It is in this respect that women are at the very junction of the 'flesh and spirit'; the point where mind and body are in potential conflict – this is the crucial area of that dominance of the material over the intellectual in the duality which is characteristic of the ideology of the period. It is Sue, and not Jude, who is the primary site of that 'deadly war waged between flesh and spirit' of which Hardy speaks in his Preface (p. 27).[30] In Jude, the two are constantly juxtaposed, the dominance of his sexuality displacing the dominance of his intellectual ambitions and vice-versa in a continuing series. Jude's sexuality is a disruptive force in a way that it has not previously been for Hardy's male characters; there is no question here – except in Jude's tortured self-questioning after the death of his children – of a predatory male sexuality destroying a weaker and more vulnerable female through her sexuality, but rather of a sexual nature in itself disturbing, partly because it is so largely beyond the conscious processes of decision and intention. When Jude first meets Arabella his intentions and wishes are overmastered by his sexual attraction toward her; the phrase used in ms. is 'in the authoritative operation of a natural law' (ms. f. 36), but this is cancelled and a less scientific phrase finally substituted – 'in commonplace obedience to conjunctive orders from head-quarters' (p. 63). It is this episodic 'battle' of Jude's which gives the novel its similarly episodic form, in which there is a repeated pattern of the abrupt confrontation of his inner life with his material situation: his meditation over the well is broken by the strident tones of his aunt (p. 35), his sympathies with the hungry birds are interrupted by Farmer Troutham's clacker (p. 39), and his recitation of his intellectual attainments is answered by the slap of a pig's penis against his ear (p. 61); from this point on, the dons of Christminster temporarily give way to the Donnes of Cresscombe. Jude's attempt to unite the two through his marriage founders with the significant image of Arabella's fingermarks, hot and greasy from lard-making, on the covers of his classic texts. His wavering thereafter between the two women enacts the alteration of dominance within himself. Points of crisis and transition are marked by Jude's personalised *rites de passage*: his burning of his books, auctioning of his furniture, removing his pillow from the double bed, and so on.[31]

Kate Millett argues that Sue is the 'victim of a cultural literary convention (Lily and Rose)' that cannot allow her to have both a mind and sexuality.[32] The very persistence with which Jude attempts to bring Sue to admit her sexuality into their relation-ship suggests that this is too simple an account of the self-evident contrast of Sue and Arabella. Hardy seems to have been making conscious use of the convention *within* the figure of Sue; her name means 'lily', and there is symbolism in the scene in which Jude playfully forces her into contact with the roses of which she says ' "I suppose it is against the rules to touch them" ' (p. 308).[33] It is interesting to note, by the way, that in the year of *Jude*'s publication, Hardy was collaborating with Florence Henniker on a story where the heroine's name, Rosalys, seems consciously to draw together the two symbolic traditions.[34]

For Sue, mind and body, intellect and sexuality, are in a complex and disturbing interdependence, given iconic representation in her twin deities, Apollo and Venus, which she transmutes for Miss Fontover – prefiguring the later collapse of her intellect and repudiation of her sexuality – into the representative of religious orthodoxy, St. Peter, and the repentant sexual sinner, St. Mary Magdalen. Further, there are the complementary images of Sue as 'a white heap' on the ground after her desperate leap from her bedroom window (p. 242), and as a 'heap of black clothes' on the floor of St. Silas after the death of her children (p. 358); as victim of her sexuality and as victim of religious ideology, she is the arena of their conflict. Her intellectual education throughout the novel runs alongside her emotional involvements: the undergraduate who lent her his books and wanted her to be his mistress; Phillotson who gives her chaperoned private lessons in the evenings; and, of course, Jude, with whom she spends much of her time in discussion. But in each case, sexuality is a destructive, divisive force, wrecking the relationship and threatening the precarious balance in Sue's life between her intellectual adventurousness and her sexual reserve. Her relationship with Jude involves her in the involuntary physiological processes of conception, pregnancy and childbirth, and these in turn enforce upon her a financial and emotional dependence on Jude which destructive for both of them.

Sue, then, is at the centre of this irreconcilability of 'flesh' and 'spirit'; yet she is constantly distanced from the novel's centre of consciousness by the careful manipulation of points of view. A variety of interpreters interpose between her and the reader – Phillotson, Widow Edlin, even Arabella; but chiefly, of course, Jude. There is a kind of collusion between him and the narrator, which is most evident in the scene of Jude's first walk round Christminster, when he sees the phantoms of past luminaries of the university; the actual names are withheld from the reader as if to convey the sense of a shared secret between narrator and character. This collusion enables us to follow the movements of Jude's thoughts and actions – the narrator's examination of his consciousness is authoritative. Sue, on the other hand, is, as John Bayley remarks, consistently *exhibited*;[35] she is pictorialised, rendered in a series of visual images which give some accuracy to Vigar's descriptions of the novel as employing a ' "snapshot" method'.[36] Sue's consciousness is opaque, filtered as it is through the interpretations of Jude, with all their attendant incomprehensions and distortions; it is this that makes of her actions impulses, of her confused and complex emotions flirtation, and of her motives 'one lovely conundrum' (p. 156).[37] The histories of Jude and Sue are, in some respects, remarkably similar, and yet she is made the instrument of Jude's tragedy, rather than the subject of her own. In a sense the reader's knowledge of her exists only through the perceiving consciousness of Jude, and so it is that after his death, she is not shown at all; Arabella takes on Jude's role of interpreting her to us. The effect of this distancing is to give what is openly a man's picture of a woman; there is no attempt, as there is with Tess Durbeyfield, to make her consciousness and experience transparent, accessible to authoritative explanation and commentary. She is resistant to appropriation by the male narrator, and so the partiality of the novel is not naturalised.

It is often said that Sue's 'frigidity' brings about not only her own tragedy, but also – and in this view more importantly – Jude's.[38] In fact, this tragedy follows upon not merely the sexual consummation of their relationship, but Sue's assimilation, through her parenthood, into a pseudo-marriage. Once she has children, she is forced to live with Jude the economic life of the couple, and gradually to reduce her opposition to marriage to formalism by pretending to marry Jude and adopting his name. It is motherhood – her own humiliation by the respectable wives who hound her and Jude from their work, Little Father Time's taunting by his schoolmates – that convinces her that ' "the world and its ways have a certain worth" ' (p. 368; this is an insertion in the first edition), and so begins her collapse into ' "enslavement to forms" ' (p. 405). For the anti-marriage theme of the novel is not entirely concerned with legally or sacramentally defined marriage, though these play a significant role, and it differs again here from most of the contemporary New Woman fiction. In most cases (as in Grant Allen, for example) it is merely the legal aspect that is attacked, while a 'free union' which duplicates the marital relationship in every respect but this is seen as a radical alternative. Even for a radical feminist theorist like Mona Caird, it is the inequality of the terms on which the contract is based that is the root of the problem:

The injustice of obliging two people, on pain of social ostracism, either to accept the marriage-contract as it stands, or to live apart, is surely self-evident. . . . [I]f it were to be decreed that the woman, in order to be legally married, must gouge out her right eye, no sane person would argue that the marriage-contract was perfectly just, simply because the woman was at liberty to remain single if she did not relish the conditions. Yet this argument is used on behalf of the present contract, as if it were really any sounder in the one case than in the other.[39]

Her solution is to propose a more flexible and personalised contractual relationship. Jude and Sue experience the same sense that predetermined social forms, however they may be for other people, cannot suit ' "the queer sort of people we are" ' (p. 299); they regard themselves unequivocally as the argument from exception, despite various intimations that they are simply precursors of a general change of feeling. It is curious that this argument contradicts the general tendency of the attack on marriage, for if they are exceptional in their relation- ship, it is in their 'perfect . . . reciprocity' (p. 221), their ' "extraordinary sympathy, or similarity" ' (p. 245). Their Shelleyan vision of themselves as twin souls, two halves of a single whole, is a version of Romanticism which is in conflict with the attack on marriage as enforcing a continuing and exclusive commitment; the same contradiction is apparent in Shelley's *Epipsychidion* itself, an important source for *Jude*.[40] Sue and Jude see themselves as giving freely just this kind and degree of commitment, embodying in a 'purer', because uncon- strained, form the very ideal of marriage; indeed, they often talk of their relationship precisely *as* a marriage, and refer to each other as 'husband' and 'wife'. Other relationships of this kind are perceived by them as invariably gross and degrading – the cowed and pregnant bride who marries her seducer ' "to escape a nominal shame which was owing to the weakness of her character" ', the boozy, pock-marked woman marrying ' "for a lifetime" ' the convict whom she really wants ' "for a few hours" ' (pp. 297–8). Their own relationship, however, they perceive as refined and singled out, its sexuality as merely the symbol of its spirituality. But, in the course of the novel, they are forced to recognise that their relationship is not transcen- dant of time, place, and material circumstance, as they have tried to make it; their Romantic delusion gives way, leaving Jude cynical, but in Sue's case leading on into the ideology of

legalised and sacramental marriage that her experiences have
led her to respect. Ironically, it is a debased Romantic version
that concludes the book, through Arabella's final statement that
' "She's never found peace since she left his arms, and never will
again till she's as he is now!" ' (p. 413). Sue comes to see in
Phillotson her husband in law, as Tess comes to see in Alec her
husband in nature; the logic is only apparently opposite, for in
both cases it is underpinned by that sense of the irrevocability of
commitment which is inculcated by the ideology of marriage.
Jude illustrates how a relationship conceived by its protagonists
as in opposition to marriage cannot help becoming its replica –
that it is in the lived texture of the relationship that the
oppression resides, and not in the small print of the contract.
The 'alternative' relationship proves ultimately no alternative
at all, for its material situation presses upon it to shape it into a
pre-existing form. Jude and Sue escape none of the oppressions
of marriage, but they incur over and above these the penalties
reserved for transgressors against it. There is no form for the
relationship to take except those named and determined by the
very form that they seek to transcend: unless it is marriage, it is
adultery or fornication. It is in this sense that Jude comes to see
that he too is one of ' "that vast band of men shunned by the
virtuous – the men called seducers" ' (p. 352).

In a sense, then, *Jude the Obscure* offers a challenge to
contemporary reformist feminism. It challenges in particular
the notion of the home or the love-relationship as a protected
zone, beyond the reach of existing material and ideological
structures, which could be reformed by individual acts of will
and intention. Jude comes finally to see himself and Sue as
martyred pioneers: ' "Perhaps the world is not illuminated
enough for such experiments as ours! Who were we, to think we
could act as pioneers!" ' (p. 360). They show rather the unimaginable nature of female-male relations as they would exist
outside the economic and ideological pressures which wrench
the relationship back into pre-determined forms of marriage,
just as Hardy's novel is wrenched back finally into pre-existing
fictional forms; but it is part of the strength of *Jude* that it makes
visible the violence of those wrenchings, and gives a sense of the
energy which cannot be wholly contained within those forms.
The novel points, too, to the crucial role of parenthood, and so

of the nuclear family, in enforcing the marital model, for it is when Little Father Time arrives that the relationship is forced to adapt, economically and in appearance, to the conventional marital couple. There are two references, very radical in their time, to the necessity for socialised childcare, though without challenging the existing sex-role division. In the first, Phillotson tells Gillingham that ' "I don't see why the woman and the children should not be the unit without the man" ' (p. 247); in the serial text, he argues in more detail that ' "I don't see why society shouldn't be reorganized on a basis of Matriarchy – the woman and the children being the unit without the man, and the men to support the women and children collectively – not individually, as we do now." '[41] Later, Jude raises the same question when confronted with the possibility that Arabella's son need not necessarily be also his:

> "The beggarly question of parentage – what is it, after all? What does it matter, when you come to think of it, whether a child is yours by blood or not? All the little ones of our time are collectively the children of us adults of the time, and entitled to our general care" (p. 288).

It is interesting that, although in 1892 Hardy had written to Alice Grenfell that he did not support women's suffrage,[42] by 1906 he had changed his mind, largely on the grounds that women would take on a more progressive role in introducing socialised childcare:

> . . . the tendency of the women's vote will be to break up the present pernicious convention in respect of manners, customs, religion, illegitimacy, the stereotyped household (that it must be the unit of society), the father of a woman's child (that it is anybody's business but the woman's own except in cases of disease or insanity).[43]

In the light of this, it is not surprising that, while Sue's sexuality all but destroys her, Arabella's is the very guarantee of her survival. She, neither enigma nor conundrum, is clear-sighted about her means of economic survival, and barters her sexuality accordingly. She runs an ironically parallel course to Sue Bridehead's in her rejection of one husband and finding of another, her (temporary) sublimation of her sexuality into religiosity, her loss of her child, and her eventual return to her first husband. Her education, carried out largely by her work-mates, parallels and undercuts the more formalised self-

education of both Jude and Sue, forming part of the collision in
the novel between 'dogma', 'doctrines', 'principles' – in short,
formal education – and 'instincts', 'impulse', 'inclinations' –
the complexities and contingencies of personal experience.

Arabella is always connected with both sexuality and
fecundity. The scene of her first meeting with Jude, even more
overtly symbolic in the texts of the serial and first edition, is
suggestive of a literal seduction. In this earlier version, Jude is
timorous, picking up the pig's penis with the end of his stick,
and averting his eyes while he offers it to Arabella. She responds
in this way: 'She, too, looked in another direction and took the
piece as though ignorant of what her hand was doing.'[49] In
subsequent editions, this is replaced by her 'sway[ing] herself
backwards and forwards on her hand' (p. 63)! After this, the
scene of the actual seduction seems redundant; it continues,
however, the emphasis on breasts which frequently accompanies Arabella's appearances in the novel.[45] The egg which she is
hatching between her breasts introduces the idea of fertility into
the self-evident sexuality of the scene. She is a kind of surrogate
mother for the orphan Jude; at his unexpected re-meeting with
her in the bar, he reacts as though he had been 'whisked. . . back
to his milk-fed infancy' (p. 217). Yet it is Sue who becomes a
mother, not only of her own children, but also of Arabella's
son, while Arabella herself, for all the implied multiplicity of
her sexual involvements, never plays a maternal role. This is
crucial, given the way in which this role precipitates Sue into her
' "enslavement to forms" ' (p. 405); and there is a hint that it is
not simply coincidental that Arabella's sexual 'freedom' is
preserved. Before her marriage to Jude, she meets Physician
Vilbert; she 'had been gloomy, but before he left her she had
grown brighter' (p. 80). Since the idea of obliging Jude to marry
her has been her intention from the outset, it is unclear whether
she has obtained from the physician a simple piece of advice –
pretend to be pregnant – or whether, pregnant in fact, she has
got from him some of those ' "female pills" ' which he had
earlier asked the boy Jude to advertise in payment for the
grammars he never brings (p. 52). 'Female pills' was at this time
a widely-understood euphemism for abortifacients. Arabella,
then, is perhaps able to safeguard herself from the consequences
of her sexuality, at least in the form of unwanted children, and

so to resist some of the more urgent economic and ideological pressures which push women back into nuclear family units.

A. O. J. Cockshut considers *Jude the Obscure* a refutation of contemporary feminist thought, and Sue Bridehead an illustration of Hardy's pessimism about women's attempts to defy the inexorable, 'natural' limitations of their sex; he concludes that 'The attempt to turn Hardy into a feminist is altogether vain'.[46] He is right, I think, in seeing the novel as in conscious dialogue with both feminist and anti-feminist fiction of its time; but his interpretation of the novel's role in this dialogue is, surely, entirely mistaken. Sue's 'breakdown' is not the sign of some gender-determined constitutional weakness of mind or will, but a result of the fact that certain social forces press harder on women in sexual and marital relationships, largely by virtue of the implication of their sexuality in child-bearing. Even among the apparently radical New Woman novelists, there is widespread agreement that motherhood is a divinely – and biologically – appointed mission, providing the widest and purest field for the exercise of the 'innate' moral qualities of the woman. In some anti-feminist novels – such as *A Yellow Aster* – it is the approved agent of the rebellious woman's recuperation into the fold of happy docility. Only Mona Caird[47] and Hardy, among the more widely-read novelists dealing with this issue, draw attention to its coercive role in the reproduction of the nuclear family unit. *Jude the Obscure* poses a radical challenge to contemporary reformist feminist thought in its understanding that the ' "something external" ' which says ' "You shan't love!" ' also and at the same time says ' "You shan't learn!" ' and ' "You shan't labour!" ' (p. 347).

But it is not only its challenge to the existing social and ideological formations of the period that makes *Jude the Obscure*, in Eagleton's phrase, an 'unacceptable text'.[48] It is a novel that threatens to crack open the powerful ideology of realism as a literary mode, and throws into question the whole enterprise of narrative. 'The letter killeth' – and not only Jude. Tess, too, is destroyed by letters: the text-painter's flaming sign, Joan Durbeyfield's letter of advice, Tess's own misplaced written confession, the various appeals and dununciations and warnings dispatched to Angel in Brazil. It is wholly fitting, then, that Angel should finally track down Tess once more by following the directions of the local postman! Sue Bridehead, on the other hand, is progressively reduced from a challenging articulacy to a tense and painful silence that returns her to the fold of marriage – a conclusion which ironically duplicates the death of Jude. Writing comes increasingly to resemble an instrument of death, for the women in particular. From the fatal 'letter' of fiction, Hardy will turn to the 'letter' of a poetry that memorialises.

NOTES

1 *One Rare Fair Woman: Thomas Hardy's Letters to Florence Henniker 1893–1922*, ed. Evelyn Hardy and F. B. Pinion (London, 1972), pp. 3 and 46.

2 Egerton's letter, dated 22 November 1895, is referred to in *Thomas Hardy's Correspondence at Max Gate: A Descriptive Check List*, ed. Carl J. Weber and Clara Carter Weber (Waterville, Maine, 1968), p. 56. Hardy's letter about Caird is 'To Percy Bunting,' 13 January 1890, *Collected Letters of Thomas Hardy: Volume I 1840–1892*, ed. R. L. Purdy and Michael Millgate (Oxford, 1978), p. 208.

3 *One Rare Fair Woman*, p. 8.

4 Gail Cunningham, *The New Woman and the Victorian Novel* (London, 1978), pp. 105–6.

5 'To Millicent Garrett Fawcett,' 14 April 1892, *Collected Letters*, p. 264.

6 William Roberton, *The Novel-Reader's Handbook: A Brief Guide to Recent Novels and Novelists* (Birmingham, 1899), pp. 1–2.

7 Grant Allen, *The British Barbarians: A Hill-Top Novel* (London, 1895), p. 94.

8 Richard Little Purdy, *Thomas Hardy: A Bibliographical Study* (London, 1954), p. 91.

9 Grant Allen, *The Woman Who Did* (London, 1895), p. 41.

10 *Woman Who Did*, pp. 182–90.

11 Robert Yelverton Tyrrell, *Jude the Obscure, Fortnightly Review*, 65 (1896), 858.

12 [H. G. Wells], 'Jude the Obscure,' *Saturday Review*, 82 (1896), 153.

13 'Novel Notes,' *Bookman*, 6 (1894), 24.

14 'Novel Notes,' 24.

15 For a representative selection, see *Working Class Stories of the 1890s*, ed. P. J. Keating (London, 1971).

16 E.g. 'To Florence Henniker,' 10 November 1895, *One Rare Fair Woman*, p. 47.

17 *One Rare Fair Woman*, p. 43.

18 Patricia Ingham, 'The Evolution of *Jude the Obscure*,' *Review of English Studies*, 27 (1976), 27–37 and 159–69; a decisive refutation of John Paterson's 'The Genesis of *Jude the Obscure*,' *Studies in Philology*, 57 (1960), 87–98.

19 Ward Hellstrom reads the novel in terms of Arnold in 'Hardy's Scholar-
    Gipsy,' in *The English Novel in the Nineteenth Century: Essays on the Literary
    Mediation of Human Values*, ed. George Goodin, Illinois Studies in
    Language and Literature, No. 63 (Urbana, 1972), pp. 196–213; while
    William J. Hyde reads in terms of Mill, in 'Theoretic and Practical
    Unconventionality in *Jude the Obscure*,' *Nineteenth-Century Fiction*, 20
    (1965), 155–64.
20 *One Rare Fair Woman*, p. 46.
21 'Hearts Insurgent,' *Harper's New Monthly Magazine*, European ed. 30
    (1895), 594.
22 Cf. Alan Friedman, 'Thomas Hardy: "Weddings Be Funerals"', in *The
    Turn of the Novel* (New York, 1966), pp. 70–1.
23 Cousin, or bother and sister, relationships were widely used in feminist
    fiction to contrast the treatment and expectations and experiences of
    sex-differentiated pairs; e.g. in Elizabeth Barrett Browning, *Aurora Leigh*
    (1856), and Sarah Grand's *The Heavenly Twins* (1893).
24 Cf. John Goode, 'Sue Bridehead and the New Woman,' in *Women Writing
    and Writing about Women*, ed. Mary Jacobus (London, 1979), pp. 100–13.
25 John Lucas, *The Literature of Change: Studies in the Nineteenth-Century
    Provincial Novel* (Hassocks, Sussex, 1977), pp. 188–91.
26 D. H. Lawrence, 'Study of Thomas Hardy,' in *Phoenix: The Posthumous
    Papers of D. H. Lawrence*, ed. Edward D. McDonald (1936; rpt. London,
    1961), pp. 495–510; and Kate Millett, *Sexual Politics* (London, 1971),
    pp. 130–4.
29 *Harper's*, European ed. 29 (1895), 576; and *Jude the Obscure* (London,
    1895), p. 161.
28 John Goode, 'Woman and the Literary Text,' in *The Rights and Wrongs of
    Women*, ed. Juliet Mitchell and Ann Oakley (Harmondsworth, 1976),
    p. 242.
29 See her comments on p. 186 (' "Their philosophy only recognises rela-
    tions based on animal desire" ') and p. 222 (' "they can't give it con-
    tinuously to the chamber-officer appointed by the bishop's licence to
    receive it." ').
30 Cf. Geoffrey Thurley, *The Psychology of Hardy's Novels: The Nervous and
    the Statuesque* (St. Lucia, Queensland, 1975), p. 191.
31 Cf. William H. Marshall, *The World of the Victorian Novel* (London, 1967),
    pp. 404–24.
32 *Sexual Politics*, p. 133.
33 Cf. Mary Jacobus, 'Sue the Obscure,' *Essays in Criticism*, 25 (1975),
    304–28.
34 'The Spectre of the Real,' in *In Scarlet and Grey: Stories of Soldiers and Others*
    (London, 1896), pp. 164–208.
35 John Bayley, *An Essay on Hardy* (Cambridge, 1978), p. 201.
36 Penelope Vigar, *The Novels of Thomas Hardy: Illusion and Reality* (London,
    1974), p. 193.
37 Cf. Elizabeth Langland, 'A Perspective of One's Own: Thomas Hardy
    and the Elusive Sue Bridehead,' *Studies in the Novel*, 12 (1980), 12–28.
38 E.g. Shalom Rachman, 'Character and Theme in Hardy's *Jude the*

Obscure,' *English*, 22, No. 113 (1973), 45–53; and T. B. Tomlinson, *The English Middle-Class Novel* (London, 1976), pp. 121–4.

39 Mona Caird, 'The Future of the Home,' in *The Morality of Marriage and other Essays on the Status and Destiny of Woman* (London, 1897), p. 117.

40 For an interesting account of the Shelleyan motif in the novel, see Michael E. Hassett, 'Compromised Romanticism in *Jude the Obscure*,' *Nineteenth-Century Fiction*, 25 (1971), 432–43.

41 *Harper's*, European ed. 30, 125.

42 'To Alice Grenfell,' 23 April 1892, *Collected Letters*, p. 266.

43 'To Millicent Garrett Fawcett,' 30 November 1906, Fawcett Library, London.

44 'The Simpletons,' *Harper's*, European ed. 29 (1894), 80. The serial title was changed to 'Hearts Insurgent' in subsequent instalments.

45 E.g. on pp. 62, 64, 93 and 197.

46 A. O. J. Cockshut, *Man and Woman: A Study of Love and the Novel 1740–1940* (London, 1977), p. 129.

47 See *The Daughters of Danaus* (London, 1894), pp. 341–2.

48 Terry Eagleton, 'Liberality and Order: The Criticism of John Bayley,' *New Left Review*, No. 110 (1978), 39.

Bibliography of Works Consulted

SECTION A: THOMAS HARDY

1. HARDY'S WRITINGS

a) *Fiction*

Parenthetical page-references to Hardy's fiction throughout the text, unless otherwise identified, are to the New Wessex Edition of the Novels, General Editor P.N. Furbank, published in fourteen volumes by Macmillan 1975–76:

		Original Date of Publication
1.	*Under the Greenwood Tree*, Introd. Geoffrey Grigson	1872
2.	*Far from the Madding Crowd*, Introd. John Bayley	1874
3.	*The Return of the Native*, Introd. Derwent May	1878
4.	*The Trumpet-Major*, Introd. Barbara Hardy	1880
5.	*The Mayor of Casterbridge*, Introd. Ian Gregor	1886
6.	*The Woodlanders*, Introd. David Lodge	1887
7.	*Tess of the d'Urbervilles*, Introd. P.N. Furbank	1891
8.	*Jude the Obscure*, Introd. Terry Eagleton	1895
9.	*Desperate Remedies*, Introd. C.J.P. Beatty	1871
10.	*A Pair of Blue Eyes*, Introd. Ronald Blythe	1873
11.	*The Hand of Ethelberta*, Introd. Robert Gittings	1876
12.	*A Laodicean*, Introd. Barbara Hardy	1881
13.	*Two on a Tower*, Introd. F.B. Pinion	1882
14.	*The Well-Beloved*, Introd. J. Hillis Miller	1897

I have also used the New Wessex Edition of the Stories, edited by F.B. Pinion, and published in three volumes by Macmillan in 1977:

		Original Date of Publication
1.	*Wessex Tales* and *A Group of Noble Dames*	1888 and 1891
2.	*Life's Little Ironies* and *A Changed Man*	1894 and 1913
3.	*Old Mrs Chundle* and other stories, with *The Famous Tragedy of the Queen of Cornwall*	miscellaneous

OTHER EDITIONS:

Jude the Obscure. London, 1895.

'The Spectre of the Real.' By Thomas Hardy and Florence

Henniker. In *In Scarlet and Grey: Stories of Soldiers and Others*, by Florence Henniker. London, 1896.

An Indiscretion in the Life of an Heiress. Ed. Terry Coleman. London, 1976.

SERIAL TEXTS:

The Return of the Native: Belgravia, 34 (January–December 1878).

The Woodlanders: Macmillan's Magazine, 54 and 55 (May 1886–April 1887).

Tess of the d'Urbervilles: Graphic, 44 (July–December 1891). An episode and a related sketch were published separately: 'The Midnight Baptism, A Study in Christianity,' *Fortnightly Review*, 55 (May 1891), 695–70. 'Saturday Night in Arcady,' Special Literary Supplement, *National Observer* (Edinburgh), NS 6 (14 November 1891).

Jude the Obscure: 'The Simpletons' (title for one instalment only), afterwards 'Hearts Insurgent.' *Harper's New Monthly Magazine*, European ed. 29 (1894) and 30 (1895). December 1894–November 1895.

b) *Miscellaneous*

'The Tree of Knowledge,' *New Review*, 10 (1894), 681.

Thomas Hardy's Personal Writings. Ed. Harold Orel. London, 1967.

The Early Life of Thomas Hardy 1840–1891. By Florence Emily Hardy. London, 1928.

The Later Years of Thomas Hardy, 1892–1928. By Florence Emily Hardy. London, 1930.

The Literary Notes of Thomas Hardy. Ed. Lennart A. Björk. I. *Text* and I. *Notes*. Goteborg, 1974.

c) *Letters*

'To John Lane.' 15 December 1910. Rpt. in Publisher's Note, *The Song of Songs*, by Hermann Sudermann. Trans. Beatrice Marshall. London, 1913, pp. ix–x.

Thomas Hardy's Correspondence at Max Gate: A Descriptive Check List. Ed. Carl J. Weber and Clara Carter Weber. Waterville, Maine, 1968.

One Rare Fair Woman: Thomas Hardy's Letters to Florence Henniker 1893–1922. Ed. Evelyn Hardy and F.B. Pinion. London, 1972.

Collected Letters of Thomas Hardy: Volume I 1840–1892. Ed. Richard Little Purdy and Michael Millgate. Oxford, 1978.

Parker, W.M. 'Hardy's Letters to Sir George Douglas.' *English*, 14 (1963), 218–25.

d) *Unpublished Material*
'To Millicent Garrett Fawcett.' 30 November 1906. Fawcett Library, London.
Ms of 'Jude the Obscure.' Fitzwilliam Museum, Cambridge.

2. WRITINGS ABOUT HARDY
Bayley, John. *An Essay on Hardy*. Cambridge, 1978.
Black, Clementina. Rev. of *Tess of the d'Urbervilles. Illustrated London News*, 9 January 1892, p.50.
Brick, Allan. 'Paradise and Consciousness in Hardy's *Tess.' Nineteenth-Century Fiction*, 17 (1962), 115–34.
Brooks, Jean. *Thomas Hardy: The Poetic Structure*. London, 1971.
Brown, Douglas. *Thomas Hardy*. Men and Books. London, 1954.
Carpenter, Richard. 'The Mirror and the Sword: Imagery in *Far From the Madding Crowd.' Nineteenth-Century Fiction*, 18 (1964), 331–45.
— *Thomas Hardy*. London, 1976.
Casagrande, Peter J. 'Hardy's Wordsworth: A Record and a Commentary.' *English Literature in Transition*, 20 (1977), 210–37.
— 'The Shifted "Center of Altruism" in *The Woodlanders*: Thomas Hardy's Third "Return of a Native".' *ELH*, 38 (1971), 104–25.
Crompton, Louis. 'The Sunburnt God: Ritual and Tragic Myth in *The Return of the Native.' Boston University Studies in English*, 4 (1960), 229–40.
Deen, Leonard W. 'Heroism and Pathos in Hardy's *Return of the Native.' Nineteenth-Century Fiction*, 15 (1960), 207–19.
de Laura, David J. '"The Ache of Modernism" in Hardy's Later Novels.' *ELH*, 34 (1967), 380–99.
Draffan, Robert A. 'Hardy's *Under the Greenwood Tree*,' *English*, 22 (1973), 55–60.
Drake, Robert Y., Jr. '*The Woodlanders* as Traditional Pastoral.' *Modern Fiction Studies*, 6 (1960), 251–7.
Duffin, H.C. *Thomas Hardy: A Study of the Wessex Novels, The Poems and 'The Dynasts'*. 1916; rpt. Manchester, 1937.
Eagleton, Terry. 'Thomas Hardy: Nature as Language.' *Critical Quarterly*, 13 (1971), 155–62.
— Introduction. *Jude the Obscure*. New Wessex ed. London, 1975, pp.13–23.
Ebbatson, J.R. 'The Darwinian View of Tess: A Reply.' *Southern Review*, 8 (1975), 247–53.
Eggenschwiler, David. 'Eustacia Vye, Queen of Night and Courtly Pretender.' *Nineteenth-Century Fiction*, 25 (1971), 444–54.
Ellis, Havelock. 'Concerning *Jude the Obscure*,' *Savoy*, 6 (1896), 35–49. Rpt. as *Concerning Jude the Obscure*. London, 1931.

— 'Thomas Hardy's Novels,' *Westminster Review*, 63 (1883), 334–64.

Evans, Robert. 'The Other Eustacia.' *Novel*, 1 (1968), 251–9.

Fayen, George S., Jr. 'Hardy's *The Woodlanders*: Inwardness and Memory.' *Studies in English Literature*, 1, No. 4 (1961), 81–100.

Friedman, Alan. 'Thomas Hardy: "Weddings be Funerals".' In *The Turn of the Novel*. New York, 1966, pp. 38–74.

Gerber, Helmut E., and Eugene W. Davis, ed. *Thomas Hardy: An Annotated Bibliography of Writings About Him*. An Annotated Secondary Bibliography Series on English Literature in Transition 1880–1920. Gen. Ed. Helmut E. Gerber. De Kalb, Illinois, 1973.

Goode, John. 'Sue Bridehead and the New Woman.' In *Women Writing and Writing about Women*. Ed. Mary Jacobus. pp. 100–13.

Gregor, Ian. *The Great Web: The Form of Hardy's Major Fiction*. London, 1974.

Grindle, Juliet. 'A Critical Edition of Thomas Hardy's *Tess of the d'Urbervilles*.' D.Phil. Oxford, 1974.

Guerard, Albert J. *Thomas Hardy: The Novels and Stories*. London, 1949.

Hannigan, D.F. 'The Latest Development of English Fiction.' *Westminster Review*, 138 (1892), 655–9.

Hardwick, Elizabeth. 'Sue and Arabella.' In *The Genius of Thomas Hardy*. Ed. Margaret Drabble. London, 1976, pp. 67–73.

Hardy, Barbara. Introduction. *A Laodicean*. New Wessex ed. London, 1975, pp.13–29.

Hassett, Michael E. 'Compromised Romanticism in *Jude the Obscure*.' *Nineteenth-Century Fiction*, 25 (1971), 432–43.

Hawkins, Desmond. *Thomas Hardy*. London, 1950.

Hazen, James. 'The Tragedy of Tess Durbeyfield.' *Texas Studies in Literature and Language*, 11 (1969), 779–94.

Hellstrom, Ward. 'Hardy's Scholar-Gipsy.' In *The English Novel in the Nineteenth Century: Essays on the Literary Mediation of Human Values*. Ed. George Goodin. Illinois Studies in Language and Literature, No. 63. Urbana, 1972, pp. 196–213.

Herbert, Lucille. 'Hardy's Views in *Tess of the d'Urbervilles*.' *ELH*, 37 (1970), 77–94.

Heywood, C. '*The Return of the Native* and Miss Braddon's *The Doctor's Wife*: A Probable Source.' *Nineteenth-Century Fiction*, 18 (1963), 91–4.

Holloway, John. 'Hardy's Major Fiction.' In *The Charted Mirror. Literary and Critical Essays*. London, 1960, pp. 94–107.

Howe, Irving. *Thomas Hardy*. London, 1968.

Hyde, William J. 'Theoretic and Practical Unconventionality in *Jude the Obscure*.' *Nineteenth-Century Fiction*, 20 (1965), 155–64.

Hyman, Virginia R. *Ethical Perspective in the Novels of Thomas Hardy*.

Kennikat Press National University Publication. Literary Criticism Series. Port Washington, 1975.

Ingham, Patricia. 'The Evolution of *Jude the Obscure.' Review of English Studies*, 27 (1976), 27–37 and 159–69.

'Ingram, E.V.' [Caradoc Granhim]. 'Art Literature.' *Westminster Review*, 142 (1894), 392–402.

Jacobus, Mary. 'Sue the Obscure.' *Essays in Criticism*, 25 (1975), 304–28.

—'Tree and Machine: *The Woodlanders.*' In *Critical Approaches to the Fiction of Thomas Hardy*. Ed. Dale Kramer. London, 1979, pp. 116–34.

— 'Tess: The Making of a Pure Woman.' In *Tearing the Veil: Essays on Femininity*. Ed. Susan Lipshitz. London, 1978, pp. 77–92.

Kettle, Arnold. Introduction. *Tess of the d'Urbervilles*. New York, 1966, pp. vii–xxiii. Rpt. in *Twentieth Century Interpretations of 'Tess of the d'Urbervilles.'* Ed. Albert J. LaValley. Englewood Cliffs, New Jersey, 1969, pp. 14–29.

Kozicki, Henry. 'Myths of Redemption in Hardy's *Tess of the d'Urbervilles.' Papers on Language and Literature*, 10 (1974), 150–8.

Kramer, Dale. 'Revisions and Vision: Thomas Hardy's *The Woodlanders*. Part 1.' *Bulletin of New York Public Library*, 75 (1971), 195–230.

— 'Revisions and Vision: Part II. Years to Maturity.' *Bulletin of New York Public Library*, 75 (1971), 248–82.

— *Thomas Hardy: The Forms of Tragedy*. London, 1975.

— ed. *Critical Approaches to the Fiction of Thomas Hardy*. London, 1979.

Laird, J.T. *The Shaping of 'Tess of the d'Urbervilles'*. Oxford, 1975.

Lang, Andrew. 'At the Sign of the Ship.' *Longman's Magazine*, 21 (1892), 100–106.

Langland, Elizabeth. 'A Perspective of One's Own: Thomas Hardy and the Elusive Sue Bridehead.' *Studies in the Novel*, 12 (1980), 12–28.

Lawrence, D.H. 'Study of Thomas Hardy.' In *Phoenix: The Posthumous Papers of D.H. Lawrence*. Ed. Edward D. Macdonald. 1936; rpt. London, 1961, pp. 398–516.

Lodge, David. Introduction. *The Woodlanders*. New Wessex ed. London, 1975, pp. 13–22.

— 'Tess, Nature and the Voices of Hardy.' In *Language of Fiction. Essays in Criticism and Verbal Analysis of the English Novel*. London, 1966, pp. 164–88.

Matchett, William H. '*The Woodlanders*, or Realism in Sheep's Clothing.' *Nineteenth-Century Fiction*, 9 (1955), 241–61.

May, Charles E. '*Far from the Madding Crowd* and *The Woodlanders*:

Hardy's Grotesque Pastorals.' *English Literature in Transition*, 17 (1974), pp. 147–58.

Meisel, Perry. *Thomas Hardy: The Return of the Repressed, A Study of the Major Fiction*. Yale College Series of Scholarly Essays, 12. New Haven, 1972.

Miles, Rosalind. 'The Women of Wessex.' In *The Novels of Thomas Hardy*. Ed. Anne Smith. London, 1979, pp. 23–44.

Miller, Joseph Hillis. *Thomas Hardy: Distance and Desire*. London, 1970.

— 'Fiction and Repetition: *Tess of the d'Urbervilles*.' In *Forms of Modern British Fiction*. Ed. Alan Warren Friedman. Austin, Texas, 1975, pp. 43–71.

Millgate, Michael. *Thomas Hardy: His Career as a Novelist*. London, 1971.

Morrell, Roy. *Thomas Hardy: The Will and the Way*. Kuala Lumpur, 1965.

Morris, Mowbray. 'Culture and Anarchy.' *Quarterly Review*, 174 (1892), 317–43.

Morton, Peter. '*Tess of the d'Urbervilles*: A Neo-Darwinian Reading.' *Southern Review* (Adelaide), 7 (1974), 38–50.

— '*Tess* and August Weismann: Unholy Alliance?' *Southern Review*, 8 (1975), 254–56.

Newton, William B. 'Hardy and the Naturalists: their Use of Physiology.' *Modern Philology*, 49 (1951), 28–41.

— 'Chance as Employed by Hardy and the Naturalists.' *Philological Quarterly*, 30 (1951), 154–75.

Oliphant, Margaret O.W. 'The Anti-Marriage League.' *Blackwoods*, 159 (1896), 135–49.

[—] 'The Old Saloon.' *Blackwoods*, 151 (1892), pp. 464–74.

[Page, Thomas Nelson]. 'Editor's Study. I.' *Harper's New Monthly Magazine*, 85 (1892), 152–3.

Paris, Bernard J. '"A Confusion of Many Standards": Conflicting Value Systems in *Tess of the d'Urbervilles*.' *Nineteenth-Century Fiction*, 24 (1969), 57–79.

Paterson, John. 'The Genesis of *Jude the Obscure*.' *Studies in Philology*, 57 (1960), 87–98.

— *The Making of 'The Return of the Native'*. University of California English Studies, No. 19, Berkeley, 1960.

Payne, Charles Morton. Rev. of *Tess of the d'Urbervilles*. *Dial*, 12 (1892), 424.

Preston, Harriet Waters. 'Thomas Hardy.' *Century*, NS 24 (1893), 353–9.

Purdy, Richard Little. *Thomas Hardy: A Bibliographical Study*. London, 1954.

Rachman, Shalom. 'Character and Theme in Hardy's *Jude the Obscure.' English*, 22, No. 113 (1973), 45–53.

Rev. of *Tess of the d'Urbervilles. Pall Mall Gazette*, 31 December 1891, p.3.

Rev. of *Tess of the d'Urbervilles. Review of Reviews*, 5 (1892), 19.

Riesner, Dieter. 'Über die Genesis von Thomas Hardys *The Return of the Native.' Archiv*, 200 (1963), 53–9.

Rogers, Kathleen. 'Women in Thomas Hardy.' *Centennial Review*, 19 (1975), 249–58.

Saunders, Mary M. 'The Significance of the Man-Trap in *The Woodlanders.' Modern Fiction Studies*, 20 (1974–5), 529–31.

Schweik, Robert. 'Moral Perspective in *Tess of the d'Urbervilles.' College English*, 24 (1962), 14–18.

Short, Clarice. 'In Defense of *Ethelberta.' Nineteenth-Century Fiction*, 13 (1958), 48–57.

Showalter, Elaine. 'The Unmanning of the Mayor of Casterbridge.' In *Critical Approaches to the Fiction of Thomas Hardy*. Ed. Dale Kramer, London, 1979, pp. 99–115.

Southerington, F.R. *Hardy's Vision of Man*. London, 1971.

Stanzel, Franz K. 'Thomas Hardy: *Tess of the d'Urbervilles.' In Der moderne englische Roman: Interpretationen*. Ed. Horst Oppel. Berlin, 1965, pp. 34–48.

Steig, Michael. 'Art Versus Philosophy in Hardy: *The Woodlanders.' Mosaic* 4, No. 3 (1971).

Tanner, Tony. 'Colour and Movement in *Tess of the d'Urbervilles.' Critical Quarterly*, 10 (1968), 219–39.

Thurley, Geoffrey. *The Psychology of Hardy's Novels: The Nervous and the Statuesque*. St. Lucia, Queensland, 1975.

Trail, George Y. 'The Consistency of Hardy's Sue: Bridehead Becomes Electra.' *Literature and Psychology*, 26 (1976), 61–8.

Trent, W.P. 'The Novels of Thomas Hardy.' *Sewanee Review*, 1 (1892), 1–25.

Tyrrell, Robert Yelverton. '*Jude the Obscure.' Fortnightly Review*, 65 (1896), 857–64.

'Urban, Sylvanus.' 'Table Talk.' *Gentleman's Magazine*, NS 49 (1892), 321.

Vigar, Penelope. *The Novels of Thomas Hardy: Illusion and Reality*. London, 1974.

Weber, Carl J. 'Hardy and *The Woodlanders.' Review of English Studies*, 15 (1939), 330–3.

[Wells, H.G.] 'Jude the Obscure.' *Saturday Review*, 82 (1896), 153.

Williams, Merryn. *Thomas Hardy and Rural England*. London, 1972.

—, and Raymond Williams. 'Hardy and Social Class.' In *Thomas*

Hardy: The Writer and his Background. Ed. Norman Page. Writers and their Background. London, 1980, pp. 29–40.

Woolfe, Virginia. 'Thomas Hardy's Novels.' *Times Literary Supplement*, 19 January 1928, 33–4. Rpt. 'The Novels of Thomas Hardy.' In *The Second Common Reader*. London, 1932, pp. 245–57.

Wotton, George E. 'Ideology and Vision in the Novels of Thomas Hardy.' D. Phil. Oxford, 1980.

SECTION B: THE LITERARY CONTEXT

I. FICTION

Adams, Francis. *A Child of the Age*. London, 1894.

Allen, Grant. *The Woman Who Did*. London, 1895.

— *The British Barbarians, A Hill-Top Novel*. London, 1895.

Barry, Rev. William. *The New Antigone: A Romance*. 3 vols. London, 1887.

— *The Two Standards*. London, 1898.

Beaumont, Mary. *The New Women*. London, 1895.

Brooke, Emma Frances. *A Superfluous Woman*. 3 vols. London, 1894.

Browning, Elizabeth Barrett. *Aurora Leigh*. London, 1856.

Caird, Mona. *The Wing of Azrael*. 3 vols. London, 1889.

— *The Daughters of Danaus*. London, 1894.

Clapperton, Jane Hume. *Margaret Dunmore: or, A Socialist Home*. London, 1888.

'Cleeve, Lucas' [Adelina G.I. Kingscote]. *The Woman Who Wouldn't*. London, 1895.

Craik, Dinah Maria Mulock. *The Woman's Kingdom. A Love Story*. 3 vols. London, 1869.

'Cross, Victoria' [Nivien Corey]. 'Theodora. A Fragment.' *Yellow Book*, 4 (1895), 156–88.

— *The Woman Who Didn't*. London, 1895.

Dalton, Henry Robert S. *Lesbia Newman*. London, 1889.

Darcy, Ella. *Monochromes*. London, 1895.

Dix, Gertrude. *The Girl from the Farm*. London, 1895.

Dixie, Lady Florence. *Redeemed in Blood*. London, 1889.

— *Gloriana; or, the Revolution of 1900*. London, 1890.

Dixon, Ella Hepworth. *The Story of a Modern Woman*. London, 1894.

Dowie, Ménie Muriel. *Gallia*. London, 1895.

'Egerton, George' [Mary Chavelita Dunne Golding Bright]. *Keynotes*. London, 1893.

— *Discords*. London, 1894.

— *Symphonies*. London, 1897.

— *Fantasias*. London, 1898.

— *A Leaf from the Yellow Book: The Correspondence of George Egerton*. Ed. Terence de Vere White. London, 1958.

Flaubert, Gustave. *Madame Bovary. Moeurs de Province*. 2 vols. Paris, 1857.

Gissing, George. *Isabel Clarendon*. 2 vols. London, 1886.

— *The Odd Women*. 3 vols. London, 1893.

— *In the Year of Jubilee*. 3 vols. London, 1894.

— *The Whirlpool*. London, 1897.

— *Letters of George Gissing to Members of his Family*, collected and arranged by Algernon and Ellen Gissing. London, 1927.

Goethe, Johann Wolfgang von. *Die Wahlverwandtschaften. Ein Roman*. 2 vols. Tübingen, 1809.

Graham, Kenneth. *The Headswoman*. London, 1898.

'Grand, Sarah' [Frances Elizabeth McFall]. *Ideala*. London, 1888.

— *The Heavenly Twins*. 3 vols. London, 1893.

— *The Beth Book*. London, 1897.

Grundy, Sydney. *The New Woman. An Original Comedy in Four Acts*. London, 1894.

Henniker, Florence. *In Scarlet and Grey: Stories of Soldiers and Others*. London, 1896.

Holdsworth, Annie E. *Joanna Trail, Spinster*. London, 1894.

Ibsen, Henrik. *The Lady from the Sea*. Trans. Michael Meyer. London, 1960.

— *Hedda Gabler*. Trans. Michael Meyer. London, 1962.

'Iota' [Kathleen Mannington Caffyn]. *A Yellow Aster*. 3 vols. London, 1894.

James, Henry. *The Bostonians*. London, 1886.

[Johnstone, Edith]. *A Sunless Heart*. 2 vols. London, 1894.

Keating, Peter, ed. *Working Class Stories of the 1890s*. London, 1971.

Kenealy, Arabella. *Dr. Janet of Harley Street*. London, [1893].

— *The Honourable Mrs. Spoor*. London, [1895].

— *A Semi-Detached Marriage*. London, 1899.

Linton, Eliza Lynn. *The Rebel of the Family*. 3 vols. London, 1880.

Meredith, George. *Rhoda Fleming*. 3 vols. London, 1865.

— *Diana of the Crossways*. 3 vols. London, 1885.

— *One of our Conquerors*. 3 vols. London, 1891.

Miller, George Noyes. *The Strike of a Sex*. London, [1895].

Moore, Frank Frankfort. *'I Forbid the Banns.' The Story of a Comedy which was Played Seriously*. 3 vols. London, 1893.

Moore, George. *A Drama in Muslin: A Realistic Novel*. London, 1886.

— *A Mere Accident*. London, 1887.

— *Esther Waters: A Novel*. London, 1894.

Murray, Henry. *A Man of Genius*. 2 vols. London, 1895.

Papillon, E.T. *Alleyne: A Story of a Dream and a Failure*. London, 1894.

Platt, William. *Women, Love, and Life*. London, 1895.

'Raimond, C.E.' [Elizabeth Robins]. *George Mandeville's Husband*. London, 1894.

Robins, Elizabeth. *Votes for Women*. London, 1905.

'Rutherford, Mark' [William Hale White]. *Clara Hopgood*. London, 1896.

Schreiner, Olive ('Ralph Iron'). The Story of an African Farm. 2 vols. London, 1883.

Shaw, George Bernard. *The Irrational Knot; Being the Second Novel of his Nonage*. London, 1905.

Smith, John. *Platonic Affections*. London, 1896.

'Smudgiton, Borgia.' 'She-Notes.' *Punch*, 106 (1894), 109 and 129.

Street, George Slythe. *Episodes*. London, 1895.

— *The Wise and the Wayward*. London, 1896.

Syrett, Netta. *Nobody's Fault*. London, 1896.

Voynich, Ethel. *The Gadfly*. London, 1897.

Warwick, H. Sidney. *Dust O'Glamour; and Some Little Love-Affairs*. Bristol, [1897].

Wotton, Mabel F. *Day-Books*. London, 1896.

2. CRITICISM

Addleshaw, Percy. Rev. of *The Woman Who Did*, by Grant Allen. *Academy*, 47 (1895), 186–7.

Chapman, Elizabeth R. *Marriage Questions in Modern Fiction, and Other Essays on Kindred Subjects*. London, 1897.

Courtney, William L. *The Feminine Note in Fiction*. London, 1904.

Crackanthorpe, B.A. 'Sex in Modern Literature.' *Nineteenth Century*, No. 218 (1895), pp. 607–16.

Crackanthorpe, Hubert. 'Reticence in Literature: Some Roundabout Remarks.' *Yellow Book*, 2 (1894), 259–69.

Cunningham, Gail. *The New Woman and the Victorian Novel*. London, 1978.

Decker, Clarence R. 'Zola's Reputation in England.' *PMLA*, 49 (1934), 1140–53.

Eastwood, M. 'The New Woman in Fiction and in Fact.' *Humanitarian*, 5 (1894), 375–9.

'Egerton, George' [Mary Chavelita Dunne Golding Bright]. 'A Keynote to "Keynotes"'. In *Ten Contemporaries: Notes Toward their Definitive Bibliography*. Ed. 'John Gawsworth' [Terence Armstrong]. London, 1952, pp. 57–60.

Ellmann, Richard, ed. *Edwardians and Late Victorians*. English Institute Essays 1959. New York, 1960.

Fawcett, Millicent Garrett. '"The Woman Who Did".' *Contemporary Review*, 67 (1895), 625–31.

Fernando, Lloyd. 'The Radical Ideology of the "New Woman".' *Southern Review* (Adelaide), 2 (1967), 206–22.

— 'Gissing's Studies in Vulgarism: Aspects of his Anti-Feminism.' *Southern Review*, 4 (1970), 43–52.

— *'New Women' in the Late Victorian Novel*. Pennsylvania, 1978.

Fletcher, Ian, ed. *Meredith Now: Some Critical Essays*. London, 1971.

— assoc. ed. *Decadence and the 1890s*. Stratford-upon-Avon Studies. Ed. Malcolm Bradbury and David Palmer. Vol. 17. London, 1979.

Frierson, William C. 'The English Controversy over Realism in Fiction 1885–1895.' *PMLA*, 43 (1928), 533–50.

Gibbons, Tom. *Rooms in the Darwin Hotel: Studies in English Literary Criticism and Ideas 1880–1920*. Nedlands, Western Australia, 1973.

Goode, John. *George Gissing: Ideology and Fiction*. Vision Critical Study. London, 1978.

Gorsky, Susan R. 'Old Maids and New Women: Alternatives to Marriage in Englishwomen's Novels, 1847–1915.' *Journal of Popular Culture*, 7 (1973), 68–85.

Gosse, Edmund. *Questions at Issue*. London, 1893.

Griest, Guinevere L. *Mudie's Circulating Library and the Victorian Novel*. London, 1970.

Harris, Wendell V. 'John Lane's Keynotes Series and the Fiction of the 1890s.' *PMLA*, 83 (1968), 1407–13.

— 'Egerton: Forgotten Realist.' *Victorian Newsletter*, No. 33 (1968), pp. 31–5.

Harvey, H.E. 'The Voice of Woman.' *Westminster Review*, 145 (1896), 193.

Hogarth, Janet E. 'Literary Degenerates.' *Fortnightly Review*, 63 (1895), 586–98.

James, Henry. *Letters of Henry James*. Ed. Percy Lubbock. 2 vols. London, 1920.

Kettle, Arnold. 'E.L. Voynich: A Forgotten English Novelist.' *Essays in Criticism*, 7 (1957), 163–74.

Lucas, John. *The Literature of Change: Studies in the Nineteenth-Century Provincial Novel*. Hassocks, Sussex, 1977.

May, James Lewis. *John Lane and the Nineties*. London, 1936.

Moore, George. *Literature at Nurse, or Circulating Morals*. London, 1885.

'"New" Art at the Old Bailey.' *Speaker*, 11 (1895), 403–04.

Noble, James Ashcroft. 'The Fiction of Sexuality.' *Contemporary Review*, 67 (1895), 490–8.

'Novel Notes.' *Bookman*, 6 (1894), 24–5.

'Philisitine, The' [J.A. Sterry?]. *The New Fiction (A Protest Against Sex-Mania), and Other Papers*. London, 1895.

Poole, Adrian. *Gissing in Context*. London, 1975.

'Recent Novels.' *Spectator*, No. 3, 483 (1895), pp. 431–3.

Roberton, William. *The Novel-Reader's Handbook: A Brief Guide to Recent Novels and Novelists*. Birmingham, 1899.

[Scott, H.S., and E.B. Hall]. 'Character Note. The New Woman.' *Cornhill*, NS 23 (1894), 365–8.

Shaw, George Bernard. *The Quintessence of Ibsenism*. London, 1891.

— *The Sanity of Art: An Exposure of the Current Nonsense about Artists being Degenerate*. London, 1908.

Slater, Edith. 'Men's Women in Fiction.' *Westminster Review*, 149 (1898), 571–7.

Stead, W.T. 'The Novel of the Modern Woman.' *Review of Reviews*, 10 (1894), 64–74.

— 'The Book of the Month. "The Woman Who Did." By Grant Allen,' *Review of Reviews*, 11 (1895), 177–90.

Stubbs, Patricia. *Women and Fiction: Feminism and the Novel 1880–1920*. Brighton, 1979.

Stutfield, Hugh. 'Tommyrotics.' *Blackwoods*, 157 (1895), 833–45.

— 'The Psychology of Feminism.' *Blackwoods*, 161 (1897), 104–17.

Sutherland, J.A. *Victorian Novelists and Publishers*. London, 1976.

Waugh, Arthur. 'Reticence in Literature.' *Yellow Book*, 1 (1894), 201–19.

SECTION C: GENERAL BIBLIOGRAPHY

Acton, William. *The Functions and Disorders of the Reproductive Organs in Childhood, Youth, Adult Age, and Advanced Life Considered in their Physiological, Social, and Moral Relations*. 1857; 3rd ed., London, 1862.

— *Prostitution, Considered in its Moral, Social and Sanitary Aspects in London and Other Large Cities, & c*. London, 1857.

Allbutt, Dr Henry Arthur. *The Wife's Handbook*. London, 1886.

Althusser, Louis. *Lenin and Philosophy and Other Essays*. Trans. Ben Brewster. London, 1970.

Aveling, Edward. *Darwinism and Small Families*. London, 1882.

Banks, J.A. and Olive. *Feminism and Family Planning in Victorian England*. Studies in Sociology. Liverpool, 1964.

Barker-Benfield, B. 'The Spermatic Economy: A 19th Century View of Sexuality.' *Feminist Studies*, 1 (1972), 45–74.

Barthes, Roland. *s/z*. Paris, 1970.

Belsey, Catherine. *Critical Practice*. New Accents. Gen. Ed. Terence Hawkes. London, 1980.

Bennett, Tony. *Formalism and Marxism*. New Accents. London, 1979.

Bishop, J.P. *New Commentaries on Marriage, Divorce, and Separation*. 2 vols. London, 1891.

Bloch, Iwan. *A History of English Sexual Morals*. Trans. W.H. Forstern. London, 1936.

Branca, Patricia. *Silent Sisterhood: Middle-Class Women in the Victorian Home*. London, 1975.

British Parliamentary Papers: Marriage and Divorce, 3. Shannon, 1971.

Burniston, Steve, and Chris Weedon. 'Ideology, Subjectivity and the Artistic Text.' In *Working Papers in Cultural Studies*, 10 (1977). Rpt. as *On Ideology*. Centre for Contemporary Cultural Studies. London, 1978, pp. 199–229.

Caird, Mona. *The Morality of Marriage, and Other Essays on the Status and Destiny of Woman*. London, 1897.

Carpenter, Edward. *Love's Coming-of-Age. A Series of Papers on the Relations of the Sexes*. Manchester, 1896.

Carter, Robert Brudenell. *On the Pathology and Treatment of Hysteria*. London, 1853.

Charteris, Hon. Evan. *Life and Letters of Sir Edmund Gosse*. London, 1931.

Clapperton, Jane Hume. *Scientific Meliorism and the Evolution of Happiness*. London, 1885.

Cockshut, A.O.J. *Man and Woman: A Study of Love and the Novel 1740–1940*. London, 1977.

Cominos, Peter T. 'Late-Victorian Sexual Respectability and the Social System.' *International Review of Social History*, 8 (1963), 18–48 and 216–50.

— 'Innocent Femina Sensualis in Unconscious Conflict.' In *Suffer and Be Still*. Ed. Vicinus. pp. 155–72.

Cook, Lady. *Talks and Essays*. 4 vols. London, [1897].

— *A Check and Libertines: And, A Father's Responsibility, An Unnamed Vice, One of the Evils of Society, Virtue*. London, [1900?].

Conway, Jill. 'Stereotypes of Femininity in a Theory of Sexual Evolution.' In *Suffer and Be Still*. Ed. Vicinus. pp. 140–54.

Darwin, Charles. *On the Origin of Species by Means of Natural Selection*. London, 1859.

— *The Descent of Man, and Selection in Relation to Sex*. 2 vols. London, 1871.

Drysdale, C.R. 'Socialistic Malthusians: A Review.' *Malthusian*, 21 (1897), 89–90.

Duffin, Lorna. 'The Conspicuous Consumptive: Woman as an

Invalid.' In *The Nineteenth-Century Woman: Her Cultural and Physical World*. Ed. Lorna Duffin and Sara Delamont. London, 1978, pp. 26–56.

Eagleton, Terry. *Criticism and Ideology: A Study in Marxist Literary Theory*. London, 1976.

— Rev. of *Truth and Ideology*, by Hans Barth. *Notes and Queries*, NS 25 (1978), 361–2.

— 'Liberality and Order: The Criticism of John Bayley.' *New Left Review*, No. 110 (1978), 29–40.

Eliot, T.S. *After Strange Gods: A Primer of Modern Heresy*. The Page-Barbour Lectures at the University of Virginia, 1933. London, 1934.

Ellis, Havelock. *Man and Woman: A Study of Human Secondary Sexual Characters*. London, 1894.

— *The New Spirit*. London, 1890.

Ellmann, Mary. *Thinking About Women*. 1968; rpt. London, 1979.

'Ethelmer, Ellis' [Elizabeth Wolstenholme-Elmy]. *Woman Free*. London, 1893.

Ferrerro, Guglielmo. *The Problem of Woman from a Bio-Sociological Point of View*. Turin, 1893.

— and Cesare Lombroso. *La donna delinquente, la prostituta e la donna normale*. Turin, 1893.

Figlio, Karl. 'Chlorosis and Chronic Disease in Nineteenth-Century Britain: the Social Constitution of Somatic Illness in a Capitalist Society.' *Social History*, 3 (1978), 167–97.

Finn, Frank. 'Some Facts of Telegony.' *Natural Science*, 3 (1893), 436–40.

Foucault, Michel. *La volonté de savoir*. Vol. I of *Histoire de la sexualité*. Paris, 1976.

Gamble, Eliza Burt. *The Evolution of Woman: An Inquiry into the Dogma of her Inferiority to Man*. London, 1894.

Geddes, Patrick, and J. Arthur Thomson. *The Evolution of Sex*. London, 1889.

Gorham, Deborah. 'The "Maiden Tribute of Modern Babylon" Re-examined: Child Prostitution and the Idea of Childhood in late-Victorian England.' *Victorian Studies*, 21 (1978), 353–79.

'Graduate, A.' *A Lecture to Young Men on the Preservation of Health and the Personal Purity of Life*. London, 1885.

Graves, Charles L. *Life and Letters of Alexander Macmillan*. London, 1910.

Halliday, George. 'Social Darwinism: A Definition.' *Victorian Studies*, 14 (1971), 389–405.

Hansson, Laura Marholm. *Modern Women*. Trans. Hermione Ramsden. London, 1896.

Hardwick, Elizabeth. 'Seduction and Betrayal.' In *Seduction and Betrayal: Women and Literature*. London, 1974, pp. 177–208.

Harper, Charles G. *Revolted Woman: Past, Present, and to Come*. London, 1894.

Harrison, Frederic. 'The Emancipation of Women.' *Fortnightly Review*, 56 (1891), 437–52.

Harvey, H.E. 'Science as a Moral Guide.' *Westminster Review*, 149 (1898), 186–93.

Heilbrun, Carolyn G. *Towards Androgyny: Aspects of Male and Female in Literature*. London, 1973.

Henriques, Fernando. *Modern Sexuality*. Vol. III of *Prostitution and Society*. London, 1968.

Hynes, Samuel. *The Edwardian Turn of Mind*. London, 1968.

Jacobus, Mary, ed. *Women Writing and Writing about Women*. London, 1979.

Klein, Viola. *The Feminine Character: History of an Ideology*. International Library of Sociology and Social Reconstruction. London, 1946.

Le Gallienne, Richard. *Retrospective Reviews: A Literary Log*. 2 vols. London, 1896.

Lerner, Laurence. *The Truthtellers: Jane Austen, George Eliot, D.H. Lawrence*. London, 1967.

Linton, Eliza Lynn. *The Girl of the Period*. London, 1883.

— 'Partisans of Wild Women.' *Nineteenth Century*, 31 (1892), 455–64.

Logan, William. *The Great Social Evil: Its Causes, Extent, Results, and Remedies*. London, 1871.

MacDonald, Robert H. 'The frightful Consequences of Onanism: Notes on the History of a Delusion.' *Journal of the History of Ideas*, 28 (1967), 423–31.

Machery, Pierre. *A Theory of Literary Production*. Trans. Geoffrey Wall. London, 1978.

— and Etienne Balibar. 'Literature as an Ideological Form: Some Marxist Propositions.' *Oxford Literary Review*, 3 (1978), 4–12.

Mackintosh, Robert. *From Comte to Benjamin Kidd: the Appeal to Biology or Evolution for Human Guidance*. London, 1899.

Marcus, Steven. *The Other Victorians: A Study of Sexuality and Pornography in Mid-Nineteenth Century England*. London, 1966.

Marholm, Laura. *The Psychology of Woman*. Trans. Georgia A. Etchison. London, 1899.

Marshall, William H. *The World of the Victorian Novel*. London, 1967.

Marx, Eleanor, and Edward Aveling. *The Woman Question*. London, 1886.

Marxist-Feminist Literature Collective. 'Women's Writing: *Jane Eyre, Shirley, Villette, Aurora Leigh.*' In *1848: The Sociology of Literature*. Proceedings of the Essex Conference on the Sociology of Literature July 1977. Ed. Francis Barker and others. Essex, 1978, pp. 185–206.

McLaren, Angus. *Birth Control in Nineteenth-Century England*. London, 1978.

Miller, George Noyes. *After the Strike of a Sex or, Zugassent's Discovery*. London, 1896.

Miller, John Hawkins. '"Temple and Sewer": Childbirth, Prudery and Victoria Regina.' In *The Victorian Family: Structure and Stresses*. Ed. Anthony S. Wohl. London, 1978, pp. 23–43.

Miller, Joseph Hillis. *The Form of Victorian Fiction*. University of Notre Dame, Ward-Phillips Lectures in English Language and Literature, Vol. 2. Notre Dame, 1968.

Millett, Kate. *Sexual Politics*. London, 1971.

Mitchell, Juliet. *Psychoanalysis and Feminism*. Harmondsworth, 1974.

—, and Ann Oakley, ed. *The Rights and Wrongs of Woman*. Harmondsworth, 1976.

Neuman, R.P. 'Masturbation, Madness and the Modern Concepts of Childhood and Adolescence.' *Journal of Social History*, 8 (1975), 1–27.

Newman, Francis William. *The Corruption Now Called Neo-Malthusianism. With Notes by Dr E. Blackwell*. London, 1889.

Nordau, Max. *Degeneration*. London, 1895.

Pearsall, Ronald. *The Worm in the Bud: the World of Victorian Sexuality*. London, 1969.

Pearson, Karl. *The Ethic of Freethought: A Selection of Essays and Lectures*. London, 1888.

'Prostitution.' *Westminster Review*, 53 (1850), 448–506.

Purcell, E. '*Degeneration*. By Max Nordau.' *Academy*, 47 (1895), 475–6.

Quilter, Harry, ed. *Is Marriage a Failure?* London, 1888.

Rev. of *The Functions and Disorders of the Reproductive Organs*, by William Acton. *London Medical Review*, 3 (1862), 145.

Robertson, John M. *Socialism and Malthusianism*. London, 1885.

Romanes, George J. 'Mental Differences between Men and Women.' *Nineteenth Century*, 21 (1887), 654–72.

Rover, Constance. *Love, Morals, and the Feminists*. London, 1970.

Rowbottom, Sheila, and Jeffrey Weeks. *Socialism and the New Life: The Personal and Sexual Politics of Edward Carpenter and Havelock Ellis*. London, 1977.

Schwartz, Gerhart S. 'Devices to Prevent Masturbation.' *Medical Aspects of Human Sexuality*, 7 (1973), 141–53.

Scott, Clement. 'An Equal Standard of Morality.' *Humanitarian*, 5 (1894), 353–5.

Searle, Geoffrey. *Eugenics and Politics in Britain 1900–1914*. Science in History, No. 3. Leyden, 1976.

Shelley, Percy Bysshe. *Complete Poetical Works*. Ed. Neville Rogers. Vol. 1 *1802–1813*. Oxford, 1972.

Showalter, Elaine. *A Literature of their Own: British Women Novelists from Brontë to Lessing*. London, 1977.

— 'Towards a Feminist Poetics.' In *Women Writing and Writing About Women*. Ed. Jacobus, pp. 22–41.

— and English Showalter. 'Victorian Women and Menstruation.' In *Suffer and Be Still*. Ed. Vicinus. pp. 38–44.

Stead, W.T. 'The Maiden Tribute of Modern Babylon.' *Pall Mall Gazette*, July 1885.

Stedman Jones, Gareth. *Outcast London: A Study in the Relationship between Classes in Victorian Society*. Oxford, 1971.

Stockham, Alice Bunker. *Karezza. Ethics of Marriage*. Chicago, 1896.

Swiney, Francis. *The Bar of Isis, or the Law of the Mother*. London, 1907.

Taylor, Gordon Rattray. *Sex in History*. Past in the Present. London, 1953.

Thomas, Keith. 'The Double Standard.' *Journal of the History of Ideas*, 20 (1959), 195–216.

Tissot, Samuel A.A.D. *L'onanisme: dissertation sur les maladies produites par la masturbation*. 10th ed. Toulouse, 1875.

Tomlinson, T.B. *The English Middle-Class Novel*. London, 1976.

Trudgill, Eric. *Madonnas and Magdalens: the Origins and Development of Victorian Sexual Attitudes*. London, 1976.

Ussher, R. *Neo-Malthusianism: An Enquiry into that System with Regard to its Economy and Morality*. London, 1898.

van Ghent, Dorothy. *The English Novel: Form and Function*. 1953; rpt. New York, 1960.

Vicinus, Martha, ed. *Suffer and Be Still: Women in the Victorian Age*. London, 1973.

Williams, Raymond. *The English Novel from Dickens to Lawrence*. London, 1970.

Woodhull Martin, Victoria C. *The Rapid Multiplication of the Unfit*. London, 1891.

Index